Rethinking Business and Management

Rethinking Business and Management

Global Transformations in the Digital Age

Hamid Yeganeh

Rethinking Business and Management:
Global Transformations in the Digital Age

Cover design by Hamid Yeganeh

Interior design by Exeter Premedia Services Private Ltd., Chennai, India

First published in 2026 by
Business Expert Press, LLC
222 East 46th Street, New York, NY 10017
www.businessexpertpress.com

ISBN-13: 978-1-60649-643-5 (paperback)
ISBN-13: 978-1-60649-645-9 (e-book)

International Business Collection

First edition: 2026

10 9 8 7 6 5 4 3 2 1

EU SAFETY REPRESENTATIVE
Mare Nostrum Group B.V.
Doelen 72
4831 GR Breda
The Netherlands
gpsr@mare-nostrum.co.uk

Description

Rethinking Business and Management **offers a timely and critical examination of how business and management are being reshaped by digitalization, globalization, and deep socio-economic change.** As contemporary capitalism becomes increasingly driven by intangible assets, data, digital platforms, and financial power, this book challenges conventional assumptions about how markets, organizations, and managerial authority operate.

Bringing together insights from political economy, organization studies, and marketing, the book explores the rise of the intangible and sharing economies, shifting patterns of work marked by flexibility and precarity, and the growing influence of moral and political discourses such as *woke capitalism*. It examines how multinational corporations adapt within a fragmented yet highly interconnected global system, and how platform-based organizations and data-driven personalization are redefining both management practices and consumer identities.

The book also addresses the intensifying entanglement between digital technologies and finance, showing how fintech, platforms, and digital infrastructures are transforming investment, payment systems, and the distribution of economic power. Throughout, it foregrounds the implications of these transformations for inequality, governance, and the future of capitalism itself.

Combining analytical rigor with a critical perspective, *Rethinking Business and Management* provides readers with a coherent framework for understanding the forces reshaping business today. It is an essential resource for scholars, students, and practitioners seeking to navigate—and rethink—the contemporary business landscape..

Contents

PART 1
Socioeconomic Shifts

CHAPTER 1

The Rise of the Intangible Economy

The Rise of Intangible Assets

From the 19th century until about three decades ago, businesses concentrated their investments on physical assets. At the turn of the 21st century, however, investments shifted markedly toward intangible assets. According to McKinsey Global Institute (Hazan et al. 2021), by 2019 intangibles accounted for 40 percent of total investment in the United States and 10 European economies, up from 29 percent in 1995. This transformation was propelled by globalization and digitalization, which raised the importance of intellectual property, brand value, and knowledge-based resources (Haskel and Westlake 2018). Intangibles now form an increasingly large share of company value and are essential to competitiveness (see Figure 1.1).

The shift is striking in market data. Between 1982 and 1998, the value of tangible assets on S&P 500 balance sheets dropped from an average of 62 percent of market value to only 15 percent (Di Tommaso et al. 2004). Even major disruptions, including financial crises, have not slowed intangible investment (Hazan et al. 2021). The COVID-19 pandemic accelerated this trend, as firms heavily invested in intangibles outperformed others in the postpandemic period. Based on estimates, in 2018–2019, top-performing companies with a median growth rate of 20 percent invested 2.6 times more in intangibles than low-performing firms, which grew at just 3 percent (Hazan et al. 2021). In sectors where knowledge is central, such as financial services, the gap rises to five to seven times. These findings highlight the strong link between intangible capital and higher growth. Executive surveys also suggest that momentum will continue: three-quarters of respondents in North America and Europe expect

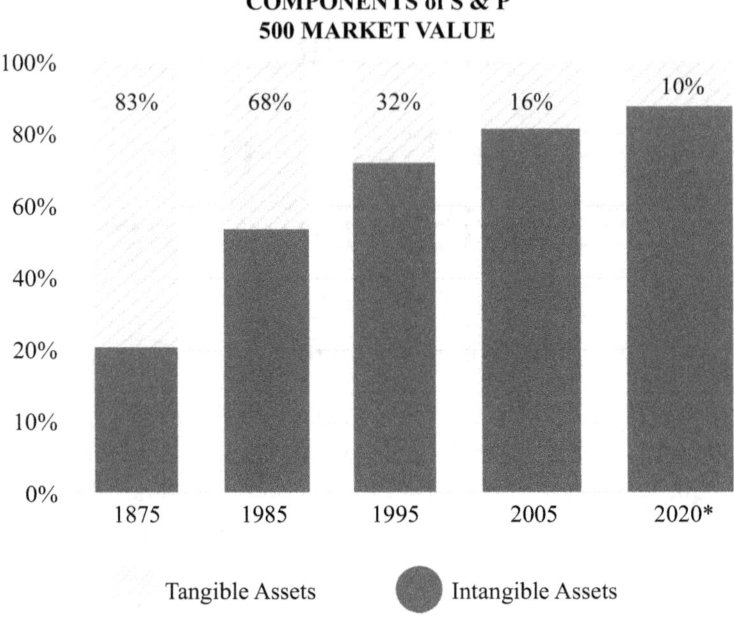

SOURCE: OCEAN TOMO, LLC INTANGIBLE ASSET MARKET VALUE STUDY, 2020
*INTERIM STUDY UPDATE AS OF 7/1/2020

Figure 1.1 S&P500 Market Value: The phenomenal growth of intangible assets

Source: OCEAN TOMO, 2020

intangible investments to increase (Hazan et al. 2021). Human capital, innovation, and social capital are now widely recognized as the key drivers of competitiveness at both the firm and national levels. Institutions such as the European Union and the Organization for Economic Cooperation and Development (OECD) emphasize their role in knowledge creation, entrepreneurship, and long-term growth (Bianchi and Labory 2004).

The rise of intangibles signals a structural shift in value creation. Companies no longer rely solely on producing and selling physical goods, but increasingly generate returns through the development, protection, and application of intangible resources. In our current knowledge-driven economy, productivity and growth are inseparable from these assets. The rise of intangible capital is reshaping the broader economic and social landscape. Intangibles share distinctive features: they are knowledge-intensive, highly scalable, prone to spillovers, and often involve sunk costs, synergies, risks, and uncertainties. Their growth has far-reaching consequences, altering organizational structures, driving geographic clustering, widening gaps between industry leaders and laggards, and complicating accounting and valuation methods. They also foster monopolistic strategies, speculation, and financial instability, while fueling intangible consumption and deepening social inequality (Yeganeh 2024).

The Meaning of Intangible Assets

The definition of intangible assets has long been debated, and most descriptions remain abstract, offering limited practical guidance for practitioners and researchers. Various terms such as intangible assets, intangible capital, intangible resources, intellectual capital, and intellectual property are often used interchangeably.

In general, assets are everything a company owns that has monetary value. Understanding the composition and classification of assets is crucial for financial management and reporting, as different categories serve distinct purposes in supporting operations, growth, and strategy. Assets are typically divided into four broad categories:

1. **Current Assets**: These are assets expected to be sold, consumed, or converted into cash within one year or the business's operating cycle. They include cash, accounts receivable, inventory, and short-term investments, and are vital for liquidity and day-to-day operations.
2. **Fixed Assets**: Also called noncurrent or long-term assets, these include machinery, equipment, plants, and properties with a useful life exceeding one year. Fixed assets are essential for production and long-term operations, and their cost is depreciated over time to account for wear and tear.
3. **Investments**: These include holdings in stocks, bonds, or other securities, representing ownership in different firms or financial instruments. Depending on intent and holding period, investments may be classified as short-term or long-term.
4. **Intangible Assets**: Unlike the other categories, intangible assets lack physical substance yet hold significant economic value. Often referred to as "intellectual capital," they include patents, copyrights,

trademarks, software, proprietary knowledge, customer relationships, and brand reputation. Though intangible, these assets play a central role in building competitive advantage and ensuring long-term success.

While some authors prefer "intellectual capital" to describe these resources, the concepts frequently overlap. Intellectual capital generally refers to the knowledge, skills, and intellectual property that contribute to a firm's value, even when not fully reflected on the balance sheet. Increasingly, it is recognized as a critical driver of innovation, performance, and competitiveness.

Scholars have proposed several definitions of intangibles, most of which emphasize their forward-looking nature. We may describe intangible assets as knowledge that can be converted into profit or as "claims to future benefits" that lack physical or financial form (Sullivan 2000; Lev 2001). This perspective underscores their role in creating value through innovation, organizational design, and human capital practices. Intangibles often interact with tangible and financial assets to generate corporate growth.

The Financial Accounting Standards Board (FASB) similarly characterizes intangible assets as noncurrent, nonfinancial claims to future benefits without physical or financial substance. The OECD provides a complementary definition, highlighting intangible assets as nonphysical, nonfinancial resources relevant to commercial activities and transferable between independent parties under comparable conditions (Helderman and Sporken 2012). More broadly, intangible assets are immaterial resources that are renewable, dynamic, and often enhanced through use. Unlike physical assets, intangible assets do not diminish when consumed. Still, they may increase in utility or value through knowledge accumulation, organizational learning, and network effects.

Types of Intangible Assets

The classification of intangible assets is a complex task due to the diverse definitions and perspectives surrounding them. Various researchers have proposed different categorizations, contributing to a broad spectrum of classifications. Despite the use of varied terminology, a common thread runs through many scholars, who often affirm a classification into three overarching categories: human capital, customer capital, and structural capital (Kaufmann and Schneider 2004). Sullivan offers a more detailed breakdown, separating intellectual capital into three distinct categories: human capital, which is related to employees; intellectual assets, which result from human capital; and legally protected intellectual property. These categories are interconnected, underscoring the dynamic interplay among the different facets of intellectual capital. We may present another perspective by proposing a classification into employee competence and internal and external structures (Sveiby 1997). Accordingly, intangibles are fundamentally rooted in an organization's personnel, further highlighting the role of human capital.

We may classify intangible assets into three broad categories, namely: (1) computerized information, (2) innovative property, and (3) economic competencies (see Table 1.1). The computerized information category includes investments that involve putting information into computers to make them useful in the long run. Examples cited are software (both purchased and self-developed) and databases. It notes the growing importance of big data in various industries. The innovative property category includes research and development (R&D) and other product and service development forms, including design and creative endeavors. It also consists of the rights associated with these innovations. The economic competencies category covers investments that do not involve innovation or computers. It requires knowledge embedded in firm-specific human and structural resources. The subcategories include marketing and branding, organizational capital, and company-specific training.

We need to bear in mind that each type of investment can generate intellectual property rights (IPR), such as R&D patents and entertainment copyrights (Haskel and Westlake 2018). IPR vary by country; not all investment forms can be patented in every jurisdiction. Focusing solely on patenting does not provide a complete picture of innovation metrics. Many statistical agencies now treat these spending categories as investments. Still, this treatment is relatively recent and can be inconsistent across countries. The recognition of database investment is noted as an example of inconsistency.

Table 1.1 Classification of intangible assets

Broad category	Type of investment	Type of legal property that might be created	Treated as an investment in national accounts?
Computerized information	Software development Database development	Patent, copy-right, design IPR, trademark, other copyright, other	Yes, since the early 2000s. Recommended in SNA 1993, but OECD suggests uneven imple-mentation.
Innovative property	R.D. Mineral exploration Creating entertain-ment and artistic originals Design and other product development costs	Patents, design IPR Patents, other Copyright, design IPR Copyright, design IPR, trademark	Yes, recommended in SNA 2008 and introduced gradually since then. Yes, in the EU, in the U.S., since 2013. No
Economic competencies	Training Market research and branding Business process reengineering	Other Copyright, trademark Patent, copyright, other	No No No

Source: Haskel and Westlake 2018

The Distinctive Features of Intangibles

As shown in Table 1.2, intangible assets have specific essential characteristics that distinguish them from conventional assets.

Knowledge Content

Intangible assets are widely understood to be rooted in knowledge, a central element common across different categories of intangibles (Di Tommaso et al. 2004; Stewart 1997). From a neoclassical perspective, firms engage in collaboration broadly to diffuse the risks inherent in generating technological knowledge. Knowledge itself displays three defining characteristics. First, it functions as a public good: once produced, its creator cannot fully control it, nor can its use be easily restricted, making it ill-suited to traditional market mechanisms. Second, the creation of knowledge is

Table 1.2 The distinctive features of intangible assets

Feature	Description	Examples/Implications
1) Knowledge Content	Intangibles contain explicit or implicit information.	Knowledge: Is unsuitable for conventional markets It cannot be fully appropriated Is a public good Its creation is uncertain Involves economies of scale.
2) Nonscarcity (Nonrivalry)	Intangibles are not scarce, and their opportunity costs are minimal.	Intangibles are immaterial and almost unlimited.
3) Limited Tradability	Intangibles lack organized and active markets.	They involve: High transaction costs Informal contacts and transactions Trust and relationships.
4) Risk and Information Asymmetries	Intangibles are uncertain and nebulous.	Uncertain financial performance. Fear of imitation.
5) High Scalability	Intangibles can be produced in mass.	They can be scaled almost infinitely.
6) Low or Zero Marginal Cost	Intangibles are cheap to reproduce.	They do not involve the significant cost of reproduction.
7) High Initial Investment	Intangibles require substantial initial investment.	Barriers to entry are significant.
8) Network Effects	Intangibles gain value after application.	The networks of Uber drivers, Airbnb hosts, and Instagram users gain value after use.
9) Sunken Costs	Intangibles cannot be recovered if decisions are reversed.	Intangible assets are challenging to sell and are often specific to the firm that owns them.
10) Spillovers	One company's intangibles benefit other businesses.	Intangibles are nonrivalrous, nonexcludable, and fluid.
11) Synergies	Existing intangibles create new and more valuable intangibles.	The effects of intangibles are compounded as they are combined, making them more valuable than individual assets.
12) Partial Excludability (Contested Ownership)	Intangible ownership is less protected.	Firms struggle to internalize intangibles through effective strategies.

(Continued)

Table 1.2 The distinctive features of intangible assets (Continued)

Feature	Description	Examples/Implications
13) Shared/Multiple Consumption	They can be shared and concurrently utilized by multiple consumers.	Justifies business approaches like franchising or licensing. Businesses can reach diverse audiences simultaneously.
14) Environmental Sustainability	Intangible assets do not significantly contribute to the depletion of finite natural resources.	Intangibles minimize the need for physical resources and contribute to environmental conservation.

intrinsically uncertain; outcomes are difficult to predict, and the process often involves significant variability. Third, knowledge production benefits from economies of scale, meaning that average costs decline as more knowledge is generated (Arrow 1972). Intangible assets embody all three of these features. As public goods, the knowledge embedded in intangibles is nonrivalrous and nonexcludable; once generated, it can be shared and used by multiple actors without being depleted. This openness, however, limits innovators' ability to capture the full economic value of what they create, since exclusivity cannot be taken for granted. The uncertainty surrounding knowledge generation introduces further risk, distinguishing intangible investments from those in tangible assets, where outcomes tend to be more stable and predictable. Finally, economies of scale in knowledge production imply that greater or more collaborative efforts reduce per-unit costs, reinforcing the collective and cumulative nature of knowledge development (Yeganeh 2024).

Nonscarcity (Nonrivalry)

Physical, human, and financial assets face rivalry and struggle (Lev 2001). In contrast, intangible assets exhibit nonrivalry and minimal opportunity costs. This unique characteristic stems primarily from the nature of intangible assets, which are characterized by substantial fixed (sunk) costs and marginal costs that are typically negligible or zero. Intangible assets are costly to create initially but relatively inexpensive to reproduce (Desrochers 2001). The substantial fixed costs associated with intangible asset creation denote the investments required upfront. Once developed, however, these assets often incur minimal additional costs for reproduction. This cost structure contributes to the nonrivalrous nature of intangible assets, as their reproduction does not incur the same expenses as the initial creation. In practice, this characteristic influences firms' strategic decisions on the control and management of intangible assets. Given the potential for simultaneous global utilization of these assets, companies frequently choose to centralize power and management at a single headquarters. Centralization enables efficient coordination, ensuring optimal use of intangible assets across diverse markets without redundant investments in separate management structures.

The notion of nonrivalry in intangible assets implies that using them does not diminish their availability to others. Unlike physical or human resources, where one entity's utilization may limit access to others, multiple entities can employ intangible assets without significant competition or depletion.

Limited Tradability

Determining legal ownership of intangible assets poses a more elusive challenge than that of tangible assets, and even the existence of IPR does not always provide clear boundaries for the appropriation of such assets. Despite these complexities, it is noteworthy that intangible asset markets do exist (Lev 2001). However, what sets intangibles apart is the absence of organized, active marketplaces with numerous participants and transparent pricing mechanisms, a characteristic that distinguishes them from other asset classes. The lack of well-defined markets for intangible assets does not mean they are excluded from economic exchange; their transactions take a distinctive form. The high transaction costs associated with intangibles necessitate a departure from traditional market structures. Instead, exchanges involving intangible assets often occur through informal contacts facilitated by frequent interactions and a foundation of trust between parties. This informal mode of exchange acknowledges the challenges in establishing formal marketplaces and the need for a nuanced approach to intangible asset transactions. The limited tradability of intangibles aligns with classical literature that confirms the imperfections of a free market in the realm of knowledge and information (Stiglitz 1985).

In part, failures in establishing organized markets for intangibles can be attributed to the inherent difficulty in crafting comprehensive contracts that adequately address the nuanced outcomes associated with intangible assets (Teece 1998).

Risk and Information Asymmetries

Creating intangible assets through education, R&D, and innovation is notably associated with uncertainty. The transmission of intangibles, protected by property rights, introduces heightened risk, primarily due to the inherent information asymmetry associated with these assets. Challenges in identifying and quantifying intangibles give rise to principal–agent conflicts among parties exchanging such assets. Moreover, managing intangible assets is an exceptionally uncertain process, often akin to navigating in the dark (Lev 2001). The knowledge-intensive nature of most intangibles contributes to the risk factor. Predicting outputs from nonphysical inputs becomes challenging, making it difficult for firms to capture returns from essentially intangible assets (Feldman 2002). The commercial innovation risk is further compounded by the fear of imitation, which can limit the returns an innovator obtains from their creative efforts.

While intangible assets have the potential to generate future economic benefits, such as revenue, cost savings, or advantages derived from their application, recognizing and measuring these assets requires specific criteria. These criteria include assessing the probability of expected future economic benefits flowing to the entity and ensuring the reliable measurement of the asset's cost. Managerial judgment plays a crucial role in assessing the degree of certainty surrounding the anticipated flow of future economic benefits.

High Scalability

Intangible assets possess a distinctive characteristic known as scalability, setting them apart from physical assets. This feature means that intangible assets can be utilized repeatedly and simultaneously across multiple locations or instances with minimal additional cost once created or acquired. Examples of scalable intangible assets include operating manuals, software applications, and product designs for jet engines. Scalability often encourages more firms to enter markets, potentially leading to industry concentration dominated by a few large companies. In markets where assets are highly scalable, a winner-takes-all dynamic often emerges, making it challenging for competitors to establish a significant presence. Unlike physical assets that degrade and wear out over time, certain intangible assets, such as Google's data and algorithms or Coca-Cola's brand, can scale without diminishing value. This resilience contributes to these assets' enduring significance and value in an evolving economic environment. In the intangible economy, where costs do not rise directly in proportion to revenues, businesses strive to achieve scale and maximize revenue. Creating truly differentiated intangible assets becomes crucial in ensuring that the revenue generated from scale effectively manages costs. This emphasis on differentiation underscores the importance of developing unique and valuable intangible assets that set a business apart from competitors, thereby contributing to sustained success and market competitiveness.

Low or Zero Marginal Cost

Low or zero marginal cost refers to the situation in which the cost of producing each additional unit becomes negligible or approaches zero. This concept particularly applies to intangible products, where the initial creation of the asset incurs a significant investment. However, the cost of duplicating or distributing additional units is minimal. Examples of intangible products with zero or near-zero marginal cost include digital media, software, online educational materials, e-books, apps, music, electronic artwork, and information in general. For example, once a song, movie, or book is created digitally, making additional copies for distribution incurs minimal cost. Online platforms, streaming services, and e-book stores can replicate and deliver these products to unlimited users without incurring high extra costs. Software applications, especially those distributed digitally, often have zero marginal cost. Once the initial development is complete, making copies for users or distributing updates involves negligible expenses. Open-source software, in particular, can be freely duplicated and shared. Like software, mobile applications have low marginal costs once the development is finished. App developers can distribute their creations to millions of users through app stores without incurring substantial per-download costs. Once data or information is collected and organized, the cost of providing access or distributing that information to additional users is minimal. This issue applies to databases, research reports, and various informational products.

High Initial Investment

The characteristic of high initial investment in intangibles is marked by substantial costs incurred during the early stages of creating intellectual property. This feature is evident across diverse industries, including pharmaceuticals, software development, and entertainment. It reflects the significant financial commitment required before realizing tangible economic benefits.

Pharmaceutical companies invest substantial sums in their product pipeline, including research, development, and clinical trials. The costs are incurred well before the possibility of commercialization, covering the extensive efforts to discover, test, and secure regulatory approvals for new drugs. This high initial investment is a calculated risk, with the expectation that successful drugs will offset the costs associated with unsuccessful ones. Software firms allocate considerable person-hours and financial resources to develop new software products. Even seemingly simple programming features can demand several thousand hours of testing and development. The iterative nature of software development involves continuous refinement, which contributes to high initial costs before a product is ready for release. Movie and television studios face substantial expenses in producing content, covering script development, casting, filming, postproduction, and marketing. While blockbuster hits like Titanic and Harry Potter yield significant returns, the average revenue for films can be considerably lower than the production costs. The industry adopts a portfolio approach, where successful projects aim to compensate for less profitable or unsuccessful ones. In creative fields, such as songwriting and inventions, the apparent simplicity of a successful creation often opposes years of experimentation and investment. The initial investment includes the costs of failed attempts, low-pay periods, and the acquisition of skills and knowledge that contribute to the eventual success of the creation. The infrequent big successes support the more frequent small losses, forming a portfolio strategy for managing the inherent risks of creative endeavors. The notion of a portfolio is central to how industries view their intangible assets. It acknowledges that not every creative endeavor or innovative project will yield significant financial returns. Instead, the successes are expected to outweigh the costs of numerous attempts, creating a sustainable, profitable overall intellectual property portfolio (Yeganeh 2024).

Network Effects

Network effects occur when the value of a particular asset rises in proportion to the number of users engaging with it. This phenomenon is inherently rooted in demand-side dynamics, with intangible assets often deriving value from synergies with other intangibles, thus generating self-reinforcing loops. Platforms are prime examples of intangible value creators, demonstrating this concept by attracting users who contribute more data and enabling superior algorithms. This aspect, in turn, enhances the platform's overall appeal, creating a cycle that attracts new customers and partners (EDGE 2022). Notable examples include the networks of Uber drivers, Airbnb hosts, and Instagram users, as well as the foundational standards of the World Wide Web.

The positive feedback loop of network effects amplifies the utility or value of an asset as its user base grows. However, it is crucial to note that network effects are not universally positive and can lead to congestion, particularly in technologies such as high-speed cable Internet. The influx of additional users may negatively impact access speed for existing users. It is imperative to distinguish network effects from economies of scale, as the latter refers to supply-side advantages that lead to cost savings with increased production scale. In contrast, network effects arise from heightened demand and a growing user base, influencing the asset's utility or value.

Sunken Costs

Sunken costs are investments that cannot be recovered quickly if a business reverses a decision. Recouping costs associated with intangible assets poses a greater challenge than those for tangible assets. Unlike tangible assets such as machinery and vehicles, which can be sold relatively quickly in the event of bankruptcy, intangible assets such as brand reputation and operational procedures pose a more difficult hurdle to liquidation. This complexity arises because intangible assets are often tied to a company's unique identity, making them less attractive to potential buyers. Unlike tangible assets, which can be mass-produced and standardized, intangible assets are often bespoke and tailored to the specific needs of the company that owns them. This specificity renders them less interchangeable between businesses and diminishes their marketability. The sale of intangible assets, such as knowledge and know-how, further complicates the requirement for formal IPR for protection. Intangible assets may lack active buyers; even when they do, the transaction process is often complicated and demanding.

The challenges associated with recovering intangible assets are exacerbated by their company-specific nature. Many intangible assets are closely aligned with the distinctiveness of the firm that possesses them, rendering them less valuable or relevant to other entities. This uniqueness not only limits their market potential but also adds complexity to the sale process, making it less straightforward than for tangible assets.

Spillovers

Spillovers occur when intangible investments by one company inadvertently confer benefits on other businesses, often without the original company's intent. A quintessential illustration of intangible assets characterized by substantial spillover effects is R&D investments. R&D endeavors generate nonrivalrous ideas, meaning that using the concept does not deplete its availability to others, and nonexcludable, implying that it is challenging to prevent others from using the idea unless legally protected. The domains where spillovers are prominent include product design, marketing strategies, organizational innovation, and employee training.

These spillover effects occur when investments made by one company influence or inspire other firms in the same industry, creating a ripple effect of knowledge diffusion and innovation.

In contrast to the well-established laws and norms governing the ownership of physical assets that have evolved over thousands of years, the legal framework and norms surrounding intangible asset ownership are relatively recent. This nascent stage in the development of intangible asset ownership laws makes them more contested and uncertain, introducing complexities and challenges in determining the rightful ownership and protection of intangible assets. The dynamic nature of spillovers of intangible investments highlights the complex interplay between companies within an industry. As intangible assets become increasingly pivotal in the contemporary business environment, navigating the evolving ownership laws and norms is essential for companies seeking to harness the benefits of spillovers while addressing the challenges posed by the ambiguous nature of intangible asset ownership.

Synergies

Synergies refer to the strategic integration of existing ideas and innovations to create novel technologies and products. The process of technological advancement often hinges on integrating and synthesizing preexisting ideas and technologies. The evolution of ideas follows a dynamic pattern of exchange, in which the combination of diverse concepts and technologies catalyzes the generation of new, more valuable innovations, resulting in a pyramid of progressive advancements. The root of this phenomenon lies in recognizing that the true potential of innovation is unleashed when diverse ideas converge. The synergy achieved by combining these disparate elements transcends the sum of individual assets, thereby amplifying their overall value. This interconnected web of ideas indicates the collaborative nature of technological progress. It confirms how the convergence of varied concepts fuels innovation. Notably, synergies between intangible assets possess an intriguing quality of unpredictability, often transcending traditional domain boundaries. These synergies' cross-domain nature adds dynamism and complexity to the innovation environment, as breakthroughs can emerge from unexpected intersections of knowledge and expertise.

Moreover, the interplay between intangible and tangible assets in technological innovation is pivotal. Information technologies, exemplified by computers and smartphones, showcase the dance between intangible investments and tangible assets. The harmonious integration of intangible software, algorithms, and user interfaces with the physical hardware of computers and smartphones exemplifies the symbiotic relationship between these asset categories, underscoring the holistic approach necessary for technological advancement.

The concept of synergies implies the collaborative, iterative nature of innovation, underscoring that the whole is often more significant than the sum of its parts. Recognizing and harnessing synergies as industries evolve becomes paramount for organizations aiming to stay at the forefront of technological progress.

Partial Excludability

While the ownership of specific intangibles, such as a company's brands or various forms of intellectual capital, enjoys well-established legal recognition and protection, the ownership status of other intangibles, particularly a firm's labor force and human capital, is comparatively less secure. Moreover, certain intangible assets, such as a customer base, exist outside the firm's legal boundaries, posing challenges in establishing exclusive ownership. Despite companies' efforts to internalize these valuable sources through strategies that foster enduring connections between employees and consumers (Di Tommaso et al. 2004), ownership dilemmas persist. For example, investments in employee training and development, though beneficial to the firm, create a situation in which the advantages of a skilled workforce extend beyond the organization itself. Trained employees, upon changing jobs, carry their enhanced skills and knowledge to other companies, thereby contributing to the broader societal benefit (Di Tommaso et al. 2004; Lev 2001). In intangible asset management, informal and formal institutions play a pivotal role in deriving value from stored intangible assets by enforcing excludability. In managing intangible assets, excludability is often formalized and enforced by legal systems through mechanisms such as patents, copyrights, and noncompete clauses.

Shared/Multiple Consumption

Intangible assets possess a distinct quality of shareability, allowing them to be concurrently utilized by multiple consumers. This characteristic finds a suitable illustration in events such as musical concerts or sports gatherings, where the experience is available to thousands of spectators in the physical venue. It simultaneously reaches millions of viewers through television and Internet broadcasts. This feature (simultaneous consumption) has considerable strategic significance, justifying business approaches such as franchising or licensing. Businesses may leverage the expansive reach of intangible assets to reach diverse audiences simultaneously. For instance, a sports franchise may franchise its brand or license its events, enabling multiple entities to capitalize on the shared experience offered by the sporting events. This approach broadens the audience base and creates avenues for revenue generation by making the intangible asset accessible to a wide range of consumers. Recognizing the simultaneous consumption feature becomes a cornerstone for business strategies aimed at rapid growth. Franchising, for example, enables businesses to expand their reach by having third-party operators replicate their successful models. On the other hand, licensing allows enterprises to grant others the right to use specific elements of their intangible assets, expanding the assets' impact across various markets.

Environmental Sustainability

The transition to an intangible economy strongly aligns with sustainability principles, as intangible assets do not significantly contribute to the depletion of finite natural resources. Unlike their tangible counterparts, which often require raw materials and contribute to environmental degradation through resource extraction and manufacturing processes, intangible assets, by virtue of their nonmaterial nature, have a smaller ecological footprint. The shift toward digitization, especially in industries where physical testing and prototyping are essential, enhances efficiency and contributes to environmental conservation. Simulating complex procedures, such as aircraft engine tests, on digital platforms reduces the need for physical prototypes. This reduction in physical testing conserves resources and significantly curtails greenhouse gas emissions associated with traditional manufacturing and testing processes. By leveraging the power of information processes over physical ones, industries in the intangible economy demonstrate a forward-thinking approach that enhances efficiency and innovation, actively mitigates environmental impact, and promotes a more sustainable, ecologically responsible business paradigm.

References

Arrow, K.J. 1972. *Economic Welfare and the Allocation of Resources for Invention*, pp. 219–236. Macmillan Education U.K.

Bianchi, P., and Labory, S. 2004. The Political Economy of Intangible Assets. In: *The Economic Importance of Intangible Assets*, pp. 25–48.

Desrochers, P. 2001. Geographical Proximity and the Transmission of Tacit Knowledge. *The Review of Austrian Economics* 14, no. 1, pp. 25–46.

Di Tommaso, M., Paci, D., and Schweitzer, S. 2004. Clustering of Intangibles. In *The Economic Importance of Intangible Assets*, pp. 73–102. Routledge

EDGE, D. 2022. *The Great Transition*. DXC Leading Edge.

Feldman, M.P. 2002. The Internet Revolution and the Geography of Innovation. *International Social Science Journal* 54, no. 171, pp. 47–56.

Haskel, J., and Westlake, S. 2018. *Capitalism Without Capital: The Rise of the Intangible Economy*. Princeton University Press.

Hazan, E., Smit, P.S., Woetzel, A.J., Cvetanovski, B., Krishnan, M., and Gregg, B. 2021. *Getting Tangible about Intangibles*. McKinsey Global Institute.

Helderman, L., and Sporken, E. 2012. International Revision of the Special Considerations for Intangibles in Chapter VI of the OECD Transfer Pricing Guidelines and Related Provisions. *International Transfer Pricing Journal* 19, no. 6, pp. 383–390.

Kaufmann, L., and Schneider, Y. 2004. Intangibles: A Synthesis of Current Research. *Journal of Intellectual Capital* 5, no. 3, pp. 366–388.

Lev, B. 2001. *Intangibles: Management, Measurement, and Reporting*. The Brookings Institution.

Stewart, T.A. 1997. *Intellectual Capital: The Wealth of Organizations*. Doubleday/Currency.

Stiglitz, J.E. 1985. Information and Economic Analysis: A Perspective. *The Economic Journal* 95(Supplement), pp. 21–41.

Sullivan, P.H. 2000. *Value-Driven Intellectual Capital: Converting Intangible Corporate Assets into Market Value*. John Wiley & Sons.

Sveiby, K.E. 1997. *The New Organizational Wealth: Managing and Measuring Knowledge-Based Assets*. Berrett-Koehler Publishers.

Teece, D.J. 1998. Capturing Value from Knowledge Assets: The New Economy, Markets for Know-How, and Intangible Assets. *California Management Review* 40, no. 3, pp. 55–79.

Yeganeh, H. 2024. *Business and Management in the Age of Intangible Capitalism*. Business Expert Press.

CHAPTER 2

The Sharing Economy

The Rise of the Sharing Economy

The sharing economy, also known as the collaborative economy, has become one of the most transformative forces of the 21st century, reshaping the way societies consume, own, and organize work. By allowing people to share, rent, or trade assets such as homes, vehicles, and skills, this new economic model has disrupted established industries while creating novel economic, social, and cultural dynamics that challenge conventional business practices.

The concept of the "sharing economy" emerged in the early 2000s, signaling a paradigm shift toward access-based consumption. It is rooted in *collaborative consumption,* the reinvention of traditional behaviors such as renting, lending, or swapping through technology-enabled networks (Botsman and Rogers 2010). This shift blurs the conventional boundaries between producers and consumers, giving rise to crowd-based capitalism, an economic order in which digital platforms mediate trust, reputation, and value creation (Sundararajan 2016). These platforms not only facilitate transactions but also cultivate networks of mutual dependence, transforming isolated market exchanges into community-oriented systems of participation and reputation.

Several factors underpin the expansion of the sharing economy. Technological advances, particularly mobile and platform technologies, have enabled the creation of large-scale, trust-based systems that connect millions of users. Sociocultural shifts have encouraged a move away from ownership toward access, reflecting changing attitudes toward consumption and sustainability. Meanwhile, economic pressures such as stagnating wages and high asset prices have made collaborative consumption an attractive alternative to traditional markets. These platforms reduce transaction costs, expand market reach, and match supply and demand more efficiently, illustrating the broader logic of network effects in the digital age (Hamari et al. 2016; Yeganeh 2021).

The growth of the sharing economy has been extraordinary. According to GlobeNewswire (2024), its global value stood at USD 366.2 billion in 2024 and is expected to reach USD 1.4 trillion by 2030, representing a compound annual growth rate of 24.8 percent. Business Research Insights (2024) projects even faster expansion, from USD 260.36 billion in 2024 to USD 3.19 trillion by 2033, a compound annual growth rate of 32.1 percent. Such figures reflect the sector's rapid institutionalization within the digital economy and its capacity to generate new markets, employment patterns, and consumption habits (Figure 2.1).

Adoption among consumers is widespread. A Pew Research Center (2016) study found that 72 percent of American adults had used at least one shared or on-demand service. Yet, awareness of the terminology remains limited: only 27 percent recognized the term "sharing economy," and just 11 percent were familiar with "gig economy" (Expert360 2024). This paradox, high usage but low conceptual awareness, illustrates how deeply integrated these services have become in daily life. For many consumers, engaging in peer-to-peer exchange through platforms such as Uber or Airbnb feels natural and convenient rather than revolutionary, even though it represents a major structural transformation of capitalism itself.

Uber and Airbnb exemplify the global reach and impact of the sharing economy. Founded in 2009, Uber operates in roughly 10,500 cities

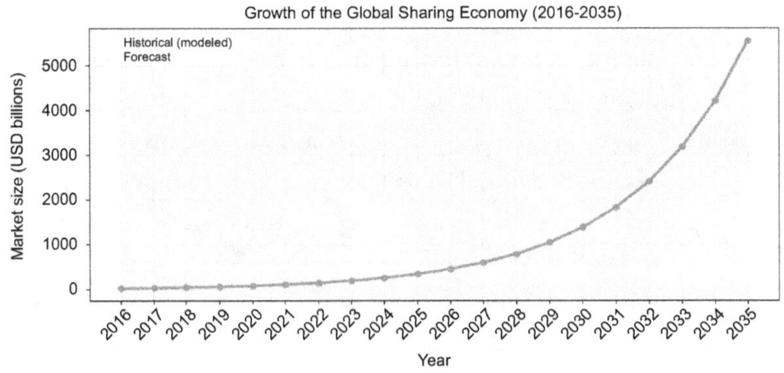

Figure 2.1 Growth of the global sharing economy (2016–2035)

Source: Author's calculations and visualization based on Business Research Insights (2024).

across nearly 70 countries, serving around 180 million monthly active users through more than 6 million drivers and couriers (The *Wall Street Journal* 2025). In the second quarter of 2025, the company completed 3.3 billion trips, generating USD 46.8 billion in gross bookings and USD 12.65 billion in revenue, with net profits reaching USD 1.36 billion. Similarly, Airbnb, founded in 2008, now leads the home-sharing sector, offering more than 8 million listings across 220 countries, supported by 5 million hosts and over 200 million users (DemandSage 2025). In 2024, Airbnb earned USD 11.1 billion in revenue, and by mid-2025, it maintained an operating margin of approximately 23 percent (Finimize 2025). These examples illustrate how platform-based firms can achieve remarkable efficiency and profitability while owning few physical assets.

The economic logic driving the sharing economy lies in its ability to reduce marginal production costs to nearly zero (Rifkin 2014). Digital platforms leverage underutilized resources such as spare rooms, vehicles, or equipment to create additional value without new material production. This efficiency aligns with sustainability objectives, as it encourages resource sharing and reduces waste. Consequently, the sharing economy not only reconfigures economic relationships but also challenges the ownership-driven consumption paradigm that has dominated industrial capitalism.

Yet the sharing economy's implications extend far beyond economics. It is also a cultural and social phenomenon that reshapes trust, identity, and community in digital environments. Peer-review systems, reputation scores, and user feedback have become mechanisms of decentralized governance, replacing institutional regulation with community-driven accountability (Schor 2020). However, this apparent democratization conceals deep inequalities. Many participants, particularly gig workers, face precarious employment conditions. While they benefit from flexibility, they often lack benefits, job stability, and bargaining power. This shift represents a new form of "platform capitalism," where digital networks redistribute risk from corporations to individuals while capturing value at the top.

Moreover, digital intermediation concentrates enormous power in the hands of platform owners who control algorithms, data, and pricing mechanisms. The sharing economy thus operates as both a decentralizing and centralizing force: it democratizes market access. Still, it simultaneously reinforces corporate dominance (Kenney and Zysman 2016). This paradox underscores the ambivalent nature of digital capitalism, at once liberating and exploitative, empowering yet unequal. The next stage in the evolution of the sharing economy will likely be marked by deeper technological integration. Blockchain and decentralized ledgers offer new ways to facilitate trust without centralized intermediaries. Tokenization allows assets from property to intellectual creations to be digitally fractionalized and traded securely, further expanding access and liquidity. When combined with artificial intelligence (AI), these technologies may enable more efficient resource allocation, predictive pricing, and personalized user experiences, enhancing both economic efficiency and inclusivity.

Platformization and Network Effects

The rise of the sharing economy has been inseparable from the emergence of digital platforms and technological infrastructures that mediate interactions among users, producers, and consumers on a massive scale. These platforms, such as Uber, Airbnb, and DoorDash, do not merely facilitate transactions; they redefine how value is created, distributed, and controlled in the modern economy. The process of *platformization*, the transformation of industries, markets, and social practices around digital platforms, has become one of the defining features of 21st-century capitalism. Central to this transformation are *network effects*, the self-reinforcing dynamics that make platforms more valuable as they attract more users, leading to market concentration and the rise of platform monopolies.

Platformization represents a fundamental shift from traditional business models toward digital intermediation. Unlike conventional firms that produce and sell goods or services directly, platforms create ecosystems where users, service providers, and developers interact and generate value collaboratively. Platforms are "digital infrastructures that enable two or more groups to interact," capturing and monetizing those interactions through data extraction, algorithmic pricing, and transaction fees (Srnicek 2017). In the sharing economy, companies such as Uber, Airbnb, and DoorDash epitomize this model. They do not own cars, rooms, or restaurants; instead, they own the digital interface, the technological and data-driven system that connects millions of independent participants around the world (Figure 2.2).

The power of platformization lies in its scalability and efficiency. Platforms can expand globally with minimal physical infrastructure, relying on software architectures that automate matching, coordination, and payment processes. Platforms have transformed social and economic life into programmable networks governed by algorithms and data flows (van Dijck et al. 2018). This transformation blurs traditional boundaries between producers and consumers, employers and workers, and even between public and private domains. Individuals simultaneously become users, data sources, and value creators. At the same time, ownership and control of the ecosystem remain concentrated in the hands of platform operators.

The rapid expansion of digital platforms is primarily driven by *network effects*, a concept that captures how a product or service becomes more valuable as more people use it. Katz and Shapiro (1985) define network effects as the phenomenon in which "the utility that a user derives from consumption increases with the number of other users consuming the same good." Network effects manifest in two primary forms. *Direct network effects* occur when the value of participation increases simply because more users join the platform, as seen in communication or social media

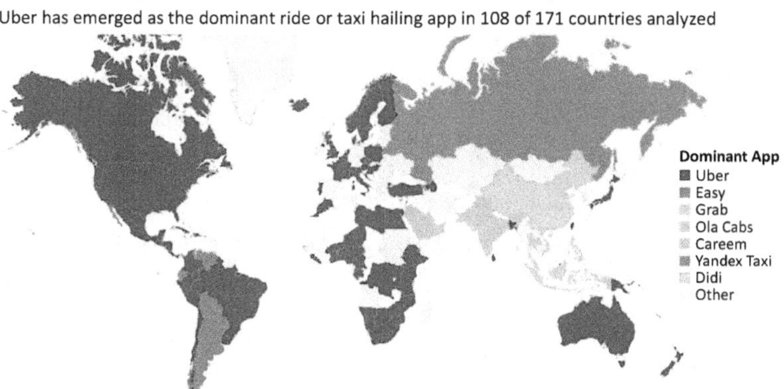

Figure 2.2 Uber's global reach: Uber operates in 108 countries

Source: Author's calculations and visualization.

networks. *Indirect network effects* arise when the growth of one group (e.g., Uber drivers) enhances the value for another (e.g., passengers), creating positive feedback loops. The more drivers join Uber, the shorter the waiting times for riders; the more riders use the app, the higher the potential earnings for drivers. This circular dynamic not only accelerates user adoption and fosters rapid growth but also tends to produce "winner-takes-all" outcomes, where a few large platforms dominate entire markets.

While network effects can enhance innovation and user experience, they also lead to market concentration and monopolistic power. Once a platform reaches critical mass, it becomes tough for new competitors to gain traction. This self-reinforcing process creates high entry barriers and consolidates market power among a small number of dominant actors. Uber, Airbnb, and DoorDash exemplify this trajectory: each leveraged early growth, aggressive pricing, and extensive global expansion to entrench its position as a quasi-monopoly in its respective sector.

The dominance of digital platforms has far-reaching social and economic implications. On the one hand, platformization democratizes access to income-generating opportunities by enabling individuals to monetize their assets or skills easily. On the other hand, it creates new forms of dependency and precarity. Gig workers, though classified as independent contractors, are subject to algorithmic management, variable pay, and limited social protections, leaving them vulnerable to instability and exploitation (Schor 2020). At a systemic level, platform concentration undermines market fairness and local autonomy. Platformization extends beyond economics to reshape governance, culture, and communication, embedding corporate logics into the fabric of everyday life (van Dijck et al. 2018). When network effects produce monopolistic dominance, platforms effectively act as private regulators of the digital commons, setting prices, controlling visibility, and dictating terms of participation.

Addressing the inequalities created by network effects requires new approaches to governance and competition policy. Traditional antitrust frameworks, which focus primarily on price competition, are ill-equipped to handle digital markets where services are often free, and value resides in user data. Scholars such as Srnicek (2017) and Zuboff (2019) advocate for stronger regulatory oversight to ensure data transparency, fair labor standards, and interoperability across platforms. Emerging technological solutions, such as decentralized platforms built on blockchain, seek to redistribute power and reduce reliance on centralized intermediaries, though such alternatives remain experimental.

Datafication and Algorithmic Control in the Sharing Economy

Datafication is the process of converting human behavior, social interactions, and economic activity into quantifiable data. When combined with algorithmic control, it produces a new form of governance in which trust, reputation, and coordination are managed through automated systems rather than through human judgment or institutional authority. Within digital platforms such as Uber, Airbnb, and Amazon, data-driven mechanisms, including ratings, user reviews, recommendation algorithms, and dynamic pricing, increasingly replace traditional managerial oversight. Together, these mechanisms form an emerging mode of algorithmic governance in which control is exercised through data, computation, and automation. Every click, transaction, or movement recorded by sensors and mobile devices becomes a data point that feeds into complex algorithmic systems. These systems enable platforms to predict and influence user behavior with exceptional speed and precision (Mayer-Schönberger and Cukier 2013).

This transformation extends far beyond commercial activity. Zuboff describes this development as surveillance capitalism, an economic order in which human experience becomes the raw material for predictive analytics and behavioral modification (Zuboff 2019). Data in this context does not simply describe behavior; it actively shapes it by feeding back into algorithms that determine what content, prices, or options individuals encounter. Through this process, datafication transforms people into data subjects, continuously monitored, evaluated, and guided within algorithmic ecosystems that regulate social and economic interactions.

Algorithmic governance marks a profound reconfiguration of power and coordination. In the platform economy, algorithms mediate trust and reputation through automated feedback infrastructures. On services such as Uber or Airbnb, reputation is quantified through user reviews and star ratings that function as digital proxies for credibility. A high rating signals reliability, while a low score can restrict or even terminate participation in the market. This dynamic reflects the rise of algorithmic power, the ability of computational systems to categorize, prioritize, and shape social reality (Beer 2017).

Trust, once grounded in personal relationships or institutional authority, becomes a measurable and continuously updated data metric. These systems appear transparent, yet the underlying processes that generate evaluations remain hidden within proprietary algorithms. Users are therefore governed by invisible forms of assessment that reward or penalize behavior without clear explanation. This logic extends to pricing and coordination as well. In the gig economy, platforms such as Uber deploy algorithmic management systems that determine fares, assign routes, and monitor performance. Drivers receive instructions, activity tracking, and performance evaluations from an automated manager rather than from a human supervisor. Similar systems operate in e-commerce, content moderation, and digital advertising, where algorithms organize enormous volumes of interactions without direct human oversight.

The efficiency of these systems lies in their scalability and speed. Algorithms process large quantities of data instantaneously and coordinate supply and demand with far more precision than traditional bureaucratic systems. Predictive analytics enhances logistics, resource allocation, and personalization, creating gains in productivity and convenience. Yet this efficiency comes at a high cost. Algorithmic systems do more than facilitate coordination; they govern behavior through incentives, nudges, and penalties. The claim of neutrality often masks structural biases embedded in data sets, which can lead to discriminatory outcomes that disproportionately affect marginalized groups (Eubanks 2018). Gig workers may be excluded from platforms due to opaque performance metrics. At the same time, consumers are guided toward profit-maximizing content by recommendation systems that restrict diversity and choice.

This broader dynamic is known as platform governance, a system in which algorithms act simultaneously as market participants and as regulators. They determine eligibility for participation, set rules of engagement, and enforce compliance through automated means (Gillespie 2014). In this environment, individuals must manage their digital reputations to maintain visibility and access to economic opportunities. The result is a self-regulating order in which social discipline emerges not from law or hierarchy but from algorithmic evaluation.

This transformation introduces a new politics of visibility and power. Although users appear empowered by access to information and choice, absolute control resides with those who design and own the algorithms. As Pasquale argues in The Black Box Society, these systems operate with minimal transparency, making it nearly impossible for individuals or regulators to understand how decisions are made (Pasquale 2015). The logic of platform capitalism prioritizes efficiency and profit, often at the expense of fairness and accountability. Algorithmic sorting and reputation scoring create new hierarchies of visibility and value. Those with high ratings or favorable data profiles gain advantages, while others face diminishing opportunities or complete invisibility. In this way, algorithmic control digitizes and intensifies social inequality while maintaining an appearance of objectivity.

Addressing these challenges requires ethical and regulatory frameworks that promote transparency, accountability, and human oversight. Policies such as the European Union General Data Protection Regulation represent initial attempts to reassert human agency within automated systems. At the same time, alternative models of data governance are emerging. Cooperative and decentralized platforms seek to redistribute data ownership to users and promote data justice—a principle aimed at restoring collective control over digital resources and resisting the monopolization of information (Couldry and Mejias 2019).

The Changing Nature of Labor, Consumption, and Ownership

The rise of digital platforms and the sharing economy has transformed how people work, consume, and relate to material possessions. Two significant developments define this transformation. The first is the blurring of labor and consumption. The second is the shift from ownership to access. Together, these changes illustrate how digital capitalism restructures economic processes, cultural values, and social identities. In a world mediated by platforms, individuals function simultaneously as workers and consumers, often described as prosumers. At the same time, access to goods and services increasingly replaces ownership as the primary mode of economic participation. These trends dissolve long-standing boundaries between production and consumption, property and use, and work and leisure, ushering in a new phase of economic and cultural life built on flexibility, participation, and connectivity.

The blurring of labor and consumption is one of the most striking features of the digital economy. In the industrial era, production and consumption were distinct activities. Factories produced goods, and consumers purchased them. Digital platforms have merged these roles by allowing users to generate value while consuming services. Alvin Toffler described this hybrid figure as the prosumer, someone who consumes and produces simultaneously (Toffler 1980). Platforms such as Uber, Airbnb, and Etsy exemplify this dynamic. A car owner who drives for Uber is not only a user of a technological service but also a provider of mobility. A homeowner renting out space through Airbnb transforms a private residence into a commercial asset. Activities once understood as private acts of consumption now double as productive labor (Yeganeh 2021).

This convergence offers autonomy and entrepreneurial possibilities, yet it also introduces new forms of insecurity. Juliet Schor argues that while the sharing economy promotes empowerment and flexibility, it masks the instability of platform-based labor, which often lacks benefits, protections, and a predictable income (Schor 2020). Gig work fragments employment into isolated tasks that depend on fluctuating demand and opaque algorithms. Users perform unpaid activities that sustain platforms, such as rating drivers, writing reviews, and uploading content. These tasks are framed as voluntary, but are essential for platform operation. This dynamic can be described as free labor, a form of unpaid digital activity that generates immense value for corporations by producing data and engagement (Terranova 2000).

The culture of self-entrepreneurship further shifts economic risk onto individuals. Instead of stable employment with collective protections, participants become independent contractors responsible for their own tools, taxes, and welfare. Sharing economy platforms externalize costs while internalizing profits, turning individuals into precarious microentrepreneurs whose livelihoods depend on systems that exploit their contributions (Scholz 2017). At the same time, identity becomes tied to platform performance. Maintaining high ratings and a favorable online profile becomes necessary for visibility and continued opportunity. Self-presentation becomes digital labor, a continuous effort to appear competent, reliable, and agreeable.

Parallel to the blurring of labor and consumption is a cultural movement away from ownership toward access. In the industrial age, ownership signified stability, success, and identity. Homes, cars, and collections served as markers of achievement and belonging. Digitalization and platform intermediation have shifted priorities toward access-based consumption. The ability to use goods and services when needed is valued more than permanent possession. Jeremy Rifkin argues that the traditional capitalist ideal of ownership is giving way to an economy in which access becomes the primary mode of participation (Rifkin 2014).

Access-based models now shape nearly all spheres of daily life. Streaming services such as Spotify, Netflix, and Apple Music provide entertainment without ownership. Uber and Zipcar offer mobility without owning a car. Airbnb enables travel without property ownership—consumption shifts from acquiring a thing to experiencing a service. Consumers increasingly value convenience, flexibility, and mobility over the prestige once attached to owning material goods (Bardhi and Eckhardt 2012). Younger generations, in particular, view ownership as burdensome. Debt, maintenance, and permanence restrict mobility and adaptability, whereas access offers freedom and responsiveness to change.

This transition is driven by cultural preferences and structural conditions. Urbanization, rising housing costs, and environmental concerns make ownership less practical or desirable for many. Access-based consumption is promoted as efficient and sustainable because it maximizes the use of shared resources. Yet these models also concentrate power in platform corporations that control access, pricing, and data flows. Users enjoy convenience, but ownership and control of underlying assets remain centralized. The appearance of democratization often masks a more profound asymmetry in information and authority.

The shift from ownership to access also changes how individuals construct meaning and identity. In a possession-based society, people expressed identity through material belongings. In the access-based economy, identity is shaped through experiences, memberships, and networks. Zygmunt Bauman describes this condition as liquid modernity, a state defined by change, movement, and disposability (Bauman 2007). Individuals navigate life through temporary engagements rather than permanent commitments, reflecting the logic of digital platforms that promote constant renewal and continuous engagement. The blurring of labor and consumption and the rise of access-based consumption are deeply interconnected. Both are driven by platforms that mediate interactions, coordinate resources, and convert participation into data and value. Platforms merge labor and consumption into a single activity of use. Engaging with a platform generates utility for the user and data for the corporation. The driver, the renter, the reviewer, and the streamer all participate in a continuous cycle of production and consumption regulated by algorithms.

The Consequences of the Sharing Economy

The sharing economy has emerged as one of the most transformative forces in contemporary capitalism, reshaping the ways people work, consume, and interact. This new economic logic promises efficiency, flexibility, and empowerment by leveraging underused resources and democratizing access to markets. Yet, alongside its opportunities lie significant challenges: the erosion of traditional labor protections, regulatory gaps, new forms of inequality, and questions about long-term sustainability. The consequences of the sharing economy, therefore, span multiple dimensions: economic, social, environmental, and ethical, revealing both its potential and its pitfalls.

Employment and Labor Market

The sharing economy has created new avenues for employment and income generation. Digital platforms enable individuals to earn part- or full-time income by transforming personal assets such as cars or homes into productive resources. Many Uber drivers, for example, appreciate the ability to work during their free hours, thanks to flexible schedules that let them balance other jobs or studies. Similarly, Airbnb hosts can generate additional income by renting spare rooms or entire properties. This flexibility is one of the most celebrated features of the sharing economy, granting individuals autonomy over when and how they work while offering consumers convenient, on-demand access to services (Yeganeh 2021).

These models also challenge the traditional "nine-to-five" labor structure and the rigid separation between work and personal life. They have introduced new modes of earning that modernize labor markets and reshape the concept of work itself. However, this shift also exposes weaknesses in existing social systems. Because many sharing economy participants operate as independent contractors rather than employees, they fall outside the traditional economy's safety nets. Pension systems, health care benefits, and labor protections once tied to stable employment are becoming increasingly obsolete. As this new form of work expands, governments face pressure to rethink the regulatory foundations of the labor market. Moreover, the sharing economy disrupts conventional industries and tax systems. Platforms often operate outside established frameworks, offering services at lower prices that attract customers away from incumbents such as hotels and taxis. While this increases consumer choice and competition, it can reduce government revenues and strain public services. Peer-based rating systems, which act as decentralized trust mechanisms, also shift regulatory responsibility from institutions to individuals. Although they promote accountability, they are susceptible to bias and manipulation.

Despite its promise of empowerment, the sharing economy has also introduced new forms of labor exploitation. Critics argue that the rhetoric of flexibility masks profound power asymmetries between platforms and workers. Uber drivers or delivery couriers, for example, often have little control over pricing, work conditions, or job security. Platforms use algorithms to allocate work, monitor performance, and even determine pay, creating opaque systems that are difficult to challenge or regulate. Classifying workers as "independent contractors" allows companies to avoid providing fundamental rights, such as minimum wages, insurance, or paid leave. As a result, many gig workers earn modest wages, cover their own operational costs, and shoulder the financial risks of illness, accidents, or unemployment. As supply grows, competition intensifies, forcing workers to accept lower pay and longer hours. For those who rely on gig work as their primary source of income, this insecurity can be psychologically and economically devastating. Work relations governed by algorithms are impersonal and one-sided, eroding workers' bargaining power and fragmenting collective solidarity.

This form of precarious labor represents a significant shift in the structure of capitalism. While industrial-era workers faced physical exploitation in factories, today's digital workers confront algorithmic exploitation through constant surveillance, ratings, and unpredictable workloads. Labor has become more individualized, fragmented, and invisible embedded in everyday consumption activities rather than confined to the factory or office.

Environmental Sustainability

One of the most frequently cited advantages of the sharing economy is its contribution to environmental sustainability. Traditional economic systems are built on continuous production and consumption, placing immense pressure on natural resources and generating waste, emissions, and pollution. The sharing economy, by contrast, encourages more efficient use of existing goods. When people share vehicles, rent tools, or exchange household items, fewer resources are required to produce new goods. The French Environment and Energy Management Agency estimates that shareable goods represent nearly one-third of household waste, suggesting that expanding sharing practices could dramatically reduce environmental burdens. In this way, the sharing economy embeds ecological protection into economic activity. Green consumption becomes an inherent feature of the business model rather than an external moral obligation. Car-sharing programs reduce the number of privately owned vehicles; home-sharing promotes more efficient use of space; and clothing rental platforms limit overproduction in the fashion industry. Yet, these benefits depend on how sharing is practiced. In some cases, the convenience and affordability of shared services stimulate *additional* consumption, more travel, more deliveries, and more energy use, offsetting potential gains. The challenge is to ensure that the sharing economy genuinely promotes sustainability rather than serving as a new form of consumer expansion.

A Utopian Vision, Disruption, and Emerging Risks

Governments and cities are beginning to adapt to the rapid expansion of the sharing economy. Taxation rules, employment classifications, insurance requirements, and safety standards are gradually being clarified, pushing the sector from its informal and disruptive origins toward greater formalization and institutional recognition. At the same time, a new phase is emerging: blockchain and tokenization now enable decentralized peer-to-peer exchanges without dominant intermediaries. This experimental Web3 sharing economy promises greater transparency, shared ownership, and reduced reliance on platforms. Beyond transportation and housing, the model is also expanding into health care, education, finance, and business-to-business services, giving rise to hybrid forms of crowdsourcing, peer production, and collaborative consumption that create an increasingly complex landscape of digital intermediation (Yeganeh 2021).

Some thinkers interpret these developments as a step toward a post-capitalist or even utopian future. Jeremy Rifkin (2014) argues that as sharing grows and production costs approach zero, the very meaning of ownership may diminish. In this optimistic vision, goods and services become abundant and nearly free, allowing societies to satisfy material needs with minimal resource use. Although this outlook highlights the transformative potential of digital sharing, it remains largely speculative. The current reality, dominated by profit-oriented platforms, suggests not the disappearance of capitalism but its reconfiguration into a data-driven system in which ownership and control concentrate in a small number of platform monopolies.

As with any disruptive innovation, the sharing economy unsettles established institutions and industries. Platforms often grow faster than the regulatory systems designed to oversee them. Airbnb has been criticized for bypassing hotel licensing and safety requirements. At the same time, Uber has faced bans or restrictions in major cities such as Paris, Berlin, London, and New York due to disputes over labor classification, insurance, and passenger safety. This regulatory lag creates friction between innovation and public accountability. Policymakers must navigate a tricky balance, encourage entrepreneurship while protecting workers, consumers, and communities.

The rise of the sharing economy also introduces significant vulnerabilities. Activities that fall outside traditional legal structures expose users and providers to increased physical, financial, and legal risks. Property damage among Airbnb hosts, safety threats posed by ride-share drivers, and privacy breaches resulting from extensive data collection illustrate these dangers. Algorithmic rating systems can reinforce social biases, disadvantaging visible minorities or low-income individuals who are perceived as less trustworthy. Although trust underpins peer-to-peer exchanges, it is unevenly distributed and often shaped by opaque algorithms.

Despite these risks, the sharing economy offers meaningful benefits, especially for low-income and underserved groups. Lowering barriers to access allows individuals to use goods and services they might otherwise find unaffordable. Travelers can stay in private homes at a lower cost, and families without cars can rely on ride-sharing for mobility. Peer-to-peer platforms support microentrepreneurship, strengthen local connections, and enhance community resilience. Whether these benefits can be sustained in the long run, however, remains uncertain.

References

Bardhi, F., and Eckhardt, G.M. 2012. "Access-based Consumption: The Case of Car Sharing." *Journal of Consumer Research* 39, no. 4, pp. 881–898.

Bauman, Z. 2007. *Liquid Times: Living in an Age of Uncertainty*. Polity.

Beer, D. 2017. *The Data Gaze: Capitalism, Power and Perception*. Sage.

Botsman, R., and Rogers, R. 2010. *What's Mine is Yours: The Rise of Collaborative Consumption*. Harper Business.

Business Research Insights. 2024. "*Sharing Economy Market Size, Share, Growth, and Industry Analysis, by Type, by Application, and Regional Forecast to 2035*." *Business Research Insights*. https://www.businessresearchinsights.com/market-reports/sharing-economy-market-100134

Couldry, N., and Mejias, U. 2019. *The Costs of Connection: How Data is Colonizing Human Life and Appropriating it for Capitalism*. Stanford University Press.

DemandSage. 2025. Airbnb Statistics 2025.

Eubanks, V. 2018. *Automating Inequality: How High-Tech Tools Profile, Police, and Punish the Poor*. St. Martin's Press.

Expert360. 2024. "Gig Economy Insights."

Finimize. 2025. "Airbnb Q2 2025 Earnings Report."

Gillespie, T. 2014. "The Relevance of Algorithms." In *Media Technologies: Essays on Communication, Materiality, and Society*, eds. T. Gillespie, P. Boczkowski, and K. Foot, 167–194. MIT Press.

GlobeNewswire. 2024. "Sharing Economy Market Forecast to 2030."

Hamari, J., Sjöklint, M., and Ukkonen, A. 2016. "The Sharing Economy: Why People Participate in Collaborative Consumption." *Journal of the Association for Information Science and Technology* 67, no. 9, pp. 2047–2059.

Katz, M.L., and Shapiro, C. 1985. "Network Externalities, Competition, and Compatibility." *The American Economic Review* 75, no. 3, pp. 424–440.

Kenney, M., and Zysman, J. 2016. "The Rise of the Platform Economy." *Issues in Science and Technology* 32, no. 3, pp. 61–69.

Mayer-Schönberger, V., and Cukier, K. 2013. *Big Data: A Revolution that will Transform how We Live, Work, and Think*. Houghton Mifflin Harcourt.

Pasquale, F. 2015. *The Black Box Society: The Secret Algorithms that Control Money and Information*. Harvard University Press.

Pew Research Center. 2016. "Shared, Collaborative, and on Demand: The New Digital Economy."

Rifkin, J. 2014. *The Zero Marginal Cost Society*. Palgrave Macmillan.

Schor, J. 2020. *After the Gig: How the Sharing Economy got Hijacked and How to Win it Back*. University of California Press.

Scholz, T. 2017. *Uberworked and Underpaid: How Workers are Disrupting the Digital Economy*. Polity Press.

Shapiro, C., and Varian, H.R. 1999. *Information Rules: A Strategic Guide to the Network Economy*. Harvard Business School Press.

Srnicek, N. 2017. *Platform Capitalism*. Polity Press.

Sundararajan, A. 2016. *The Sharing Economy: The End of Employment and the Rise of Crowd-Based Capitalism*. MIT Press.

Terranova, T. 2000. "Free Labor: Producing Culture for the Digital Economy." *Social Text* 18, no. 2, pp. 33–58.

The Wall Street Journal. 2025. "Uber Q2 2025 Earnings Highlights."

Toffler, A. 1980. *The Third Wave*. Bantam Books.

van Dijck, J., Poell, T., and de Waal, M. 2018. *The Platform Society: Public Values in a Connective World*. Oxford University Press.

Yeganeh, H. 2021. "An Analysis of Factors and Conditions Pertaining to the Rise of the Sharing Economy." *World Journal of Entrepreneurship, Management and Sustainable Development* 17, no. 3, pp. 582–600.

Zuboff, S. 2019. *The Age of Surveillance Capitalism*. PublicAffairs.

CHAPTER 3

The Age of Structural Stress

Debt, Demography, and Political Upheaval

The Rising Public Debt

Rising public debt has become one of the defining economic features of the 21st century. Public debt refers to the total liabilities a government owes to external creditors, such as foreign investors and multilateral institutions, as well as to internal creditors, including domestic banks, corporations, and citizens. While governments have always borrowed to finance wars, infrastructure, and social programs, the scale and persistence of contemporary debt accumulation mark a significant break from historical patterns. The acceleration of public borrowing after the 2008 global financial crisis, the unprecedented fiscal interventions during the COVID-19 pandemic, and ongoing pressures from geopolitical conflict, inflation, and slowing growth have entrenched high debt as a structural condition of the global economy. The United States exemplifies these developments, offering a window into both the benefits and risks of modern fiscal expansion (Reinhart and Rogoff 2010; IMF 2024).

A range of structural drivers underpins the long-term rise in public debt. A central force is the increasing reliance on debt-financed fiscal policy to stabilize economic cycles and preserve social welfare. During downturns, governments often deploy expansive stimulus packages, infrastructure spending, and welfare transfers to support households and firms. Such measures soften recessions and prevent more serious economic damage, but they frequently sustain expenditures far beyond available revenues, thereby generating chronic deficits (Krugman 2020). This pattern has gradually normalized countercyclical borrowing as a routine tool of governance rather than an exceptional response to crisis.

Demographic change further amplifies fiscal strain. Aging populations in advanced economies have expanded pension and health care obligations while shrinking the working-age tax base that funds them. Countries such as Japan, Italy, and the United States face long-term structural imbalances between their social commitments and their fiscal capacity (Bloom et al. 2015). As more citizens retire and fewer contribute to payroll taxes, governments increasingly rely on borrowing to sustain welfare systems. Debt thus becomes a mechanism of intergenerational transfer, redistributing the fiscal burden of today's commitments to future taxpayers.

Monetary policy has also played a pivotal role in enabling debt expansion. Throughout the 2010s, ultralow interest rates and, in some regions, negative rates made borrowing extraordinarily cheap. Governments issued large quantities of long-term debt under the assumption that economic growth would reliably exceed interest payments (Blanchard 2019). This environment gave the impression that high debt levels were manageable and even benign. Yet the inflationary surge after 2021, fueled by supply chain disruptions, war-related shocks, and expansive fiscal support, forced central banks to sharply tighten policy. As interest rates rose, the cost of servicing existing debt increased dramatically, exposing how vulnerable many governments had become to shifts in global monetary conditions.

Major crises have further accelerated debt accumulation. The 2008 financial crash required extensive bank bailouts, liquidity provisions, and stimulus packages to avert systemic collapse (Reinhart and Rogoff 2011). The COVID-19 pandemic produced even more dramatic fiscal responses, as governments worldwide deployed trillions in relief spending to sustain incomes, stabilize firms, and fund public health systems (OECD 2023). These interventions not only prevented catastrophic economic fallout but also entrenched historically high debt-to-GDP ratios across advanced and emerging economies.

Globally, public debt reached roughly 93 percent of world GDP in 2024, up from 70 percent in 2007 (IMF 2024). Advanced economies carry record-high burdens, while many emerging markets face rising default risks amid rising borrowing costs. Countries such as Sri Lanka,

Zambia, and Ghana have already undergone restructuring, highlighting the limits of fiscal expansion in developing contexts (Figures 3.1 and 3.2). No country illustrates these dynamics more clearly than the United States. The U.S. national debt exceeded $34 trillion in 2024, surpassing the size of the entire economy (U.S. Treasury 2024). In 2007, it stood at roughly $9 trillion. According to Congressional Budget Office projections, absent substantial reform, federal debt could reach $50 trillion by 2034, nearly 130 percent of GDP (CBO 2024). Key contributors include defense spending, rising health care costs, large entitlement programs, and mounting interest payments. By 2025, annual interest expenditures alone are expected to surpass $1 trillion (CBO 2024). Decades of structural deficits recorded in 46 of the past 50 years reflect a bipartisan reluctance to reconcile spending and revenue, reinforcing what some scholars call a model of "borrowed prosperity" (Eichengreen 2021).

Public debt is not inherently detrimental. When directed toward productive investments such as infrastructure, education, and technological development, it can stimulate growth, improve living standards,

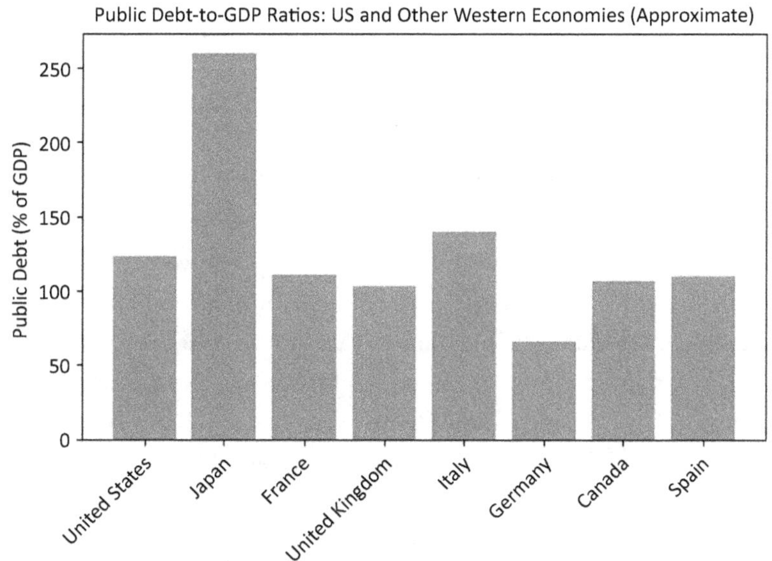

Figure 3.1 Public debt-to-GDP ratios for the United States and other developed/western economies

Source: Authors, based on data from the International Monetary Fund (IMF), World Bank, OECD Economic Outlook.

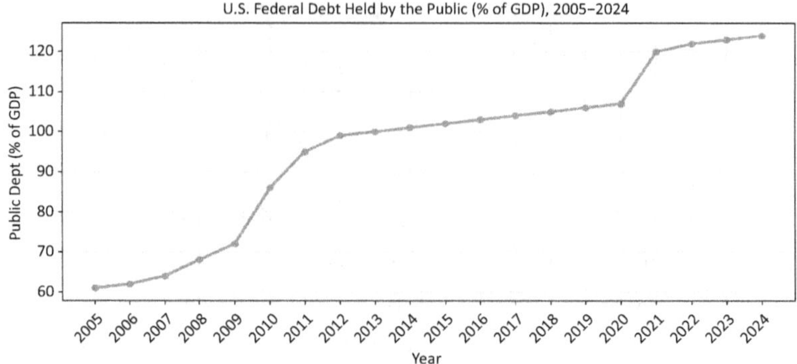

Figure 3.2 The surge of the U.S. public debt-to-GDP in 20 years

Source: Authors, based on data from the International Monetary Fund (IMF), World Bank, OECD Economic Outlook.

and support long-term competitiveness. Borrowing during recessions also prevents deeper contractions and stabilizes employment. However, debt becomes risky when it consistently grows faster than the underlying economy. High debt ratios increase fiscal vulnerability by raising interest burdens and reducing the fiscal space available for future shocks. The resulting "crowding-out effect" can displace spending on productive investments, undermining long-term growth (Cecchetti et al. 2011). Excessive reliance on central bank financing can also fuel inflation, particularly when structural supply constraints limit productive capacity (Blanchard 2019).

The implications of U.S. debt extend far beyond domestic concerns. Because the dollar serves as the world's primary reserve currency, U.S. Treasury securities are a cornerstone of global financial stability. Foreign governments, including China and Japan, hold substantial U.S. debt, which not only sustains international liquidity but also creates mutual vulnerabilities. A sudden loss of confidence in U.S. fiscal management could disrupt global capital markets and trigger widespread economic turbulence (Obstfeld and Rogoff 2009). Several emerging forces are reshaping the future of public debt. Geopolitical tensions are driving increases in defense spending across the United States, Europe, and Asia. The climate transition requires massive investment in renewable infrastructure, green technologies, and resilient energy systems estimated at $4–5 trillion annually through mid-century (World Bank 2023).

Postpandemic adjustments, including efforts to maintain subsidies and welfare programs amid higher interest rates, add further strain. These factors suggest that high debt is no longer a temporary condition but an enduring feature of advanced capitalist economies (Stiglitz 2019).

Aging Populations

Population aging, defined by a rising proportion of older individuals alongside a declining share of younger cohorts, has emerged as one of the most consequential structural forces shaping the global economy. This transformation is driven by sustained declines in fertility and continued gains in life expectancy. It is most noticeable in advanced economies such as the United States, Japan, and Western Europe. While demographic aging reflects profound human progress in health and longevity, it simultaneously introduces far-reaching challenges for economic growth, fiscal sustainability, and business strategy in the 21st century.

As fertility rates fall and life expectancy rises, the median age of societies increases steadily. In nearly all advanced economies, fertility rates have dropped below the replacement level of 2.1 births per woman. Recent estimates place fertility at approximately 1.6 in the United States, around 1.3 in Italy, and below 1.0 in South Korea (World Bank 2023). At the same time, advances in medicine, nutrition, and public health have extended life expectancy beyond 80 years across much of the Organization for Economic Cooperation and Development (OECD) (United Nations 2024). The combined effect is a widening demographic imbalance, with a shrinking workforce supporting a growing retired population. In the United States, the share of individuals aged 65 and older increased from 11 percent in 1980 to nearly 17 percent in 2024, and is projected to reach 22 percent by 2050 (U.S. Census Bureau 2024). Japan represents an even more advanced stage of aging, with almost 30 percent of its population now aged 65+, the highest proportion globally (OECD 2024) (Figure 3.3).

These demographic shifts carry substantial fiscal and macroeconomic implications. Aging societies face expanding pension and health care obligations while the tax base supporting these systems grows more slowly or contracts. In the United States, Social Security and Medicare

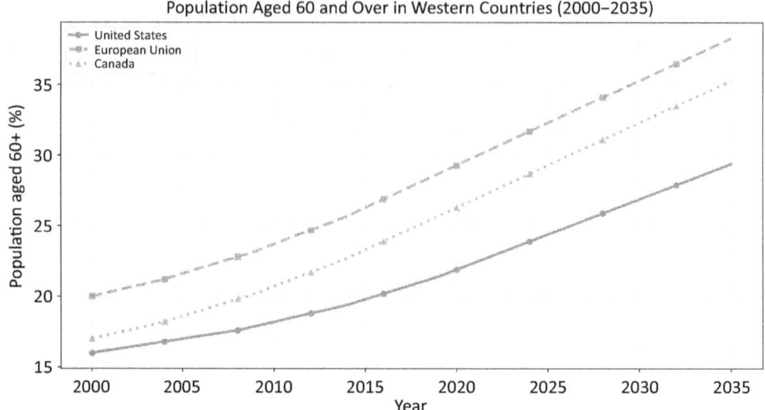

Figure 3.3 A comparison of aging populations in the United States, the European Union, and Canada

Source: Author's based on the United Nations reports.

already account for more than one-third of federal expenditures, and projections by the Congressional Budget Office (2024) indicate that age-related spending will continue to outpace economic growth. Across Europe, pension expenditures typically range from 12 to 15 percent of national income, with even higher levels observed in countries such as Italy and France (OECD 2024). As these commitments expand, governments face rising deficits, rising public debt, and diminished fiscal flexibility, raising concerns about the long-term sustainability of welfare-state arrangements.

From a growth perspective, population aging is commonly associated with slower economic expansion and weaker productivity dynamics. A declining labor force reduces potential output unless counterbalanced by higher immigration, automation, or significant gains in technological efficiency. Aging also reshapes consumption patterns. Older households tend to spend less on durable goods and more on health care, personal services, and housing. This reallocation of demand often favors sectors with lower measured productivity growth, thereby reinforcing structural constraints on overall economic performance. Demographic aging also influences global financial conditions. Older populations generally save less and display a stronger preference for safe assets, contributing, before the inflationary episode of the early 2020s, to a prolonged decline in real interest rates across advanced economies. As retirees draw down savings and institutional investors seek long-duration, low-risk instruments, capital markets adjust toward lower yields and heightened liquidity preferences (Blanchard 2019; Yeganeh 2024).

Financial institutions face distinct challenges in aging societies. Pension funds, insurance companies, and asset managers must increasingly align long-term liabilities with stable, income-generating assets. As life expectancy rises, payout periods lengthen, intensifying the demand for reliable returns over extended horizons. This dynamic has sustained strong global demand for sovereign bonds, particularly United States Treasuries and German government bonds, while also exposing institutions to valuation risks when interest rates increase. In response, financial innovation has expanded, with life-cycle funds, annuities, and longevity-linked instruments gaining prominence as mechanisms to manage extended retirement horizons.

For firms, population aging reshapes both labor supply and consumer demand. Labor shortages are becoming more visible in sectors such as health care, manufacturing, construction, and technology. To sustain output, companies increasingly rely on automation, AI, and robotics. Japan's leadership in industrial automation reflects a strategic response to its demographic constraints. Firms in the United States and Europe are similarly adapting workforce strategies by introducing flexible employment arrangements, retraining initiatives, and hybrid work models to retain older workers. What was once framed primarily as a social consideration has become an essential component of competitive strategy.

On the demand side, the expansion of the so-called silver economy is particularly significant. Older consumers constitute one of the fastest-growing and, in many cases, wealthiest demographic groups in advanced economies. Their expenditure patterns emphasize pharmaceuticals, medical devices, wellness services, financial planning, accessible transportation, and age-appropriate housing. OECD projections (2024) suggest that the global silver economy could surpass 15 trillion dollars by 2030. Firms that adapt to this structural shift by developing accessible products, health technologies, and independent living services are well-positioned to capture expanding market opportunities. The trend also creates attractive investment prospects in health care, real estate, biotechnology, elder care services, and digital health platforms.

The United States illustrates both the opportunities and vulnerabilities associated with demographic aging. Although its outlook is more favorable than that of Europe or Japan, largely due to immigration, fiscal pressures are intensifying as Social Security, Medicare, and health care costs grow faster than public revenues. The labor force participation rate among individuals aged 65 and older has nearly doubled since 1990, reflecting both evolving retirement norms and economic necessity (Bureau of Labor Statistics 2024). At the same time, health care expenditures are projected to approach 25 percent of GDP by 2050 (Centers for Medicare and Medicaid Services 2024). Japan, by contrast, illustrates the long-term macroeconomic consequences of deep and persistent aging, including population decline, deflationary pressures, ultralow interest rates, and the highest public debt-to-GDP ratio in the world, exceeding 250 percent.

Youth Bulges and Population Growth in Africa and South Asia

While advanced economies are increasingly constrained by population aging and demographic stagnation, regions such as Africa and South Asia are experiencing the opposite dynamic. Rapid population growth combined with expanding youth cohorts is transforming their economic and social landscapes. This shift carries significant developmental promise, but it also entails serious risks, depending on how effectively these societies educate, employ, and integrate young people into productive economic activity.

Youth bulges typically emerge when mortality rates decline while fertility remains high, producing population structures heavily weighted toward individuals under 30. This pattern is particularly noticeable in Sub-Saharan Africa and South Asia, where fertility rates commonly range between three and five births per woman, far exceeding levels observed in Europe, East Asia, and North America (United Nations 2024). At the same time, improvements in nutrition, health care, and sanitation have sharply reduced infant and child mortality. The result is a rapidly growing young population with the potential to reshape global labor markets, consumption patterns, and economic trajectories.

United Nations projections indicate that Africa's population will double from approximately 1.4 billion in 2024 to nearly 2.8 billion by 2050, making it the world's fastest-growing region (United Nations 2024). South Asia, which includes India, Pakistan, Bangladesh, Nepal, and Sri Lanka, will remain the world's largest population center. By mid-century, Africa and South Asia together are expected to account for nearly half of the global population under the age of 25. This demographic structure creates the possibility of a demographic dividend, a period during which a large working-age population can accelerate economic growth through higher productivity, increased savings, and expanded investment. However, this dividend materializes only when job creation, education, and institutional capacity keep pace with demographic change.

The economic potential associated with these youth cohorts is substantial. The demographic dividend is supported by historical experience in East Asia, where countries such as South Korea, Taiwan, and Singapore successfully transformed favorable age structures into rapid industrialization and technological advancement (Bloom et al. 2015). Africa and South Asia now face a comparable turning point. In India, more than 65 percent of the population is under the age of 35, and the labor force grows by roughly 12 million workers each year, reinforcing ambitions to become a global hub for manufacturing and digital services (World Bank 2023). In Sub-Saharan Africa, where the median age is just 19 and over 60 percent of the population is under 25, the region is projected to have the largest labor force in the world by 2050, surpassing both China and India (African Development Bank 2023) (Figure 3.4).

Yet demographic opportunity does not guarantee economic success. Without adequate education systems, dynamic labor markets, and effective governance, youth bulges can instead generate unemployment, social unrest, and political instability. In many countries across Africa and South Asia, youth unemployment rates exceed 30 percent. As Cincotta (2017) notes, societies characterized by large cohorts of unemployed or underemployed young men face elevated risks of conflict, radicalization, and authoritarian political responses. The Arab Spring illustrated how

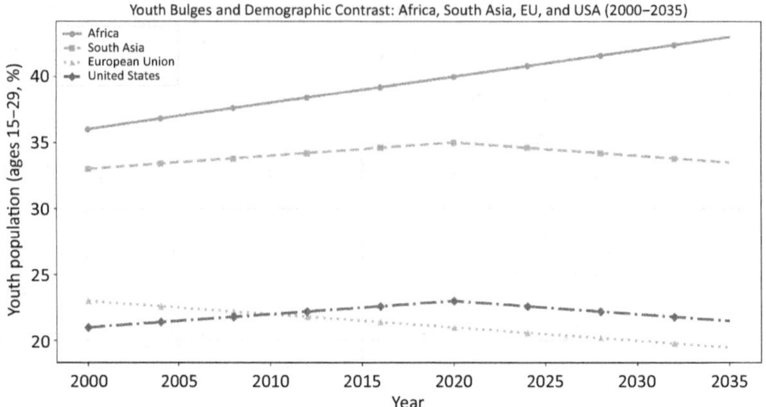

Figure 3.4 A comparison of young population in Africa, South Asia, the European Union, and the United States

Source: Author's calculations and visualization based on United Nations World Population Prospects and World Bank demographic indicators.

educated, yet economically marginalized, youth can become powerful agents of political disruption.

Structural economic constraints further complicate the situation. Many economies in Africa and South Asia remain heavily dependent on low-productivity agriculture and informal employment. In countries such as India, Pakistan, and Bangladesh, more than 80 percent of workers are employed in the informal sector, while subsistence farming continues to dominate large parts of Sub-Saharan Africa (World Bank 2023). Manufacturing growth has often been uneven and insufficient to absorb the millions of new labor market entrants each year. Education systems, meanwhile, frequently suffer from limited funding, uneven quality, and weak alignment with labor market needs. As a result, many young people enter adulthood without the technical, digital, or vocational skills demanded by an increasingly globalized, technology-intensive economy.

Rapid urbanization intensifies these pressures as cities across Africa and South Asia are expanding at unprecedented rates. United Nations estimates suggest that Africa's urban population will triple by 2050, with metropolitan areas such as Lagos, Kinshasa, and Nairobi each exceeding 20 million residents (United Nations 2024). South Asian megacities, including Dhaka, Karachi, and Mumbai, already face severe congestion, pollution, housing shortages, and infrastructure strain.

While urbanization can foster innovation and economic dynamism, poorly managed urban growth often exacerbates inequality, informality, and social fragmentation.

Despite these challenges, youth bulges carry significant implications for business and finance. Young populations constitute vast and growing markets for consumer goods, digital services, financial products, education, and health care. Africa's digital economy alone could reach over 700 billion dollars by 2050, driven by a technologically fluent generation and widespread mobile connectivity (World Bank 2023). Mobile payment systems such as M-Pesa in Kenya, along with the expanding fintech and start-up ecosystems in countries such as Nigeria, Ghana, and Rwanda, illustrate the capacity of young entrepreneurs to bypass traditional infrastructure constraints. In South Asia, rapid growth in digital payments, online education, and electronic commerce reflects high smartphone penetration and the expansion of a young middle class.

For multinational corporations, Africa and South Asia are increasingly attractive locations for manufacturing and service outsourcing, particularly as part of strategies to diversify supply chains beyond China. India and Bangladesh have already become central nodes in global manufacturing networks. However, persistent challenges in political stability, governance quality, energy supply, and regulatory uncertainty continue to limit the long-term investment potential.

Demographic dynamics in these regions also carry important geopolitical consequences. A young and expanding population can underpin future economic and military influence, as reflected in India's growing global role. Africa's demographic ascent is likely to strengthen its voice in international trade, climate negotiations, and technological adoption. At the same time, if economic opportunities fail to keep pace with demographic momentum, rising youth dissatisfaction may intensify migration pressures toward Europe and the Middle East, alter regional security dynamics, and strain global governance frameworks.

Currency Shifts and Dedollarization

The global monetary system, long anchored by the U.S. dollar, is undergoing a gradual yet meaningful transformation. This process, commonly described as dedollarization, refers to efforts by states to reduce their dependence on the dollar in trade settlement, financial transactions, and foreign exchange reserves. Although the dollar remains the dominant currency in global finance, recent geopolitical tensions, the expanded use of sanctions, technological innovation, and the growing economic weight of emerging markets have accelerated interest in alternative monetary arrangements. Together, these developments reflect deeper structural shifts in the world economy and point toward the emergence of a more multipolar financial order.

The centrality of the U.S. dollar is rooted in historical circumstances and institutional strength. Following the Second World War, the Bretton Woods Agreement of 1944 established the dollar as the core of the international monetary system. Pegged to gold and supported by fixed exchange rates, the system consolidated American economic leadership. Even after the collapse of the gold standard in 1971, the dollar retained its dominant role, supported by the size of the U.S. economy, the depth and liquidity of its financial markets, and sustained confidence in American political and legal institutions (Eichengreen 2011). Today, roughly 60 percent of global foreign exchange reserves, close to 80 percent of international trade invoicing, and nearly 90 percent of foreign exchange transactions involve the dollar (IMF 2024). This dominance grants the United States considerable advantages, including low borrowing costs, influence over global liquidity conditions, and the ability to deploy financial sanctions as a powerful instrument of foreign policy. At the same time, it exposes other economies to U.S. monetary policy cycles, interest rate shocks, and exchange rate volatility.

Momentum toward dedollarization has intensified in recent years, particularly following the expanded use of financial sanctions. The freezing of Russian central bank reserves and Russia's exclusion from the SWIFT payment network in 2022 highlighted the geopolitical risks associated with a heavy reliance on U.S.-based financial infrastructure. In response, many countries have accelerated efforts to diversify reserve holdings, increase gold accumulation, develop alternative payment systems, and settle trade in local or nondollar currencies (OECD 2024). At the same time, the reconfiguration of global trade patterns has reinforced these trends. As China, India, and other emerging economies account for a growing share of global production and trade, the gravitational center of the world economy is shifting. China and Russia now conduct most of their bilateral trade in yuan and rubles, while India has increasingly purchased Russian oil using rupees and UAE dirhams rather than dollars (World Bank 2023). These arrangements reflect not only political considerations but also the changing distribution of economic power.

Central bank behavior further illustrates the slow erosion of dollar dominance. According to the IMF (2024), the dollar's share of global foreign exchange reserves has declined from more than 70 percent in the late 1990s to around 58 percent in 2024, the lowest level in more than two decades. Over the same period, reserve holdings of euros, yuan, and particularly gold have increased. Regional financial cooperation has also gained momentum. The BRICS countries have expanded initiatives for local-currency settlement and openly discussed the possibility of creating a shared reserve asset. Institutions such as the Asian Infrastructure Investment Bank and payment systems like China's Cross-Border Interbank Payment System (CIPS) provide alternatives that reduce dependence on U.S.-dominated financial networks.

Among existing alternatives, the euro remains the most significant, accounting for roughly one-fifth of global reserves. The Chinese yuan, while still limited by capital controls and lower liquidity, has grown steadily in international usage. It is now the fourth-most-used currency in global payments and accounts for approximately 5 percent of global foreign exchange reserves (SWIFT 2024). China's development of CIPS has facilitated yuan-based trade settlements, while the gradual rollout of the digital yuan represents an additional step toward strengthening its international monetary infrastructure.

Central bank digital currencies are further reshaping the monetary landscape. Dozens of countries, including India, Nigeria, and eurozone members, are developing or piloting digital currencies to improve payment efficiency and reduce reliance on existing dollar-centric systems. These initiatives promise faster, cheaper cross-border transactions while enhancing monetary sovereignty. At the same time, gold has experienced a strategic resurgence. Central banks in China, India, Turkey, and several emerging economies have become significant buyers, reinforcing gold's role as a hedge against currency risk and geopolitical uncertainty (World Gold Council 2024).

The economic consequences of dedollarization are complex and uneven. A reduced reliance on the dollar could gradually weaken U.S. financial dominance and erode what Valéry Giscard d'Estaing famously termed America's "exorbitant privilege" (Figure 3.5). For emerging markets, a more diversified monetary system may offer greater resilience by reducing exposure to abrupt U.S. monetary tightening. The interest rate hikes of 2022 and 2023, for example, triggered capital outflows, currency depreciation, and debt stress across many developing economies. Greater use of local currencies in trade and finance could strengthen regional integration and enhance financial autonomy. At the same time, replicating the trust, liquidity, and institutional depth of U.S. financial markets remains extremely difficult. A rapid or disorderly move away from the dollar could fragment global liquidity, raise transaction costs, and increase exchange rate volatility. For businesses and investors, the gradual emergence of monetary multipolarity introduces both risks and opportunities. Firms operating across multiple currency blocs will need more sophisticated hedging strategies and greater sensitivity to regional monetary dynamics. At the same time, expanded use of the euro, yuan, and digital currencies may reduce transaction costs in regional trade, particularly in Asia, the Middle East, and Africa. Investors may also find new opportunities

***Figure 3.5** Valéry Giscard d'Estaing, the former French president and finance minister, who coined the phrase "exorbitant privilege" referring to the unique advantages the United States derives from the dollar's role as the world's dominant reserve, invoicing, and settlement currency.*

in yuan-denominated assets, digital currency ecosystems, and alternative payment infrastructures.

Political Populism and Policy Volatility

The 21st century has seen a resurgence of political populism across diverse regions, including the United States, Europe, Latin America, Asia, and Africa. Broadly defined as appealing to "the people" in opposition to established elites and institutions, populism has reshaped political systems, public discourse, and the global business environment. This new political climate is marked by heightened uncertainty, regulatory instability, and abrupt policy reversals that undermine the predictability on which markets and corporations depend. Economic decision making is increasingly shaped by nationalist sentiment, political symbolism, and short-term electoral considerations rather than long-term strategy or institutional continuity.

Populism is deeply rooted in dissatisfaction with the uneven outcomes of globalization. Large segments of society perceive that the liberal economic order has disproportionately benefited multinational corporations and highly educated elites while eroding wages, employment security, and local cultural cohesion. As Rodrik (2018) argues, populism represents a backlash against global economic integration, driven by the perception that distant and unaccountable international institutions have weakened national sovereignty. Populist leaders mobilize these grievances by promising to restore control over borders, industries, and national decision making.

While such narratives often resonate with voters, they often translate into volatile, inconsistent economic policies. Populist governments tend to emphasize visible, immediate outcomes over sustainable, long-term reforms. This approach often involves challenging central banks' independence, renegotiating trade agreements, imposing protectionist measures, or expanding public spending ahead of elections. These actions disrupt the stable regulatory frameworks that businesses rely upon. Empirical evidence suggests tangible economic costs. Populist administrations are associated with lower investment levels, weaker productivity growth, and negative stock market reactions, reflecting heightened uncertainty and diminished confidence (Funke et al. 2020).

At the heart of the populist challenge lies a fundamental tension between democratic legitimacy and institutional stability. Populist leaders frequently claim to embody the authentic will of the people, portraying independent institutions such as courts, central banks, and regulatory agencies as obstacles to popular sovereignty. In practice, this framing often leads to the politicization and weakening of institutions designed to ensure policy continuity and credibility. Institutional erosion under populist rule is closely associated with more unpredictable policy environments and poorer governance outcomes (Guriev and Papaioannou 2020).

For firms, these dynamics translate into rising policy volatility, characterized by frequent and abrupt changes in regulations, taxation, labor laws, environmental standards, and trade rules. Such unpredictability complicates long-term planning, discourages capital investment, and increases financing costs. According to McKinsey (2023), more than 70 percent of global executives now identify political and regulatory unpredictability as a major external risk, highlighting widespread concern about the durability of the global business environment.

One of the most visible economic consequences of populism is the fragmentation of global trade. Populist governments often adopt protectionist policies such as tariffs, local content requirements, and industrial subsidies to appeal to domestic constituencies. Although politically expedient, these measures disrupt global supply chains and raise production costs. Baldwin (2022) characterizes the current phase of globalization as increasingly regionalized, driven less by efficiency and more by geopolitical alignment and resilience concerns. The U.S.–China trade conflict and the United Kingdom's withdrawal from the European Union illustrate how populist-driven decisions compel firms to reconfigure supply chains, diversify sourcing, and relocate production toward politically aligned jurisdictions. These adjustments reduce efficiency and heighten operational risk, particularly in sectors dependent on complex international inputs, including electronics, automotive manufacturing, and pharmaceuticals (World Bank 2023).

Populist policy cycles also contribute to financial instability. Governments under populist pressure often pursue expansionary fiscal policies or pressure monetary authorities to keep interest rates low, increasing the risk of inflation and currency depreciation. Populist regimes, especially in emerging markets, are associated with higher inflation rates and greater macroeconomic volatility. Financial markets tend to react swiftly to such developments. Funke et al. (2020) document that populist electoral victories are commonly followed by stock market declines and reduced foreign investment inflows, as investors demand higher risk premiums amid policy uncertainty.

Regulatory inconsistency further complicates corporate strategy. Industries may be alternately promoted or targeted depending on shifting political narratives. Energy policy, for instance, may swing between supporting fossil fuels to protect domestic employment and aggressively promoting renewable energy in response to environmental pressure. Technology firms may be celebrated as national champions at one moment and criticized for misinformation or data practices the next. This volatility forces companies to strengthen their political risk management capabilities, engage more actively with policymakers, and adopt flexible operating models. Firms with robust political risk frameworks outperform competitors in volatile environments by anticipating and adapting to policy shifts more effectively (Deloitte 2024).

Populism also influences global capital flows. The erosion of institutional credibility and policy consistency reduces the attractiveness of populist governed countries to investors. The IMF (2024) reports that foreign direct investment tends to decline during populist administrations, as capital gravitates toward jurisdictions with stricter rule of law and predictable governance. This pattern has contributed to the emergence of a governance risk premium, in which political stability and institutional quality weigh as heavily as economic fundamentals in investment decisions. As uncertainty increases, investors often seek haven assets such as gold, the U.S. dollar, and defensive equities (OECD 2024).

The Emergence of a Multipolar Global Order

The 21st century is witnessing a profound reconfiguration of global power. For much of the post–Cold War era, international relations were shaped by a unipolar structure dominated by the United States, whose military strength, technological leadership, and command over global financial institutions gave it unparalleled influence. Yet this unipolar moment is fading. Rising powers, including China, India, Brazil, Turkey, Indonesia, and regional blocs such as the African Union and the Gulf states, are asserting greater autonomy in global affairs. The resulting landscape is a multipolar global order: a system characterized by multiple centers of power, diverse governance models, and competing visions for global norms.

The roots of this transition lie in big structural changes in the world economy. One of the most significant is the redistribution of global economic power. In 1990, the G7 countries produced nearly two-thirds of global GDP; today, emerging economies contribute more than half of world output when measured by purchasing power parity (IMF 2024). China's rise has been the most dramatic: it is now the world's largest trading nation and the second-largest economy, with growing technological capabilities in AI, telecommunications, and renewable energy. India, meanwhile, is the fastest-growing major economy, with a young and expanding population that contrasts sharply with the demographic aging of Europe and Japan (World Bank 2023). Rising middle powers such as Indonesia, Mexico, and Nigeria are likewise shaping global production networks and investment flows.

The weakening dominance of Western-led global institutions is another driving force behind multipolarity. The post–World War II order anchored by institutions such as the United Nations, the International Monetary Fund (IMF), and the World Bank reflected the interests and influence of the United States and its allies. Emerging economies increasingly challenge the governance structures and perceived biases of these institutions. This shift has led to the creation of new or parallel frameworks such as the BRICS alliance, the Shanghai Cooperation Organization, and the Asian Infrastructure Investment Bank (AIIB). These institutions offer alternative channels for financing, development cooperation, and diplomatic coordination (Stuenkel 2016). Their growth marks a diversification of global governance and a gradual erosion of U.S.-centric institutional power.

Geopolitical realignments further reinforce the trend toward multipolarity. Strategic rivalry between the United States and China has become a defining feature of global politics. However, unlike the Cold War, today's world is not splitting into two coherent ideological blocs. Instead, middle powers increasingly pursue strategic autonomy, forming flexible partnerships rather than choosing sides. Countries such as India, Saudi Arabia, Türkiye, and Brazil cooperate with the United States, China, and Europe depending on issue-specific interests. This pragmatic, multivector diplomacy reduces the dominance of any single power and gives emerging states greater bargaining leverage in global affairs (Acharya 2018).

Multipolarity is also shaped by economic interdependence. Unlike earlier eras of geopolitical rivalry, today's major powers are deeply interconnected through trade, investment, supply chains, and technology. China remains a crucial market and manufacturing hub for Western firms, while Western capital markets remain essential for global finance. These interdependencies not only create incentives for cooperation but also strategic vulnerabilities. The weaponization of trade and technology, exemplified by the U.S.–China semiconductor conflict, European energy reorientation after Russia invades Ukraine, and competition over critical minerals, illustrates how economic ties can serve as instruments of geopolitical leverage.

The emergence of a multipolar order is also transforming global security dynamics. Regional powers are increasingly shaping conflict outcomes and security architectures. In the Middle East, Saudi Arabia, Iran, the UAE, and Türkiye pursue assertive foreign policies independent of U.S. preferences. In Africa, partnerships with China, Russia, and Gulf states provide alternatives to traditional Western influence. In Asia, nations navigate a complex balance between China's growing influence and U.S. security alliances. New multilateral security frameworks such as the Quad, AUKUS, and expanded BRICS cooperation reflect a security environment in which no single power can impose order and in which regional actors play decisive roles (Buzan and Wæver 2003).

The rise of multipolarity has significant implications for global governance and economic stability. On one hand, it encourages more inclusive decision making and allows nations outside the Western core to exert meaningful influence on global issues. It enables diverse development paths that reflect different cultural and institutional contexts ranging from China's state-led capitalism to India's digital governance innovations and Africa's youthful entrepreneurial ecosystems. Such pluralism can enhance resilience and creativity in addressing shared global challenges, including climate change, health crises, and digital transformation.

However, multipolarity also introduces new risks. Without a dominant stabilizing power, global coordination becomes more difficult, especially during crises. Divergent regulatory systems can fragment trade and technology networks. Competing geopolitical interests may fuel proxy conflicts, territorial disputes, and arms races. Climate governance, pandemic preparedness, and financial stability may suffer in a world where achieving consensus is harder. Moreover, the diffusion of digital and military technologies among rising states adds complexity to global risk management. Businesses and investors are already adapting to this new reality. Firms increasingly diversify supply chains, strengthen geopolitical risk assessment, and invest in emerging markets with growing consumer bases. Investors monitor currency realignments, new financial networks, and regional economic blocs. Agility, resilience, and political awareness have become essential components of corporate strategy in the multipolar era.

Deglobalization and Protectionism in the 21st Century

The early decades of the 21st century mark a turning point in the evolution of the global economy. After several decades of deepening integration characterized by free trade agreements, cross-border investment, global value chains, and liberalized financial flows, the world is now entering a period of deglobalization and rising protectionism. This shift does not represent the end of globalization but rather its reconfiguration. Driven by geopolitical tensions, economic nationalism, populist movements, and the vulnerabilities revealed by global crises, deglobalization reflects deeper transformations in the governance and distribution of global power (Rodrik 2018).

Deglobalization refers to the slowdown, stagnation, or partial reversal of cross-border flows of trade, investment, and information. Protectionism, at its core, encompasses tariffs, quotas, export controls, industrial subsidies, and localization requirements. These policies reflect growing skepticism toward open markets and a renewed emphasis on sovereignty, security, and national industrial strategy. While globalization once appeared as an inevitable outcome of technological progress, recent developments underscore its political contingency. Globalization expands or contracts according to state preferences and shifts in geopolitical power.

Several structural forces underpin the current wave of deglobalization. One of the most significant is geopolitical fragmentation. The rise of China and the intensifying strategic rivalry between Washington and Beijing have strained the foundations of the liberal economic order. The U.S.–China trade war, semiconductor export controls, and efforts to derisk supply chains demonstrate how geopolitical considerations increasingly shape economic policy (Baldwin 2022). Strategic industrial policies such as the U.S. CHIPS and Science Act, the Inflation Reduction Act, and the European Union Green Industrial Plan illustrate governments' efforts to secure technological leadership and reduce dependence on foreign suppliers.

Economic nationalism has also emerged as a powerful driver of deglobalization. Many citizens in advanced economies perceive that they have not benefited equitably from globalization. Wage stagnation, job offshoring, and deindustrialization have weakened public support for open markets. Populist leaders have capitalized on these grievances by arguing that globalization disproportionately benefits multinational corporations and economic elites. Consequently, protective trade measures have become politically attractive. The United Kingdom's withdrawal from the European Union, the United States' tariffs on steel, aluminum, and Chinese imports, and growing skepticism toward free trade agreements all reflect this shift (Funke et al. 2020).

The COVID-19 pandemic further accelerated deglobalization by exposing the fragility of global supply chains. Shortages of medical equipment, pharmaceuticals, and semiconductors highlighted the risks of relying on a limited number of foreign suppliers. Governments and firms responded by pursuing reshoring, nearshoring, and friend-shoring strategies to diversify production and enhance resilience. While these strategies improve security, they often reduce the efficiency that globalized production previously delivered. The pandemic highlighted the need to balance cost efficiency with economic security and redundancy.

Economic security has therefore become a central pillar of national strategies. States increasingly view control over critical sectors such as energy, food, semiconductors, and critical minerals as essential to sovereignty. Russia's invasion of Ukraine in 2022 intensified these concerns. Europe's rapid reduction of dependence on Russian gas, the imposition of financial sanctions, and the acceleration of clean energy investments illustrate how security considerations can override market logic. At the same time, competition over technological ecosystems, including AI, telecommunications, and electric vehicles, has strengthened protectionist impulses. Governments seek to build domestic industries, restrict foreign access to sensitive technologies, and safeguard strategic supply chains (Farrell and Newman 2019).

The rise of deglobalization is reshaping global value chains. During the era of hyperglobalization, production was fragmented across multiple countries to minimize costs. Today, firms increasingly prioritize resilience over efficiency. Supply chains are being reorganized around regional hubs such as North America, Europe, and East Asia, giving rise to what Baldwin (2019) describes as slowbalization, a moderated form of globalization characterized by slower trade growth and greater regional concentration. This shift reflects firms' efforts to mitigate geopolitical risk, manage transportation costs, and comply with evolving national regulations.

Protectionism also has significant implications for developing economies. For export-dependent countries, rising trade barriers pose new obstacles to industrialization and growth. Nations reliant on global markets for textiles, electronics, or agricultural goods face heightened vulnerability and reduced competitiveness. At the same time, deglobalization creates new opportunities. Firms seeking to diversify production away from China have increased investment in countries such as Vietnam, India, Mexico, and Indonesia, stimulating local manufacturing sectors and employment (OECD 2023). The relative winners of deglobalization will be those states capable of rapidly adapting regulations, infrastructure, and labor markets to attract and retain investment.

Financial globalization is also transforming. Cross-border capital flows have become more cautious due to geopolitical risk, higher interest rates, and supply chain uncertainty. In parallel, currency fragmentation, driven in part by efforts to reduce reliance on the U.S. dollar, is reshaping global finance. Local currency trade settlements and regional payment systems are gaining importance, contributing to a more decentralized and politically differentiated financial architecture (IMF 2024). While global financial integration is not collapsing, it is becoming more segmented and strategic.

Deglobalization and protectionism present both opportunities and risks. Greater economic diversification and strategic autonomy can enhance national resilience. Industrial policies may foster innovation, job creation, and technological upgrading. However, the costs are substantial. Protectionist measures raise prices, reduce the gains from comparative advantage, slow economic growth, and risk triggering retaliatory trade conflicts. Historical experience shows that widespread protectionism, such as during the 1930s, can intensify geopolitical tensions and undermine global economic cooperation (Irwin 2017).

References

Acharya, A. 2018. *The End of the American World Order*. Polity Press.

African Development Bank. 2023. *African Economic Outlook 2023: Mobilizing Private Sector Financing for Climate and Growth*. Abidjan: AfDB.

Baldwin, R. 2022. *The Great Convergence Revisited: Globalization in a Fragmenting World*. Harvard University Press.

Blanchard, O. 2019. "Public Debt and Low Interest Rates." *American Economic Review* 109, no. 4, pp. 1197–1229.

Bloom, D.E., Canning, D., and Fink, G. 2015. "Implications of Population Change for Economic Growth." *Oxford Review of Economic Policy* 26, no. 4, pp. 583–612.

Bureau of Labor Statistics (BLS). 2023. *Employment, Hours, and Earnings from the Current Employment Statistics Survey*. Washington, DC: U.S. Department of Labor.

Buzan, B., and Wæver, O. 2003. *Regions and Powers: The Structure of International Security*. Cambridge University Press.

Cecchetti, S., Mohanty, M., and Zampolli, F. 2011. The Real Effects of Debt. Bank for International Settlements Working Paper No. 352.

Centers for Medicare & Medicaid Services (CMS). 2024. *National Health Expenditure Projections 2023–2050*. Baltimore,

Cincotta, R. 2017. *Youth Bulge: A Demographic Dividend or a Demographic Bomb in Developing Countries?*

Congressional Budget Office (CBO). 2024. *The Budget and Economic Outlook: 2024 to 2034*. U.S. Government Publishing Office.

Congressional Budget Office (CBO). 2024. *The Budget and Economic Outlook: 2024–2034*. Washington, DC.

Deloitte. 2024. *Global Business Risk Outlook: Political Volatility and Corporate Resilience*. London: Deloitte Insights.

Farrell, H., and Newman, A.L. 2019. "Weaponized Interdependence: How Global Economic Networks Shape State Coercion." *International Security* 44, no. 1, pp. 42–79.

Funke, M., Schularick, M., and Trebesch, C. 2020. "Populist Leaders and the Economy." *Journal of Economic Perspectives* 34, no. 3, pp. 150–176.

Guriev, S., and Papaioannou, E. 2020. *Populism and the Political Economy of Macroeconomic Policy*. Centre for Economic Policy Research.

IMF. 2024. World Economic Outlook.

Irwin, D. 2017. *Clashing over Commerce: A History of U.S. Trade Policy.* University of Chicago Press.

Krugman, P. 2020. *Arguing with Zombies: Economics, Politics, and the Fight for a Better Future*. W.W. Norton.

McKinsey & Company. 2023. *Geopolitical Risk and Corporate Strategy 2023 Report*. New York: McKinsey Global Institute.

Naughton, B. 2021. *The Rise of China's Industrial Policy*. Hoover Institution Press.

Obstfeld, M., and Rogoff, K. 2009. "Global Imbalances and the Financial Crisis." *Brookings Papers on Economic Activity* 1, pp. 67–123.

Obstfeld Eichengreen, B. 2011. *Exorbitant Privilege: The Rise and Fall of the Dollar and the Future of the International Monetary System*. Oxford University Press.

(OECD). 2023. *Under Pressure: The Squeezed Middle Class*. Paris: OECD Publishing.

(OECD). 2024. *Global Financial Stability and Currency Fragmentation*. Paris: OECD Publishing. Organisation for Economic Cooperation and Development

Reinhart, C.M., and Rogoff, K.S. 2010. "Growth in a Time of Debt." *American Economic Review* 100, no. 2, pp. 573–578.

Reinhart, C.M., and Rogoff, K.S. 2011. *This Time Is Different: Eight Centuries of Financial Folly*. Princeton University Press.

Rodrik, D. 2018. "Populism and the Economics of Globalization." *Journal of International Business Policy* 1, no. 1, pp. 12–33.

Stiglitz, J.E. 2019. *People, Power, and Profits: Progressive Capitalism for an Age of Discontent*. W. W. Norton & Company.

Stuenkel, O. 2016. *Post-Western World: How Emerging Powers Are Remaking Global Order*. Polity Press.

SWIFT. 2024. *RMB Tracker: Monthly Reporting and Statistics on the Use of the Chinese Yuan*. Brussels: SWIFT Institute.

U.S. Census Bureau. 2024. *An Aging Nation: The Older Population in the United States*. Washington, DC.

U.S. Department of the Treasury. 2024. *Monthly Statement of the Public Debt of the United States*. Washington, DC.

United Nations. 2024. "World Population Prospects: 2024 Revision."

World Bank. 2023. "Global Economic Prospects."

World Bank. 2023. *Global Economic Prospects: Fragmentation and the Future of Global Value Chains*. Washington, DC: World Bank.

World Gold Council. 2024. *Gold Demand Trends Report 2024*. London: World Gold Council.

Yeganeh, H. 2024. "Conceptualizing the Patterns of Change in Cultural Values: The Paradoxical Effects of Modernization, Demographics, and Globalization." *Social Sciences* 13, no. 9, pp. 439.

CHAPTER 4

The Woke Capitalism

The Rise of Wokeism

The term "woke" has undergone a significant transformation from its origins in African American Vernacular English to its current status as a globally recognized and politically charged label. Initially, it referred to an awakened state of social and political consciousness, particularly regarding racial injustice and inequality (Shastry 2023; Sobande 2019). In the 20th century, being "woke" meant remaining alert to systemic oppression, racial discrimination, and the need for collective vigilance against social injustice. Popular definitions emphasized awareness of community issues, while the phrase "stay woke" encouraged continued attentiveness to hidden power structures, especially white supremacy and institutionalized violence. Over time, however, the term's meaning expanded in scope and application, reflecting shifting cultural contexts and ideological debates.

In contemporary usage, wokeism refers to a set of beliefs, practices, and attitudes centered on heightened sensitivity to social justice concerns, particularly those involving identity politics, power relations, and structural inequality. It extends beyond individual awareness toward collective activism that seeks to challenge norms, institutions, and cultural narratives perceived as sustaining discrimination. A "woke" individual is not merely informed but actively engaged in advocacy through political participation, digital activism, or institutional reform. As such, wokeism combines an ethical commitment to justice with a performative dimension, as individuals and organizations publicly signal moral alignment with progressive causes.

Despite its normative aspirations, the concept of "woke" has become deeply contested. In political and popular discourse, it functions as a double-edged term that can signify moral awareness while also serving as a pejorative label. Critics frequently accuse wokeism of intolerance toward dissent, ideological rigidity, and excessive intrusion into language, education, art, and personal conduct. As Fan (2019) and Shastry (2023) argue, the fragmentation of its meaning has contributed to increasing polarization. Some interpret wokeism as a necessary moral awakening, while others regard it as a new form of cultural dogmatism. This tension produces a semantic paradox in which "woke" simultaneously represents ethical consciousness and ideological excess.

As a cultural movement, wokeism has become embedded within the social, economic, and institutional structures of Western societies. It reflects the cumulative legacy of civil rights struggles, feminist movements, LGBTQ+ advocacy, and anticolonial thought, now refracted through the conditions of digital communication and global interconnectedness in the 21st century. In its contemporary form, wokeism operates not only as an individual disposition but also as an organizational and cultural framework. Government agencies, corporations, educational institutions, military organizations, and nongovernmental organizations have increasingly institutionalized woke principles through diversity, equity, and inclusion (DEI) initiatives (Foss and Klein 2023; Wright 2023). These principles are translated into corporate policies, recruitment practices, branding strategies, and public communication designed to signal social awareness and moral responsibility.

The diffusion of wokeism across major industries such as technology, entertainment, media, and retail illustrates both its cultural resonance and its economic utility. Technology firms have promoted diversity initiatives and supported racial justice organizations. Entertainment companies and streaming platforms have revised content to reflect inclusive values. At the same time, consumer brands display LGBTQ+ symbols during Pride Month or publicly endorse movements such as Black Lives Matter. This convergence of moral activism and market strategy has given rise to the concept of "woke capitalism" (Davies and MacRae 2023). In this model, corporations incorporate progressive ideals into business practices, often leveraging social causes to strengthen brand identity and consumer loyalty. Social media amplifies this process by enabling companies to project moral stances instantly and globally, converting ethical positioning into symbolic and reputational capital (Figure 4.1).

Figure 4.1 In its different forms, wokeism has been rising in the past decade

The visibility of wokeism in public debate is closely linked to global social movements. The resurgence of the Black Lives Matter movement in 2020 exemplified the emotional and moral intensity of contemporary activism (Butterworth 2021; Kendi 2023). It elevated antiracism to the center of global discourse and intensified debates around privilege, systemic bias, and representation. At the same time, feminist and LGBTQ+ movements expanded identity-based advocacy by emphasizing intersectionality as a framework for understanding overlapping forms of oppression. These developments have generated both meaningful progress and renewed cultural conflict, particularly around freedom of expression, artistic autonomy, and institutional neutrality. Conceptually, wokeism can be understood as both a moral awakening and a form of sociopolitical reordering. It embodies modernity's reflexive impulse to expose hidden hierarchies and extend recognition to marginalized groups. Yet, it also risks evolving into a quasi-religious belief system characterized by moral absolutes, symbolic rituals, and strict norms of speech and behavior (Rozado 2023; Rozado et al. 2023). In this sense, wokeism encapsulates a central paradox of modern progress.

Theoretical Foundations of Wokeism

Wokeism draws its coherence from a shared intellectual stance that privileges critical awareness, social justice, and the lived experiences of marginalized groups. Its theoretical foundations are deeply rooted in Critical Theory, Intersectionality, Postcolonialism, Critical Race Theory, Feminist Theory, and Queer Theory, each contributing distinct yet complementary insights into how power operates across social, cultural, and institutional domains.

At the core of wokeism lies Critical Theory, an intellectual tradition that emerged from the Frankfurt School in the early 20th century. Thinkers such as Max Horkheimer, Theodor Adorno, and Herbert Marcuse rejected purely positivist approaches to social analysis, arguing instead that Theory should not merely interpret the world but actively seek to transform it (Honneth et al. 2018; Thompson 2017). Critical Theory examines how dominant ideologies, cultural norms, and institutional arrangements reproduce inequality and legitimize domination. This orientation aligns closely with wokeism's normative commitment to social emancipation and its skepticism toward claims of neutrality, objectivity, or value-free knowledge. From this perspective, power is not confined to overt coercion. Still, it is embedded in language, culture, education, and everyday practices, making critical consciousness a prerequisite for social change (Wright 2023).

Intersectionality further deepens wokeism's analytical framework by emphasizing the interconnected nature of social identities and systems of oppression. Developed by Kimberlé Crenshaw, intersectionality challenges single-axis analyses of inequality by demonstrating how race, gender, class, sexuality, and other social categories interact to shape lived experiences in complex and nonadditive ways (Crenshaw 2013). Within woke discourse, intersectionality functions as both a diagnostic and ethical tool, highlighting how policies or social movements that address one dimension of inequality may inadvertently marginalize those situated at multiple intersections. By foregrounding these compounded experiences, intersectionality reinforces wokeism's insistence on inclusivity and its critique of universalist narratives that obscure structural differences.

Postcolonial Theory contributes a global and historical dimension to wokeism by interrogating the enduring legacies of colonialism, imperialism, and Eurocentrism. Postcolonial scholars argue that colonial power did not end with formal decolonization but persists through cultural hierarchies, epistemic dominance, and development paradigms that privilege Western norms and knowledge systems (Ashcroft et al. 2013). Woke perspectives draw on these insights to challenge dominant narratives in education, media, and international relations, emphasizing how language and representation continue to marginalize non-Western voices. This critique extends to global capitalism and development discourse, which are often portrayed as neutral or progressive while reproducing asymmetrical power relations rooted in colonial histories.

Critical Race Theory occupies a central place within the theoretical architecture of wokeism, particularly in its analysis of race and systemic inequality. Emerging from legal scholarship in the late 20th century, Critical Race Theory argues that racism is not an aberration but a structural feature of modern societies, embedded in legal systems, institutions, and social norms (Crenshaw et al. 1995; Delgado and Stefancic 2000).

It challenges colorblind ideologies that claim to transcend race while ignoring historical injustices and persistent disparities. A key contribution of Critical Race Theory is its conceptualization of whiteness as a form of social capital that confers material and symbolic advantages. Wokeism adopts this framework to critique both overt and subtle forms of racism, including microaggressions, and to justify activist interventions aimed at institutional reform.

Feminist Theory further informs wokeism by contesting naturalized assumptions about gender and power. Feminist scholars argue that gender is not a fixed biological essence but a socially constructed category shaped by cultural norms, institutional practices, and historical contexts (Alcoff 1996; Donovan 2012). By exposing patriarchy as a structural system rather than a collection of individual attitudes, Feminist Theory aligns with wokeism's systemic understanding of inequality. It also broadens the scope of critique to include sexuality, reproductive rights, and the regulation of bodies, while challenging heteronormative assumptions that marginalize nonconforming identities.

Queer Theory extends this critique by destabilizing binary categories of gender and sexuality altogether. Emerging in the late 20th century, Queer Theory rejects fixed identity classifications and emphasizes the fluid, performative, and socially constructed nature of sexual and gender identities (Jagose 2009; Sullivan 2003). Central to queer analysis is the critique of heteronormativity, understood as a regime of power that normalizes heterosexuality while rendering other identities deviant or invisible. Wokeism incorporates these insights to advocate for inclusivity and to question the taken-for-granted norms governing intimacy, identity, and social recognition (Figure 4.2).

Wokeism and the Moralization of Capitalism

Once defined primarily by efficiency, competition, and profit maximization, capitalism increasingly presents itself as a moral and socially conscious system. Corporations now claim to serve not only shareholders but also society, humanity, and the environment. This shift, often described as the moralization of capitalism, reflects a deliberate effort to recast business strategy in ethical terms, transforming the pursuit of profit into

Figure 4.2 Judith Butler argues that gender is not an inner essence but a social construct created through repeated, stylized actions, which they call gender performativity

an expression of social responsibility and virtue (Hanlon 2018; Wright 2023). Through ideas such as stakeholder capitalism, environmental, social, and governance investing, and purpose-driven leadership, capitalism seeks to reconcile economic gain with moral legitimacy, allowing firms to portray themselves as engines of both prosperity and progress.

Historically, capitalism was grounded in the logic of accumulation and profit. Milton Friedman's (1970) assertion that the social responsibility of business is to increase its earnings shaped corporate thinking for decades and reinforced the idea that ethics lie outside the domain of market activity. In this view, moral responsibility belonged to governments and individuals, not corporations. Over time, however, a series of structural crises challenged this narrow conception. Rising inequality, environmental degradation, financial instability, and declining trust in institutions placed growing pressure on firms to justify their social role. In response, corporations began to redefine themselves as ethically responsible actors. Capitalism has entered a moral economy in which ethical narratives and moral commitments have become central to sustaining legitimacy (Hanlon 2018). Corporate mission statements now emphasize inclusion, sustainability, and human rights, while companies such as Unilever and Microsoft position themselves as socially responsible, value-driven organizations. This transformation does not displace capitalism's foundations. Still, it reframes them, presenting profit generation as a morally defensible and socially beneficial activity.

One of the most visible expressions of this ethical reorientation is the rise of stakeholder capitalism. Promoted by institutions such as the World Economic Forum and by influential figures like Larry Fink of BlackRock, stakeholder capitalism challenges the idea that corporations exist solely to maximize shareholder value. Instead, it asserts that firms have obligations toward a broader set of stakeholders, including employees, consumers, communities, and the natural environment (Freeman 2010). In principle, this model embeds moral reasoning into corporate decision making and aligns business success with social well-being.

Closely connected to this development is the growth of environmental, social, and governance (ESG) investing. ESG frameworks assess corporate performance based on environmental impact, social responsibility, and governance standards, and have become highly influential in global financial markets. Companies with firm ESG profiles are increasingly viewed as more resilient, trustworthy, and forward-looking, attracting both investors and consumers (Eccles and Klimenko 2019). Yet critics argue that ESG often functions more as a reputational device than as a catalyst for meaningful structural change. It represents the moralization of finance itself, converting ethical considerations into measurable and tradable indicators. Within this moral economy, responsibility becomes a currency of legitimacy, while virtue is commodified through ratings, reports, and certifications.

Another key dimension of capitalism's moral turn is the rise of purpose-driven leadership. Corporate leaders increasingly present themselves as moral entrepreneurs who are motivated not only by financial performance but also by social purpose and collective welfare (Hollensbe et al. 2014). Leadership discourse now emphasizes empathy, authenticity, and ethical responsibility. This model reimagines the corporation as a socially enlightened institution guided by ethically committed leaders. Yet, as Hanlon (2018) observes, this moral entrepreneurship also serves a strategic role. It strengthens corporate legitimacy, reassures investors, and humanizes the image of capitalism without necessarily altering its underlying structures of power and inequality. Ethics thus becomes less a challenge to capitalism than a resource for its renewal, functioning as a competitive advantage in a marketplace shaped by trust, reputation, and public perception.

The Institutionalization of Virtue

We are currently witnessing the institutionalization and performance of virtue, a process through which moral discourse becomes embedded in corporate structures and communication systems. In many cases, this moral language serves symbolic and reputational functions rather than producing meaningful reform. Diversity initiatives, public statements, and social media campaigns increasingly transform morality into an administrative and aesthetic exercise, a form of corporate theater that manages public perception while leaving underlying hierarchies largely intact (Banet Weiser 2022; Fleming and Sturdy 2023).

The most visible manifestation of this process is the rise of DEI programs. Originally conceived as tools to address systemic workplace inequality, DEI initiatives have evolved into a global corporate standard. They now operate as formalized systems of policies, training modules, and reporting mechanisms that allow organizations to project ethical responsibility. Large corporations appoint chief diversity officers, conduct unconscious bias workshops, and publish annual diversity reports highlighting demographic indicators. While these practices often signal moral awareness, they have also become highly bureaucratic and procedural. Diversity functions as a form of institutional self-description, enabling organizations to claim moral virtue without confronting the deeper power relations that sustain inequality (Ahmed 2012). Inclusion becomes a ritual of compliance, focused on documenting commitment rather than redistributing authority or resources.

In many cases, DEI initiatives function more as tools of reputation management than as instruments of social transformation. They provide visible markers of ethical engagement while leaving wage structures, decision-making hierarchies, and organizational power relations essentially unchanged. Thus, diversity training often produces limited effects, as it targets individual attitudes rather than institutional mechanisms of exclusion (Noon 2020). What emerges is virtue management, the conversion of morality into a measurable and manageable component of corporate performance (Fleming and Sturdy 2023). Virtue becomes an administrative category, tracked and reported alongside financial indicators. Ethics is no longer treated as a normative aspiration but as an operational requirement.

Closely connected to this bureaucratic moralism is the phenomenon of wokewashing, the strategic use of progressive language and imagery to signal moral alignment without enacting substantive change. Similar to environmental greenwashing, wokewashing allows firms to associate themselves rhetorically with social justice causes while maintaining economic and political practices that reproduce inequality (Vredenburg et al. 2020). Corporations regularly issue statements supporting movements such as MeToo, Black Lives Matter, or Pride. Yet, these symbolic gestures often fail to translate into internal reforms. A company may celebrate Pride Month through inclusive branding while supporting political actors who oppose LGBTQ rights, or it may issue statements on racial justice while sustaining discriminatory labor practices.

Corporations present themselves as benevolent reformers while preserving their power and profitability (Giridharadas 2018). The display of virtue becomes a mechanism of legitimization, signaling that capitalism is morally aware and capable of self-correction. Corporate morality thus operates as a spectacle, a public performance designed to meet moral expectations without challenging the underlying logic of market dominance. The result is a culture of symbolic commitment, in which empathy, inclusion, and justice are simulated through communication strategies rather than embedded in institutional change.

This performance of virtue is intensified by the digital environment in which corporations now operate. Contemporary organizations exist under constant public scrutiny and must respond rapidly to online approval or condemnation. Social media has created a new form of moral accountability that is immediate, reactive, and often superficial. Corporations issue statements, apologies, or pledges within hours of public criticism, guided less by ethical deliberation than by public relations strategy and data analytics (Coombs and Holladay 2021).

Within this environment, morality is increasingly shaped by algorithms. What Wright (2023) describes as algorithmic morality refers to the way ethical behavior is defined and evaluated through online visibility, trending hashtags, and the viral circulation of outrage. Corporate virtue is measured less by the depth of reform than by its digital presence. The logic of the attention economy rewards symbolic gestures such as statements, hashtags, and inclusive advertisements rather than slow and difficult structural change. Moral credibility becomes quantified through likes, shares, and engagement metrics. The more visible the expression of solidarity or contrition, the more ethical the corporation appears.

This digital responsiveness transforms corporate ethics into crisis management. Moral gestures are deployed as protective shields against reputational risk, with social media serving simultaneously as a stage and a feedback mechanism. Corporations appear responsive and empathetic, yet their actions are often tactical rather than principled. The structure of online communication privileges speed and spectacle over reflection and accountability. What emerges is a form of moral automation, in which empathy and virtue are learned behaviors embedded within brand strategy.

Identity-Based Branding and Representation

In contemporary marketing, identity has become one of the most powerful symbolic resources that firms can mobilize. Brands no longer compete only on product features or price but increasingly on cultural meaning and social resonance. This shift reflects broader changes in consumer culture, in which individuals use brands to express who they are and how they wish to be seen. Brands function as cultural intermediaries that produce narratives helping individuals construct and communicate their sense of self, particularly as traditional anchors of identity such as religion, class, and community lose some of their structuring influence (Holt 2002). As these conventional sources weaken, brands increasingly fill the symbolic space they leave behind, shaping identity formation within market settings.

Identity-based branding builds on the assumption that consumption is inherently expressive. Individuals incorporate objects and brands into their extended selves, transforming consumption choices into performances of identity. In response, companies have embedded categories such as race, gender, sexuality, and ethnicity into their advertising narratives.

Representation thus becomes both a marketing technique and a cultural statement, allowing firms to present themselves as socially attentive and morally progressive while appealing to identity-conscious consumers.

One prominent expression of this development is brand activism, in which companies publicly align themselves with social causes such as racial justice, LGBTQ rights, environmental protection, or gender equality. Brand activism refers to corporate engagement with social and political issues that extends beyond traditional corporate social responsibility and often involves explicit value-based positioning (Kotler and Sarkar 2018). Whereas earlier marketing strategies tended to avoid politics, firms now use activism to differentiate themselves in crowded and obvious digital markets. When perceived as credible, such activism can enhance brand authenticity and strengthen emotional bonds with consumers who share similar values (Nath and Dahlen 2023).

Diverse representation in advertising plays a central role in this strategy. On one level, representation reflects wider cultural movements toward inclusion and recognition. On another, it functions as a commercial tool designed to attract consumers who are attentive to identity and social values. Inclusive branding enables firms to accumulate reputational capital by appearing socially responsible and morally engaged (Vredenburg et al. 2020). In this sense, representation becomes an intangible asset, contributing to an economic system in which symbolic and intangible value often outweighs physical production (Haskel and Westlake 2018).

Representation is not merely descriptive but performative. By showcasing diverse identities, brands communicate a particular worldview and invite consumers to align themselves with it. Purchasing a product is framed as participation in a broader project of recognition and moral affirmation. This dynamic reflects how brand culture merges market logic with identity politics, transforming visibility, empowerment, and recognition into commodified experiences (Banet-Weiser 2018).

At the same time, the transformation of identity into a marketing resource raises concerns about commodification. When identities are instrumentalized for commercial purposes, representation can become selective or superficial (Charles 2022). Identity-based branding also

Figure 4.3 Identity-based branding implies the adoption of ethical positions and acknowledging diverse social realities

intersects with political polarization. By aligning with specific identities and moral positions, brands implicitly distance or alienate other groups. Advertising messages become cultural and political signals that divide audiences along ideological lines. Moralized brand communication tends to intensify polarization, generating strong support among sympathetic consumers while provoking backlash from those who feel excluded or challenged (Eder et al. 2021). This dynamic has been visible in cases such as Nike's association with Colin Kaepernick and Bud Light's collaboration with transgender influencer Dylan Mulvaney, both of which triggered sharp political responses.

Digital media further amplifies these dynamics. Online platforms reward emotionally charged, identity-oriented content, encouraging brands to adopt moralized, affective messaging. Language infused with moral emotion spreads more rapidly on social media, giving firms strong incentives to frame communication around justice, empowerment, and recognition (Brady et al. 2017). Identity-based branding, therefore, aligns closely with the algorithmic logic of the digital economy, where visibility and engagement depend on emotional intensity (Figure 4.3).

The Political Economy of Moral Capitalism

Beneath the ethical rhetoric lies a fundamental contradiction: moral capitalism redistributes legitimacy without redistributing power or wealth. It reframes the market as a force for justice while leaving structural inequalities intact. By transforming political critique into moral compliance, moral capitalism redefines power through persuasion rather than coercion, absorbing dissent into its own ideological framework and replacing demands for redistribution with the aesthetics of virtue (Hanlon 2018; Davies and MacRae 2023).

One of the most consequential effects of this moral turn is the depoliticization of structural problems. Through the language of ethics and responsibility, capitalism converts systemic injustices into managerial challenges or matters of individual conduct. Issues such as income inequality, racial discrimination, and environmental degradation are reframed as questions of personal behavior, corporate citizenship, or responsible consumption. This dynamic reflects what Nancy Fraser identifies as progressive neoliberalism, an alliance between market liberalism and cultural progressivism that celebrates diversity and inclusion while sustaining deep economic inequality.

Within this framework, inclusion becomes a corporate slogan, sustainability becomes a branding strategy, and empowerment becomes a marketable product. Political questions are displaced by ethical narratives, shifting attention away from material redistribution toward symbolic recognition. Debates over wealth inequality give way to discussions of representation. At the same time, labor exploitation is obscured by awareness campaigns and corporate messaging. Diversity reports substitute for wage reform, and sustainability pledges stand in for binding environmental regulation. In this way, moral language conceals the underlying logic of accumulation.

This transformation illustrates capitalism's remarkable capacity to absorb critique. As Boltanski and Chiapello observed, capitalism renews itself by appropriating the moral and cultural criticisms directed against it. The social movements of the mid-20th century challenged capitalism for alienation, hierarchy, and inequality. Yet, these very values have since been repackaged as corporate virtues. Autonomy, creativity, authenticity, and justice now circulate as brand attributes rather than political demands. Moral capitalism thus functions as a mechanism of ideological containment, transforming opposition into participation and protest into marketing (Boltanski and Chiapello 2005).

Corporations now function not only as economic actors but also as symbolic figures in public life. They are praised by progressive audiences for their inclusive messaging and criticized by conservative groups for embracing what is often labeled "wokeness." This polarization has been especially visible in the United States, where brands such as Disney, Bud Light, and Target have faced public backlash for promoting diversity- or gender-related initiatives.

Despite its moral language, corporate activism is rarely driven solely by conviction. Behind each social campaign lies a logic of market segmentation. Progressive branding appeals to younger, urban, and socially liberal consumers who value ethical representation and symbolic inclusion. Corporate morality thus becomes a strategy of alignment rather than a vehicle for structural change.

The backlash against woke capitalism exposes the limits of this strategy. Many citizens perceive corporate virtue as moral arrogance imposed from above and disconnected from lived experience. Right-wing populist movements have mobilized this resentment, portraying corporate progressivism as evidence of elite moralism and cultural decay. Rather than fostering social cohesion, moral capitalism often deepens division by moralizing consumption and transforming civic disagreement into symbolic conflict.

At a deeper level, moral capitalism performs a powerful ideological function by monopolizing the language of virtue. By presenting itself as the ethical solution to global problems, capitalism preempts more radical forms of critique. To question corporate morality risks being dismissed as regressive or cynical. Moral capitalism thus establishes a form of moral monopoly in which the market is framed not only as economically necessary but also as ethically indispensable. The possibility of challenging capitalism itself is replaced by the assumption that it merely needs improvement, whether through greener practices, fairer branding, or more inclusive messaging (Wright 2023).

By integrating moral language into its own logic, capitalism transforms ethics into a mechanism of control. Critique is encouraged, but only within boundaries that pose no threat to existing structures. Activists and consumers are invited to express dissent through consumption choices, ethical purchases, and symbolic support rather than systemic confrontation. In this sense, morality becomes a tool for managing public sentiment. Capitalism now sells its own critique, packaging rebellion as lifestyle and justice as commodity (Žižek 2009).

The moral rhetoric of inclusion and sustainability thus serves two contradictory purposes. On the one hand, it humanizes capitalism by offering a vocabulary of compassion and responsibility. On the other hand, it neutralizes political resistance by converting structural demands into symbolic gestures. The same system that produces inequality legitimizes itself by claiming to oppose it. Apparent moral progress masks the persistence of material disparity. Capitalism's moral turn is therefore less an evolution toward justice than a reinvention of ideological defense, designed to preserve dominance in a morally conscious era.

The Paradoxes of Woke Capitalism

The central paradox of woke capitalism lies in its ability to perform critique while neutralizing it. By adopting the rhetoric of justice, capitalism preempts opposition and renders dissent harmless. Political conflict is transformed into corporate communication, and social reform is reframed as a branding strategy. This dynamic is evident in corporate engagement with movements such as Black Lives Matter, MeToo, or Pride. Public statements of solidarity, diversity campaigns, and symbolic gestures such as rainbow logos, feminist slogans, or climate pledges signal moral awareness. Yet these gestures rarely produce structural change. Capitalism increasingly survives not despite critique but through it, marketing rebellion as lifestyle and returning dissent in aesthetic form (Žižek 2009).

This capacity for self-absorption gives woke capitalism its resilience. Corporations can position themselves as moral leaders while reproducing the very conditions they claim to oppose. Companies that advocate racial equality rely on global supply chains marked by exploitation. Firms that promote sustainability continue to practice behaviors that contribute to environmental degradation. Organizations that celebrate gender equality often maintain wage gaps and hierarchical barriers. What appears as moral progress thus conceals a deeper continuity: the adaptation of neoliberal logic to a changing moral climate.

This adaptation operates not only at the rhetorical level but also at the ideological one. By reframing capitalism as a moral project, woke discourse shifts attention away from economic structures and toward cultural values. Problems of distribution are transformed into issues of representation. Instead of addressing wealth inequality, public debate focuses on diversity in advertising. Instead of confronting labor exploitation, attention is directed toward inclusion in leadership imagery. The moralization of capitalism converts structural conflict into matters of attitude and awareness. This substitution exemplifies what has been described as the neoliberal capture of progressivism, in which recognition replaces redistribution as the central political goal.

Another paradox of woke capitalism lies in its emotional economy. Its moral appeal relies on guilt, empathy, and the pursuit of virtue. Consumers are encouraged to express ethical commitment through market choices, turning consumption into a moral act. Companies sell not only products but also moral reassurance through fair trade goods, sustainable fashion, or carbon-neutral services. This emotional economy privatizes responsibility by redefining collective problems such as inequality, climate change, and exploitation as matters of individual morality. Rather than transforming institutions, individuals are asked to consume responsibly. In this way, capitalism addresses its legitimacy crisis by turning ethics into consumption.

The moralization of capitalism also functions as a form of governance. Corporate virtue operates as a soft mechanism of control, shaping public debate and social norms. By claiming moral authority, corporations define what counts as ethical or progressive, marginalizing alternative perspectives—criticism of corporate virtue risks being framed as intolerance or regression. Capitalism thus establishes a moral monopoly, dictating the terms of virtue and progress. It presents itself simultaneously as the cause of injustice and its solution, both the problem and the remedy. This circular logic enables capitalism to sustain itself by appearing to transcend itself (Wright 2023).

The contradictions of woke capitalism are becoming increasingly visible. As moral rhetoric intensifies, the gap between symbolic commitment and material practice grows more apparent. Public skepticism rises when diversity campaigns coexist with economic exclusion, when sustainability pledges align with environmental harm, or when ethical branding masks exploitative practices. This dissonance generates both cynicism and backlash. Progressive critics denounce corporate morality as opportunistic, while conservative movements reject it as ideological overreach. In both cases, the legitimacy of moral capitalism begins to erode.

Yet even this backlash can be absorbed. Woke capitalism's strength lies in its adaptability and its capacity to reinvent its moral narrative in response to shifting expectations. Woke capitalism may eventually give way to another ethical configuration, but the underlying mechanism will persist. Moral discourse will continue to be converted into legitimacy, critique into renewal, and ethics into economic value. The paradox of woke capitalism is therefore not temporary but structural.

References

Ahmed, S. 2012. *On Being Included: Racism and Diversity in Institutional Life*. Duke University Press.

Alcoff, L. 1996. "Feminist Theory and Social Science." In *Body Space: Destabilizing Geographies of Gender and Sexuality*, 13–27 London: Routledge.

Ashcroft, B., Griffiths, G., and Tiffin, H. 2013. *Postcolonial Studies: The Key Concepts*. Routledge.

Banet-Weiser, S. 2018. *Empowered: Popular Feminism and Popular Misogyny*. Duke University Press.

Belk, R. 1988. "Possessions and the Extended Self." *Journal of Consumer Research* 15, no. 2, pp. 139–168.

Boltanski, L., and Chiapello, E. 2005. *The New Spirit of Capitalism*. Verso.

Brady, W. et al. 2017. "Emotion Shapes the Diffusion of Moralized Content." *PNAS* 114, no. 28, pp. 7313–7318.

Butterworth, B. 2021. "What does 'Woke' mean? Origins of the Term and How the Meaning has Changed and retrieved September 30, 2021."

Coombs, W.T., and Holladay, S.J. 2021. *Digital Ethics: Corporate Response and Responsibility in the Age of Outrage*. Routledge.

Crenshaw, K. 2013. "Demarginalizing the Intersection of Race and Sex: A Black Feminist Critique of Antidiscrimination Doctrine, Feminist Theory, and Antiracist Politics." In *Feminist Legal Theories*, 23–51. Routledge.

Crenshaw, K., Gotanda, N., and Peller, G. (eds.). 1995. *Critical Race Theory: The Essential Writings that Formed the Movement*. The New Press.

Davies, W., and MacRae, D. 2023. *The New Moral Economy: Woke Capitalism and the Marketization of Ethics*. Polity Press.

Delgado, R., and Stefancic, J. (eds.). 2000. *Critical Race Theory: The Cutting Edge*. Temple University Press.

Donovan, J. 2012. *Feminist Theory: The Intellectual Traditions*. A&C Black.

Eccles, R.G., and Klimenko, S. 2019. "The Investor Revolution: Shareholders Leading on Sustainability." *Harvard Business Review* 97, no. 3, pp. 106–116.

Eder, A., Dinar, S., and Yildirim, Y. 2021. "Morality and Brand Polarization." *Marketing Letters* 32, no. 3, pp. 305–320.

Fan, J.S. 2019. "Woke Capital: The Role of Corporations in Social Movements." *Harvard Business Law Review* 9, p. 441.

Fleming, P., and Sturdy, A. 2023. "Virtue Management: The Moralization of Organizational Life." *Organization Studies* 44, no. 5, pp. 813–830.

Foss, N.J., and Klein, P.G. 2023. "Why do Companies go Woke?" *Academy of Management Perspectives* 37, no. 4, pp. 351–367.

Freeman, R.E. 2010. *Strategic Management: A Stakeholder Approach*. Cambridge University Press.

Friedman, M. 1970. *The Social Responsibility of Business Is to Increase Its Profits*—The New York Times Magazine.

Giridharadas, A. 2018. *Winners Take All: The Elite Charade of Changing the World*. Knopf.

Hanlon, G. 2018. *The Moral Economy: Why Capitalism Needs Morality*. Palgrave Macmillan.

Haskel, J., and Westlake, S. 2018. *Capitalism without Capital: The Rise of the Intangible Economy*. Princeton University Press.

Hollensbe, E., Wookey, C., Hickey, L., George, G., and Nichols, V. 2014. "Organizations with Purpose." *Academy of Management Journal* 57, no. 5, pp. 1227–1234.

Holt, D. 2022. *Cultural Strategy: Using Innovative Ideologies to Build Breakthrough Brands*. Oxford University Press.

Honneth, A., Hammer, E., and Gordon, P. 2018. *The Routledge Companion to the Frankfurt School*.

Jagose, A. 2009. "Feminism's Queer Theory." *Feminism & Psychology* 19, no. 2, pp. 157–174.

Kendi, I.X. 2023. *How to be an Antiracist*. One World.

Kotler, P., and Sarkar, C. 2018. *Brand Activism: From Purpose to Action*. Idea Bite Press.

Nath, V., and Dahlen, M. 2023. "Brand Activism and Authenticity." *International Journal of Advertising* 42, no. 1, pp. 44–62.

Noon, M. 2020. "Pointless Diversity Training: Unconscious Bias, New Racism and Agency." *Work, Employment and Society* 34, no. 4, pp. 706–718.

Rozado, D. 2023. "The Great Awakening as a Global Phenomenon." arXiv preprint arXiv:2304.01596.

Rozado, D., Al-Gharbi, M., and Halberstadt, J. 2023. "Prevalence of Prejudice-Denoting Words in News Media Discourse: A Chronological Analysis." *Social Science Computer Review* 41, no. 1, pp. 99–122.

Shastry, V. 2023. "The Merits of "Woke" Capitalism." In *The Notorious ESG: Business, Climate, and the Race to Save the Planet*, 81–101. Emerald Publishing Limited.

Sobande, F. 2019. "Woke-Washing: "Intersectional" Femvertising and Branding "Woke" Bravery." *European Journal of Marketing* 54, no. 11, pp. 2723–2745.

Sullivan, N. 2003. *A Critical Introduction to Queer Theory*. NYU Press.

Thompson, M.J. (ed.). 2017. *The Palgrave handbook of critical Theory*. Springer.

Vredenburg, J., Kapitan, S., Spry, A., and Kemper, J. 2020. "Woke Washing: What Happens When Marketing Messages Don't Match Corporate Practice." *Journal of Public Policy & Marketing* 39, no. 4, pp. 444–460.

Wright, C. 2023. "Capitalism's New Conscience: The Business of Morality." *Journal of Business Ethics* 188, no. 2, pp. 307–324.

Žižek, S. 2009. *First as Tragedy, Then as Farce*. Verso.

PART 2

Business Management and Organization

CHAPTER 5

From Market Competition to Corporate Rule

Concentration of Corporate Power and the Growing Inequality

The 21st century has witnessed a profound restructuring of global capitalism, marked by the growing concentration of economic power in the hands of a small number of multinational corporations and financial elites. This consolidation has reshaped market competition, transformed labor structures, and intensified social and economic inequalities. The widening divide between dominant firms and smaller enterprises, the erosion of local business ecosystems, the spread of lean employment models, and the expanding political influence of corporate actors form a mutually reinforcing system that amplifies inequality and weakens the institutional foundations of democratic capitalism (Autor et al. 2020; Piketty 2014).

A defining feature of contemporary capitalism is the rise of superstar firms that capture disproportionate shares of profits, innovation, and market attention. Across numerous industries, a small number of corporations dominate market share while remaining firms fragment into marginal competitors (Autor et al. 2020). These firms benefit from economies of scale, network effects, global reach, and data-driven operational models that smaller firms cannot replicate. As a result, the gap in productivity, profitability, and market power between dominant multinational corporations and typical firms has widened substantially, reinforcing inequality across the corporate world (Table 5.1).

This concentration of economic power fuels inequality at multiple levels. At the top of the income and wealth distribution, gains increasingly accrue to executives, founders, major shareholders, and financial institutions. Piketty argues that modern capitalism is characterized by

Table 5.1 The largest American companies by market capitalization in 2025

Rank	Company	Market Capitalization (Late 2025)	2025 Revenue (Estimated)
1	Nvidia	~$4.46 trillion	~$180+ billion
2	Apple	~$4.10 trillion	~$416 billion
3	Alphabet	~$3.78 trillion	~$385 billion
4	Microsoft	~$3.65 trillion	~$293 billion
5	Amazon	~$2.43 trillion	~$690+ billion
6	Broadcom	~$1.65 trillion	~$60+ billion
7	Meta Platforms	~$1.57 trillion	~$189+ billion
8	Tesla	~$1.43 trillion	~$95+ billion
9	Berkshire Hathaway	~$1.08 trillion	~$370+ billion
10	Eli Lilly	~$828 billion	~$60+ billion

Sources: Yahoo Finance (2025). Company statistics and market capitalization data.

S&P Dow Jones Indices (2025). U.S. equity market data.

a structural dynamic in which returns to capital systematically exceed returns to labor, allowing asset owners to accumulate wealth faster than wage earners (Piketty 2014). Superstar multinational corporations exemplify this pattern, as their stock valuations, dividend payouts, and executive compensation grow rapidly while wage growth for most workers remains modest. Economic rewards thus become increasingly skewed toward those with equity ownership, deepening wealth inequality within firms and across society (Piketty 2014).

The decline of small businesses further intensifies these trends. Historically, small- and medium-sized enterprises have played a central role in local employment, community stability, and economic diversification. However, globalization, digital platform dominance, and aggressive pricing strategies by large corporations have made survival increasingly difficult for smaller firms. During the COVID-19 pandemic, large numbers of small businesses closed permanently, while major corporations expanded their market reach by leveraging capital reserves, digital infrastructures, and political influence (OECD 2022). As local businesses disappear, communities lose essential sources of economic mobility and resilience, and economic activity becomes increasingly centralized in major global hubs (OECD 2022).

Labor dynamics within dominant firms also contribute to rising inequality. Many of the most valuable corporations today, particularly in technology and digital sectors, generate extraordinary revenues while employing relatively small workforces. Companies such as Google, Meta, and Apple create hundreds of billions of dollars in annual revenue with far fewer employees than the industrial giants of the 20th century. This model, in which revenue growth far outpaces employment growth, weakens the traditional link between economic expansion and job creation (Baldwin 2019). Automation, outsourcing, and digital efficiencies reduce labor demand, diminish workers' bargaining power, and widen wage disparities, allowing productivity gains to accrue primarily to shareholders rather than employees (Baldwin 2019).

Corporate political influence is another crucial mechanism that reinforces inequality. Large corporations possess the financial resources and organizational capacity to shape policy outcomes through lobbying, campaign financing, and regulatory capture. Empirical evidence shows that public policy in the United States aligns far more closely with the preferences of economic elites and business interests than with those of ordinary citizens (Gilens and Page 2014). The weakening of antitrust enforcement has enabled further consolidation in sectors such as technology, energy, agriculture, and retail, allowing firms to expand market power through mergers and acquisitions (Khan 2017). Once entrenched, this concentration of power generates a self-reinforcing cycle in which economic dominance translates into political influence, which in turn facilitates further consolidation (Gilens and Page 2014; Khan 2017).

Globalization has amplified these dynamics by enabling multinational corporations to operate beyond the effective reach of national regulatory systems. Firms can shift profits to low-tax jurisdictions, relocate production to regions with weaker labor protections, and exploit regulatory differences across countries. These practices weaken state capacity to enforce equitable taxation, protect domestic industries, and regulate corporate behavior effectively (Stiglitz 2019). Global corporate elites increasingly operate in transnational spaces. At the same time, the social and economic costs of restructuring are borne by local communities, further widening the gap between global elites and the broader population (Stiglitz 2019; Yeganeh 2020).

The implications of these developments are significant. Concentrated corporate power undermines competition, suppresses entrepreneurial activity, and erodes democratic accountability. Inequality becomes not merely an outcome of market processes but a structural feature of contemporary capitalism, reinforced by political influence, global capital mobility, and institutional arrangements favoring large firms. Regions without dominant corporations experience slower growth, stagnant wages, and declining upward mobility, contributing to social polarization and political discontent (Autor et al. 2020; Gilens and Page 2014).

Addressing these challenges requires systemic intervention. More vigorous antitrust enforcement, policies supporting small- and medium-sized enterprises, corporate tax reform, stricter limits on lobbying, and enhanced protections for workers in concentrated labor markets are essential steps toward a more balanced economic order. Given the global reach of corporate power, international cooperation is also necessary to regulate multinational corporations and close regulatory loopholes (OECD 2022; Stiglitz 2019). Without such measures, the concentration of corporate power will continue to intensify inequality, undermining economic stability and democratic legitimacy. While superstar firms have delivered remarkable innovations and efficiencies, they have also produced a monetary system in which prosperity is increasingly concentrated, competition is weakened, and inequality becomes self-perpetuating (Autor et al. 2020; Yeganeh 2020).

Platform Capitalism and Ecosystem Dependency

At the center of platform capitalism lies the platform business model itself. Major corporations such as Amazon, Google, Apple, Meta, Microsoft, Alibaba, and Tencent do not merely operate within markets, but actively create, structure, and regulate them. Platforms mediate interactions among users, advertisers, producers, and service providers, positioning themselves as indispensable intermediaries within digital economies (Srnicek 2017). Their power is reinforced by network effects, whereby the value of a platform increases as more participants join, creating self-reinforcing dynamics that favor concentration and market dominance.

Over time, these dynamics enable a small number of firms to exert control over entire ecosystems, including electronic commerce, cloud computing, mobile operating systems, and digital payments (Srnicek 2017).

This ecosystem control fundamentally alters the position of smaller firms. In traditional markets, competition was primarily based on pricing, product differentiation, or incremental innovation. Within platform ecosystems, however, firms depend on rules, algorithms, and infrastructures determined by platform owners. Millions of merchants rely on Amazon Marketplace, application developers depend on Apple App Store and Google Play, advertisers are tied to Meta and Google advertising systems, and enterprise software providers operate within Microsoft cloud environments. These relationships are inherently asymmetrical, as platforms determine access conditions, impose fees, extract data, and often compete directly with firms operating on their own infrastructure (Cunningham et al. 2021).

Such dependency enables platforms to extract new forms of economic rent. Revenue is generated through commissions, subscription fees, advertising charges, cloud services, and data monetization. These charges reflect the platforms' ability to impose terms that smaller firms have limited ability to negotiate. High application store fees, seller commissions, and advertising costs exemplify this rent extraction logic, through which platforms capture a significant share of the value created by dependent firms. As platforms expand, they become essential infrastructures through which innovation must pass, positioning themselves as unavoidable intermediaries in the value creation process (Cunningham et al. 2021).

Data occupies a central role in reinforcing platform dominance. Platforms collect vast amounts of user data, which they use to refine algorithms, personalize services, and anticipate consumer behavior. This process transforms data extraction into a core economic activity, a phenomenon often described as surveillance capitalism (Zuboff 2019). Data asymmetries create formidable barriers to entry, as dominant platforms possess informational advantages that new entrants cannot replicate. Greater data accumulation improves service quality, attracts more users, and generates further data, creating a feedback loop that entrenches market power and limits competition (Zuboff 2019).

Beyond data, platform capitalism is strengthened by the emergence of intellectual monopolies based on proprietary technologies, patents, software systems, algorithms, and technical standards. Modern multinational corporations increasingly derive value from intangible assets rather than physical capital. Intellectual monopolies allow firms to capture returns well above competitive levels by controlling access to essential knowledge and technological architectures (Pagano 2014). Search algorithms, integrated hardware and software ecosystems, enterprise operating systems, and AI frameworks illustrate how control over intellectual assets reinforces long-term market dominance and constrains potential competitors (Pagano 2014).

These intellectual monopolies shape not only markets but also the trajectory of innovation itself. Smaller firms and start-ups rarely innovate independently of dominant platforms, as they must conform to platform standards, application interfaces, and technical requirements set by incumbents. Even when disruptive innovation emerges outside these ecosystems, dominant firms may acquire potential competitors at early stages, a practice commonly described as killer acquisitions (Cunningham et al. 2021). Through such strategies, platform corporations influence which technologies scale, which markets evolve, and which innovations are absorbed or neutralized (Cunningham et al. 2021).

The global consequences of platform capitalism are substantial. Market power and wealth become increasingly concentrated in a small number of firms, while the autonomy and bargaining power of smaller companies decline. Platform dominance undermines entrepreneurial independence, weakens competition, and centralizes technological capabilities in a limited number of regions, primarily in the United States and China. Many developing economies become dependent on foreign digital infrastructures, limiting domestic technological sovereignty and exposing local markets to external regulatory and corporate decisions (Zuboff 2019; Pagano 2014).

Addressing these challenges requires a rethinking of digital governance and competition policy. More vigorous antitrust enforcement, data portability requirements, interoperability rules, and platform neutrality obligations can help rebalance market power. Regulatory initiatives such as the European Union Digital Markets Act represent attempts to constrain platform gatekeeping and restore competitive conditions. At the same time, public investment in digital infrastructure, open-source technologies, and local innovation ecosystems can reduce dependence on dominant platforms and foster more diverse technological development (Srnicek 2017).

Corporate Political Power, Regulatory Capture and Private Governance

As states confront global challenges such as climate instability, technological disruption, public health crises, and widening inequality, corporations have increasingly filled institutional gaps and asserted influence over public priorities. Through lobbying, regulatory capture, philanthrocapitalism, and private governance arrangements, business elites have expanded their authority far beyond the economic sphere. This shift reflects a fundamental transformation of political economy in which corporations no longer merely respond to rules set by governments, but actively participate in rule-making, societal agenda-setting, and global governance. As a result, core questions emerge regarding accountability, democratic legitimacy, and the distribution of power in an era where private interests increasingly shape public life (Drutman 2015; Carpenter and Moss 2014). At the center of this transformation is the expansion of corporate political power through lobbying and campaign financing. Corporations devote substantial resources to shaping regulation in their favor, influencing laws related to taxation, competition, labor standards, environmental policy, and digital governance. Corporate lobbying in the United States has evolved into a permanent political campaign, with firms spending billions annually to shape legislative and regulatory outcomes (Drutman 2015). This sustained influence contributes to regulatory capture, a condition in which regulators charged with overseeing industries become aligned with corporate interests through revolving-door employment, financial incentives, information asymmetries, and persistent political pressure (Carpenter and Moss 2014). Regulatory capture weakens oversight, undermines consumer protection, and produces policy environments that entrench dominant firms while limiting effective competition (Carpenter and Moss 2014).

The effects of corporate influence are visible across multiple sectors. Financial deregulation preceding the global economic crisis reflected extensive industry involvement in shaping regulatory frameworks. Technology firms have played a decisive role in defining privacy, competition, and digital governance regimes through continuous engagement with policymakers. Energy corporations have influenced environmental and climate policy for decades by shaping regulatory standards and delaying stricter enforcement. Beyond these formal political channels, corporations increasingly exert influence through philanthrocapitalism, defined as the strategic use of philanthropic resources to shape social agendas and public policy (Figure 5.1).

By applying market logic to social problems, philanthropic initiatives tend to advance solutions aligned with corporate interests, managerial ideologies, or technological optimism. Through foundations, impact investing, and public–private partnerships, business leaders shape education reform, public health priorities, urban development strategies, and climate initiatives. These interventions often redefine social problems in ways that favor private sector solutions while marginalizing alternative approaches rooted in public provision or democratic deliberation (McGoey 2015).

Figure 5.1 Philanthrocapitalism is an approach to social giving that applies modern business techniques and market-based strategies to solve global problems.

In global health governance, large philanthropic organizations have become highly influential actors shaping vaccine distribution strategies, research funding priorities, and institutional norms. While such interventions can yield positive outcomes, they often bypass state authority and multilateral decision-making processes, concentrating power in private hands and reducing public oversight (Youde 2019). Similar patterns appear in education, where corporate-backed reforms promote digital learning platforms and standardized assessment systems aligned with the commercial interests of technology firms. In environmental governance, corporate-led sustainability initiatives often establish voluntary standards that substitute for binding regulation while defining sustainability in market-compatible terms (McGoey 2015).

These developments reflect the broader rise of private governance, in which corporations establish rules, norms, and standards that shape social and political life: technology firms, in particular, function as quasi-sovereign actors. Digital platforms make decisions about content moderation, algorithmic visibility, misinformation policy, and data governance, which directly influence public discourse and democratic processes (Gillespie 2018). These corporations govern digital spaces used by billions of individuals worldwide, exercising forms of regulatory authority traditionally associated with states. Their decisions affect electoral dynamics, political mobilization, and the visibility of social movements, often without transparent accountability mechanisms (Gillespie 2018).

Corporate control over critical digital infrastructure further reinforces this concentration of power. Cloud computing providers operate essential systems for governments, corporations, and public institutions. Policy changes, service disruptions, or strategic decisions by these firms can generate widespread economic and political consequences. Through their control of digital ecosystems, corporations shape privacy standards, cybersecurity practices, and the development pathways of AI, frequently without meaningful democratic oversight (Nye 2021).

At the global level, corporations increasingly act as geopolitical players. Technology firms negotiate directly with governments over data localization, censorship, cybersecurity, and digital sovereignty. Financial institutions influence cross-border capital flows and macroeconomic stability, while energy corporations shape foreign policy through global supply chains and strategic investments. In this context, multinational corporations exercise structural power within systems of complex interdependence, shaping global governance outcomes alongside states (Nye 2021). The expansion of corporate power raises serious democratic concerns. Political equality is undermined when financial resources translate into disproportionate influence over public policy. Private governance lacks accountability because corporate decisions are neither democratically mandated nor subject to effective public oversight. Philanthrocapitalism enables elites to define social priorities without transparency or democratic debate. Regulatory capture further weakens governments' capacity to protect the public interest, allowing corporate actors to function as de facto policymakers in critical domains of social and economic life (Gilens and Page 2014; McGoey 2015).

Financialization of Firms, Markets, and Elites

Over the past four decades, finance has shifted from an intermediary role supporting productive investment to a dominant logic shaping corporate strategy, market dynamics, and socioeconomic inequality. Financial motives such as speculative valuation, shareholder primacy, and asset-based accumulation have increasingly displaced long-term productive capacity, innovation, and labor stability. As a result, financialization affects not only economic outcomes but also the distribution of power and resources across societies (Krippner 2011).

Financialization refers to the growing importance of financial activities, financial markets, and financial motives within the broader economy. Firms increasingly evaluate success through financial indicators such as stock price performance, shareholder returns, and capital gains. This orientation gained momentum during the 1980s amid deregulation, globalization, and an ideological shift toward market liberalism. Financial profits gradually outpaced production profits, encouraging firms to adopt strategies that enhanced short-term valuation rather than sustaining long-term productive investment (Krippner 2011).

One of the most consequential outcomes of financialization is the rise of shareholder primacy as the dominant model of corporate governance. Under this framework, firms prioritize maximizing shareholder value over workers' interests, communities, and long-term competitiveness. Agency theory played a critical role in legitimizing this orientation by framing managers as agents whose primary responsibility is to act in shareholders' interests, often through incentive structures tied to stock performance. As executive compensation became increasingly linked to share price movements, managerial incentives shifted away from productive investment toward financial engineering (Lazonick 2014).

Share buybacks provide a clear illustration of this shift. Rather than allocating profits to research, workforce development, or capital expansion, firms increasingly repurchase their own shares to raise earnings per share and boost executive compensation. Evidence shows that large corporations in the United States have devoted substantial portions of their earnings to buybacks over recent decades, diverting resources away from innovation and long-term growth. This practice exacerbates inequality by channeling financial gains primarily to shareholders and top executives rather than to employees or productive investment (Lazonick 2014).

At the market level, financialization has transformed both the composition and behavior of financial actors. The rise of large asset management firms has concentrated ownership of public corporations in the hands of a small number of institutional investors, granting them significant influence over corporate governance across global markets (Fichtner et al. 2017). Hedge funds and private equity firms pursue aggressive financial strategies, such as leveraged buyouts, debt restructuring, and asset extraction, that prioritize rapid financial returns over job stability and long-term viability (Appelbaum and Batt 2014). At the same time, high-frequency trading driven by algorithms and ultrafast execution distances market activity from underlying economic fundamentals, turning finance into a domain dominated by speed and speculation (Appelbaum and Batt 2014).

Financialization also contributes to asset bubbles, market volatility, and systemic risk. When valuations are driven more by investor sentiment, liquidity conditions, or speculative expectations than by productivity or real economic output, asset prices become increasingly detached from underlying economic activity. The global financial crisis of 2008 exposed the dangers of excessive leverage, speculative trading, and complex financial instruments disconnected from tangible assets. In the postcrisis period, expansionary monetary policies inflated asset prices across equities, bonds, and real estate, disproportionately benefiting those who already owned financial assets (Piketty 2014).

The financialization of elites represents another defining feature of this transformation. Wealth accumulation is increasingly tied to ownership of financial assets rather than wages or entrepreneurial activity. Executives and financial professionals capture a disproportionate share of economic gains through stock options, capital gains, and financial rents. Empirical evidence shows that wealth ownership has become highly concentrated, with the top segment of the population holding a substantial share of national wealth, much of it in financial form. This concentration reflects structural changes in the distribution of value rather than differences in individual productivity or effort (Piketty 2014).

Financialization also reshapes labor relations within firms. To meet investor expectations, companies increasingly pursue cost reduction strategies such as outsourcing, offshoring, automation, and flexible employment arrangements. These practices weaken job security, suppress wage growth, and shift economic risk onto workers. A growing segment of the workforce experiences precarious and insecure employment conditions as a direct consequence of financialized corporate strategies (Standing 2011). Productivity gains are increasingly captured by shareholders rather than workers, contributing to widening income inequality and reduced economic mobility (Standing 2011).

Public policy has also been deeply influenced by financialization. Governments increasingly prioritize market confidence, investor sentiment, and financial stability when designing economic policy. Central banks have assumed an expanded role in sustaining asset prices through liquidity provision, asset purchases, and prolonged low-interest rate policies. While these measures stabilize financial markets, they also inflate asset values and disproportionately benefit wealthy asset holders (Stiglitz 2012). Fiscal policy often emphasizes creditworthiness and investor expectations, leading to austerity measures that weaken public services and social protections (Stiglitz 2012).

The financialization of essential goods such as housing further illustrates these dynamics. Real estate has become a preferred asset class for institutional investors and global elites, contributing to rising housing costs, speculative investment, and displacement in urban areas. Housing increasingly functions as a financial asset rather than a social necessity, reshaping urban development patterns and limiting access to affordable shelter (Aalbers 2016).

Technological Sovereignty and Control of Critical Infrastructure

In the 21st century, technological systems underpin national security, economic growth, and democratic governance. Digital infrastructures such as cloud platforms, telecommunications networks, AI ecosystems, semiconductor supply chains, and cybersecurity frameworks have become essential to the functioning of modern societies. As these systems grow more complex and globally interconnected, questions of technological sovereignty and control over critical infrastructure have moved to the center of geopolitical strategy. Power is increasingly exercised not through territorial expansion or military dominance, but through control over technological platforms and digital dependencies. States and corporate actors now compete to shape the architecture of digital life, producing new vulnerabilities, asymmetries, and governance challenges (DeNardis 2020).

Technological sovereignty refers to a society's capacity to design, regulate, and secure the technological systems on which it depends. The European Commission defines technological sovereignty as the ability to act autonomously in the digital sphere while ensuring that critical technologies align with collective values and strategic interests (European Commission 2020). Concerns over technological sovereignty have intensified as governments recognize their growing reliance on foreign corporations for core digital infrastructures, including cloud services, AI systems, telecommunications networks, and semiconductor production. Such dependencies raise fundamental issues of autonomy, security, and resilience, particularly in a global environment marked by geopolitical rivalry and rapid technological change (European Commission 2020).

Large technology corporations lie at the center of these concerns. Firms such as Amazon, Microsoft, Google, Huawei, Apple, IBM, and Tencent operate global infrastructures deeply embedded in public and private life. Their cloud platforms host government data, financial transactions, health records, and military logistics, while their operating systems and application platforms mediate digital communication and public discourse. Their cybersecurity tools play a critical role in protecting and potentially exposing national networks. These corporations increasingly function as de facto regulators of the digital environment, shaping standards, protocols, and governance arrangements that rival or exceed the authority of nation-states (DeNardis 2020).

Cloud computing provides a clear illustration of the intersection between corporate power and state sovereignty. Governments, universities, hospitals, and firms increasingly depend on cloud services from Amazon Web Services, Google Cloud, and Microsoft Azure to store data and run essential systems. While cloud infrastructure offers efficiency and scalability, it also creates structural dependencies. Changes in pricing, service conditions, or technical disruptions can directly affect vital public services. Jurisdictional conflicts surrounding data access further complicate these dependencies, as legal frameworks such as the United States CLOUD Act raise concerns about foreign government access to sensitive national data (Schrems 2020). For states without domestic cloud capabilities, reliance on foreign providers becomes a strategic vulnerability (Schrems 2020).

Telecommunications infrastructure represents another critical arena of technological sovereignty. The controversy surrounding Huawei's participation in fifth-generation telecommunications networks highlights the geopolitical stakes embedded in technology supply chains. Several governments have restricted or prohibited the use of foreign telecommunications equipment due to concerns that vulnerabilities could be exploited for surveillance or coercion. These decisions reflect a broader recognition that control over communication networks is inseparable from national security and political autonomy (Segal 2021).

Semiconductors further reveal the fragility of global technological interdependence. Advanced chip manufacturing is concentrated among a small number of firms, including Taiwan Semiconductor Manufacturing Company, Samsung, and Intel. Disruptions to this supply chain, whether caused by geopolitical conflict, pandemics, or natural disasters, can halt production across sectors ranging from consumer electronics to defense systems. The shortages experienced during the COVID-19 pandemic exposed critical vulnerabilities in global supply chains and prompted governments to invest heavily in domestic semiconductor production and supply chain resilience (Miller and Kim 2022).

AI intensifies the stakes of technological sovereignty. AI systems rely on massive computational infrastructure, proprietary algorithms, and extensive datasets that are primarily controlled by major technology firms and technologically advanced states. These systems increasingly shape decision-making across policing, health care, finance, and public administration. Dependence on foreign AI technologies risks transferring authority over critical societal functions to external actors, making AI governance inseparable from political sovereignty (Floridi 2021).

Cybersecurity adds a layer of complexity. As energy grids, transportation systems, and financial networks become increasingly digitized, they also become more vulnerable to cyberattacks. Private technology firms often possess the technical expertise required to secure these systems, creating hybrid governance arrangements in which corporations act as indispensable partners in national security. High-profile incidents such as the SolarWinds breach demonstrated how vulnerabilities in private software can compromise government networks on a global scale, underscoring the risks of relying on external vendors for critical technological functions (DeNardis 2020).

Taken together, these dynamics generate new forms of digital dependency. States that lack domestic technological capacity become reliant on foreign infrastructures, standards, and platforms, limiting their strategic autonomy. This condition has been described as data colonialism, in which powerful actors extract value from global data flows while shaping the technological environment to their advantage (Couldry and Mejias 2019). In response, governments are pursuing strategies to strengthen technological sovereignty, including investment in national cloud infrastructures, domestic semiconductor manufacturing, data localization policies, open-source technologies, and international technological alliances. These initiatives aim to reduce dependence on foreign providers while preserving the benefits of global technological integration (European Commission 2020).

Global Expansion and Local Erosion

The expansion of multinational corporations over recent decades has fundamentally restructured the global economy by embedding local markets within extensive transnational production networks, digital platforms, and financial systems. While international firms have contributed to economic growth, technological diffusion, and market integration, their expanding reach has simultaneously weakened local economic structures, institutions, and communities. This dual process of global expansion alongside local erosion reveals a central tension within contemporary capitalism. As economic power becomes concentrated in global hubs, local foundations grow increasingly fragile, producing social, financial, and cultural consequences that shape the trajectory of globalization (Gereffi 2018).

The global footprint of multinational corporations rests on their capacity to coordinate production and distribution across multiple countries with unprecedented efficiency. Advances in logistics, information technologies, and trade liberalization have enabled firms to fragment production, centralize strategic control, and operate seamlessly across borders. Global value chains allow corporations to locate different stages of production where labor costs are lowest, regulations are weakest, or resources are most accessible, thereby maximizing efficiency and profitability (Gereffi 2018). While this system has lowered consumer prices and increased output, it has also shifted economic power away from local producers and communities toward global corporate networks that operate largely beyond local accountability (Gereffi 2018).

One of the most visible consequences of this shift is the weakening of small- and medium-sized enterprises. Historically, local businesses served as anchors of employment, innovation, and social cohesion within communities. However, they face increasing difficulty competing with multinational firms that benefit from superior access to capital, advanced technologies, global brands, and economies of scale. Empirical evidence indicates that the expansion of international retail chains and electronic commerce platforms has displaced large numbers of local businesses worldwide, particularly in retail and manufacturing sectors (UNCTAD 2020). When multinational competitors enter local markets, traditional retailers, artisans, and domestic manufacturers often experience declining revenues or are forced out altogether, reducing economic diversity and undermining local resilience (UNCTAD 2020).

Digital platforms further intensify these dynamics. Corporations such as Amazon, Google, and Meta, as well as local businesses, rely on platform algorithms, payment systems, data infrastructures, and ranking mechanisms controlled by global corporations. While such platforms can expand market access, they also extract commissions, collect valuable data, and impose rules that prioritize scalability and standardization over local autonomy. This dependency erodes local control over essential aspects of economic activity and reinforces structural reliance on global platforms (Srnicek 2017).

Labor markets are similarly affected by multinational expansion. Global competition and outsourcing often compel local firms to reduce labor costs, adopt insecure employment arrangements, or automate production processes. The growth of unstable and precarious employment has been closely linked to the restructuring of local labor markets under global competitive pressures (Standing 2011). In many regions, the offshoring of manufacturing has resulted in persistent unemployment, declining household incomes, and weakened social cohesion. Even when multinational corporations generate employment, jobs are frequently concentrated in lower wage segments of global supply chains and remain vulnerable to shifts in global demand (Standing 2011).

Local institutions face parallel pressures. Corporate tax avoidance and profit shifting erode governments' fiscal capacity to fund public goods and essential services. Multinational tax strategies deprive states of significant revenues each year, forcing local communities to shoulder heavier tax burdens or accept reductions in public investment (Zucman 2015). At the same time, governments often compete to attract multinational investment through tax incentives, regulatory concessions, and subsidies. While such strategies may produce short-term gains, they undermine long-term fiscal sustainability and weaken the regulatory autonomy of local institutions (Zucman 2015).

Cultural consequences further reflect the imbalance between global reach and local weakening. International brands, media conglomerates, and standardized retail formats diffuse homogeneous cultural products across societies, reshaping consumption patterns and urban landscapes. This process contributes to the erosion of local traditions, languages, and cultural practices, as global cultural commodities crowd out locally rooted forms of expression (Barber 1995). Although cultural exchange can enrich societies, the asymmetric power of international cultural industries often marginalizes local identities and reduces cultural diversity (Barber 1995). Systems of global private authority play an essential role in setting standards for labor practices, environmental regulation, and trade norms, thereby reducing local governments' capacity to govern autonomously in line with community needs (Cutler et al. 1999).

Despite these challenges, local weakening is not inevitable. Some regions have responded by strengthening local supply chains, investing in community-owned enterprises, promoting local procurement, and supporting cooperative business models. Others have leveraged global integration to foster local innovation, develop specialized industrial clusters, or cultivate distinctive cultural brands. The central challenge lies in balancing global openness with local resilience, ensuring that participation in the global economy does not come at the expense of local economic and social foundations (UNCTAD 2020).

References

Aalbers, M. 2016. *The Financialization of Housing*. Routledge.

Appelbaum, E., and Batt, R. 2014. *Private Equity at Work*. Russell Sage Foundation.

Autor, D., Dorn, D., Katz, L., Patterson, C., and Van Reenen, J. 2020. "The Fall of the Labor Share and the Rise of Superstar Firms." *Quarterly Journal of Economics*.

Baldwin, R. 2019. *The Globotics Upheaval*. Oxford University Press.

Barber, B. 1995. *Jihad vs. McWorld*. Times Books.

Carpenter, D., and Moss, D. 2014. *Preventing Regulatory Capture*. Cambridge University Press.

Couldry, N., and Mejias, U. 2019. *The Costs of Connection*. Stanford University Press.

Cunningham, C., Ederer, F., and Ma, S. 2021. "Killer Acquisitions." *Journal of Political Economy* 129, no. 3.

Cutler, A.C., Haufler, V., and Porter, T. 1999. *Private Authority and International Affairs*. SUNY Press.

DeNardis, L. 2020. *The Internet in Everything*. Yale University Press.

Drutman, L. 2015. *The Business of America is Lobbying*. Oxford University Press.

European Commission. 2020. Shaping Europe's Digital Future.

Fichtner, J., Heemskerk, E., and Garcia-Bernardo, J. 2017. "Hidden power of the Big Three?" *Business and Politics* 19, no. 2, pp. 298–326.

Floridi, L. 2021. *AI Ethics*. Oxford University Press.

Gereffi, G. 2018. *Global Value Chains and Development*. Cambridge University Press.

Gilens, M., and Page, B. 2014. "Testing Theories of American Politics." *Perspectives on Politics* 12, no. 3, pp. 564–581.

Gillespie, T. 2018. *Custodians of the Internet*. Yale University Press.

Khan, L. 2017. *Amazon's Antitrust Paradox*. Yale Law Journal.

Krippner, G. 2011. *Capitalizing on Crisis*. Harvard University Press.

Lazonick, W. 2014. "Profits Without Prosperity." *Harvard Business Review* 92, no. 9, pp. 46–55.

McGoey, L. 2015. *No Such Thing as a Free Gift: The Gates Foundation and the Price of Philanthropy*. Verso.

Miller, C., and Kim, J. 2022. *Chip War: The Fight for the World's Most Critical Technology*. Scribner.

Nye, J. 2021. *Do Morals Matter? Presidents and Foreign Policy from FDR to Trump*. Oxford University Press.

OECD (2022), OECD *SME and Entrepreneurship Outlook 2022*, OECD Publishing, Paris.

Pagano, U. 2014. "The Crisis of Intellectual Monopoly Capitalism." *Cambridge Journal of Economics* 38, no. 6, pp. 1409–1429.

Piketty, T. 2014. *Capital in the Twenty-First Century*. Harvard University.

Schrems, M. 2020. "Data Transfers and the CLOUD Act." *Journal of European Data Protection Law* 6, no. 4.

Segal, A. 2021. *The Hacked World Order*. PublicAffairs.

Srnicek, N. 2017. *Platform Capitalism*. Polity Press.

Standing, G. 2011. *The Precariat*. Bloomsbury Academic.

Stiglitz, J. 2012. *The Price of Inequality*. W. W. Norton.

Stiglitz, J. 2019. *People, Power, and Profits: Progressive Capitalism for an Age of Discontent*. Norton.

UNCTAD. 2020. *World Investment Report 2020*. United Nations Conference on Trade and Development.

Yeganeh, H. 2020. "A Critical Examination of the Social Impacts of Large Multinational Corporations in the Age of Globalization." *Critical Perspectives on International Business* 16, no. 3, pp. 193–208.

Youde, J. 2019. *Global Health Governance*. Polity Press.

Zuboff, S. 2019. *The Age of Surveillance Capitalism*. PublicAffairs.

Zucman, G. 2015. *The Hidden Wealth of Nations*. University of Chicago Press.

CHAPTER 6

The Emerging Trends in Work and Employment

The Slowdown in Labor Growth and Aging Workforce

The global economy is entering an era increasingly defined by population aging and the resulting slowdown in labor force growth. This demographic transformation is reshaping labor markets, economic growth trajectories, and social institutions across both advanced and emerging economies. Rising life expectancy, combined with persistently low fertility rates, has produced the fastest and most widespread aging process in human history, altering the balance between working-age populations and retirees (United Nations 2019). At present, nearly one billion people worldwide are aged 60 or older, accounting for approximately 13 percent of the global population, and this share continues to grow steadily (United Nations 2017). By mid-century, half of the world's population is expected to reside in countries where at least one-fifth of residents are 60 or older, signaling a structural shift with long-term economic consequences (United Nations 2013).

In the United States, demographic aging is advancing rapidly and is projected to intensify over the coming decades. By 2050, the population aged 65 and above is expected to reach roughly 90 million, placing increasing strain on labor markets, health care systems, and public pension programs (Lam 2011). This pattern mirrors broader trends across advanced economies, where declining fertility, longer life spans, and, in some cases, reduced immigration are reshaping population structures (Pew Research Center 2023). Historically, workforce growth in the United States averaged 2.6 percent annually in the 1970s, slowed to 1.6 percent in the 1980s, and declined further to just over 1 percent in the 1990s, even as rising female labor force participation and immigration helped offset demographic pressures (United Nations 2017). Today, these compensating forces have weakened, as female participation rates have converged mainly with those of men, limiting their ability to sustain labor supply growth.

As a result, labor force expansion is expected to continue its long-term slowdown. Projections from the United States Bureau of Labor Statistics suggest that labor force growth will average around 0.5 percent annually through 2030, a rate well below historical norms (Dubina et al. 2021). Economists caution that persistently low labor growth, if not offset by productivity gains or institutional reform, may constrain potential economic growth and intensify fiscal pressures linked to aging populations (Gordon 2016). Firms may increasingly face difficulties recruiting qualified workers, particularly during periods of economic expansion, as labor shortages become more frequent and persistent (Karoly 2004).

While demographic pressures in the United States are substantial, they are even more noticeable in several other major economies. Japan exhibits one of the highest aging rates globally, while China is entering a period of rapid workforce contraction following decades of restrictive fertility policies (Wang 2020). Across Europe, countries such as Italy and Germany face declining working-age populations and rising dependency ratios as the number of retirees grows relative to the employed population (United Nations 2013). These developments threaten long-term economic resilience and have intensified debates around immigration policy, pension reform, and the role of productivity-enhancing technologies.

In response to slowing labor force growth, advanced economies have increasingly relied on women and migrants to sustain labor supply. Over recent decades, these groups have played a critical role in offsetting demographic decline and maintaining economic activity (Lam 2011). As a result, labor markets have become more diverse in terms of age, gender, and ethnicity. Research indicates that diversity can enhance innovation, creativity, and productivity, provided that organizations adopt inclusive management practices and flexible institutional arrangements (Hunt et al. 2015).

An aging workforce also carries significant implications for workplace design, regulation, and management. Older workers face distinct physical, cognitive, and health-related challenges that may affect productivity and safety. Empirical studies show that workers aged 65 and older experience higher rates of permanent disability and workplace fatalities than younger cohorts (Karoly 2004). To address these risks, organizations must implement age-responsive strategies, including ergonomic workplace design, enhanced safety protocols, health promotion initiatives, and continuous skills development. Flexible work arrangements, remote work options, and phased retirement schemes can help retain older workers while reducing physical strain and preserving valuable institutional knowledge (Ilmarinen 2019).

At the societal level, population aging is placing increasing pressure on pension systems, health care infrastructure, and long-term care services. As the ratio of workers to retirees declines, many countries face mounting fiscal stress and difficult policy trade-offs regarding the sustainability of social welfare systems (OECD 2021). Policy responses increasingly under discussion include raising statutory retirement ages, expanding lifelong learning, encouraging higher labor force participation among older workers, increasing immigration, and investing in automation and AI to mitigate labor shortages.

Despite these challenges, population aging also presents significant opportunities. Older adults contribute experience, institutional memory, emotional intelligence, and stability to organizations and communities. Evidence suggests that multigenerational workplaces can enhance learning, decision making, and problem-solving when age diversity is effectively managed (Ng and Feldman 2015). Societies and organizations that successfully adapt to demographic aging by integrating older workers into evolving labor markets may not only mitigate economic decline but also unlock new sources of productivity and social cohesion.

Cognitive Skills and Education Attainment

The transition from an industrial economy toward a knowledge-based economy is accelerating, reshaping labor markets and redefining the skills required for economic participation. The global decline in manufacturing employment, combined with rapid advances in automation, AI, and digital technologies, has reduced demand for labor-intensive and routine jobs while expanding opportunities in technology, engineering, data science, and other knowledge-intensive fields (World Economic Forum 2023). As a result, the demand for highly skilled and educated workers continues to rise, favoring economies that can effectively cultivate, attract, and retain advanced human capital.

Across sectors, organizations increasingly seek workers capable of operating complex technological systems, developing and maintaining software, analyzing data, and managing digital networks. Beyond technical proficiency, employers are placing greater emphasis on advanced cognitive skills such as abstract reasoning, critical thinking, problem-solving, communication, and collaboration. These competencies are particularly valuable in environments characterized by uncertainty, rapid change, and interdisciplinary problem-solving (Autor et al. 2003). In addition, globalization has heightened demand for workers who can operate effectively in international contexts, collaborate in cross-national teams, and navigate diverse cultural and linguistic environments. Such capabilities enhance organizational adaptability and innovation in globally integrated markets.

These structural shifts have contributed to a persistent increase in the wage premium associated with higher levels of education and skill. Since the late 20th century, workers with postsecondary education have consistently earned significantly more than those with only secondary credentials, reflecting strong employer demand for cognitive and analytical capabilities (Goldin and Katz 2008). Between the 1970s and early 2000s, the wage premium for holding a college degree rose sharply, reinforcing incentives for individuals to pursue higher education to maintain labor market competitiveness (Day and Bauman 2000). While the precise magnitude of the premium fluctuates over time, recent evidence suggests that skill-biased technological change continues to reward workers with advanced education and adaptable skill sets (OECD 2019).

Closely linked to the rising demand for skilled labor is the expansion of educational attainment across much of the world. In both developed and emerging economies, years of schooling have increased steadily as individuals respond to the changing structure of labor demand. Higher education systems have expanded rapidly, and participation rates have grown across gender and socioeconomic groups, although access remains uneven (Barro and Lee 2015). In the United States, college completion rates among younger cohorts have risen, particularly among women, yet substantial disparities persist. African American and Hispanic populations continue to face lower average levels of educational attainment, reflecting broader inequalities in income, school quality, neighborhood conditions, and access to postsecondary institutions (Chetty et al. 2017).

Despite relatively high levels of public and private investment in education, student performance in the United States remains around the international average when compared with other advanced economies. Earlier comparisons showed that U.S. educational expenditures exceeded those of many peer countries, yet outcomes lagged behind expectations (OECD 2001). More recent assessments continue to highlight uneven achievement and wide performance gaps linked to socioeconomic status rather than overall funding levels (OECD 2022). These patterns suggest that educational challenges stem less from insufficient spending and more from structural inequalities, variation in school quality, and differences in early childhood development and social environments.

Looking ahead, technological disruption is expected to accelerate further the pace at which skills and knowledge become obsolete. Advances in AI, automation, and digital platforms are transforming occupational requirements across sectors, reducing the shelf life of technical knowledge and increasing the importance of adaptability and continuous learning. Estimates suggest that a substantial share of the knowledge acquired in technical degree programs may become outdated within a few years of graduation, underscoring the limitations of front-loaded education models that concentrate learning early in life (World Economic Forum 2023).

At the same time, technological change is creating unprecedented opportunities for education and training. The knowledge economy increasingly requires lifelong learning, with skill acquisition and renewal extending across the entire working life. In response, organizations and educational institutions are turning to digital platforms, online courses, and technology-mediated learning systems to support continuous skill development. These tools enable flexible, scalable, and cost-effective training tailored to individual needs and organizational demands (OECD 2019). Remote learning technologies also expand access to education for nontraditional students, working adults, and those in geographically remote areas.

As digital learning becomes more widespread, the boundaries between formal education, workplace training, and informal learning are increasingly blurred. Human capital development is no longer confined to schools and universities but embedded within organizations and professional networks. Economies that successfully integrate education systems with labor market needs and promote lifelong learning are likely to experience higher productivity, greater innovation, and more inclusive growth. In contrast, societies that fail to adapt risk-widening skill gaps, rising inequality, and diminished competitiveness in an increasingly knowledge-driven global economy.

The Move Toward Flattened, Fluid, and Flexible Organizations of Work

The organization of work is undergoing a profound transformation as technological forces and their associated social changes reshape how firms are structured, governed, and coordinated. Traditional hierarchical organizations based on rigid pyramidal chains of command are increasingly giving way to flatter, more fluid, and more flexible forms of organization (Davis 2016). This transition reflects the growing importance of knowledge, creativity, and intellectual property as central sources of economic value in advanced economies (Haskel and Westlake 2018). In knowledge-intensive environments, authority derived solely from formal position becomes less effective, while collaboration, expertise, and rapid decision making become more significant (Barley et al. 2017).

To adapt to these conditions, many organizations have adopted participatory management practices that distribute authority across organizational levels rather than concentrating it at the top. Empowering employees with greater autonomy and decision-making responsibility is increasingly associated with higher productivity, faster innovation, and improved organizational performance (OECD 2019). When workers are trusted to apply their specialized knowledge and professional judgment, organizations can respond more effectively to technological disruption and volatile market conditions (Autor 2019). As a result, managerial roles are shifting away from direct supervision toward coordination, facilitation, and strategic alignment.

Rising specialization has further accelerated the movement toward flexible organizational forms. Few firms can internally sustain the full range of expertise required across advanced manufacturing, software development, industrial design, business services, and human resource management. Outsourcing has therefore evolved from a peripheral cost-saving strategy into a core organizational capability (Srnicek 2017). Globalization has expanded these opportunities by enabling firms to source specialized knowledge and services across national borders, leveraging cost differentials, global talent pools, and time-zone advantages (OECD 2019). In pursuit of efficiency and adaptability, organizations increasingly fragment their value chains across multiple locations or reorganize into semiautonomous units connected by digital infrastructure (Davis 2016).

Advances in information and communication technologies have been central to enabling these decentralized structures. Cloud computing, collaborative platforms, and real-time communication tools would allow organizations to coordinate complex activities regardless of geographic proximity (Barley et al. 2017). Digital infrastructures enable modularizing work processes, monitoring outputs, and integrating activities across dispersed actors, contributing to more permeable organizational boundaries and blurred distinctions between internal employees and external collaborators (Haskel and Westlake 2018).

These structural changes are closely associated with the expansion of flexible employment arrangements, including self-employment, contract work, temporary assignments, and project-based engagements. As organizations confront rapid technological change and intensified global competition, they increasingly rely on labor arrangements that enable rapid scaling with minimal long-term commitments (Kalleberg 2018). Emerging organizational models are often structured as networks of freelancers, contractors, and semiautonomous entities connected through digital platforms rather than stable internal hierarchies (Srnicek 2017). Consequently, work is shifting from permanent organizational roles toward task-specific and project-oriented configurations (Autor 2019).

Under sustained competitive pressure, employers are increasingly turning to part-time, contingent, and contract workers to meet strategic objectives. Empirical evidence suggests that nonstandard forms of work continue to expand across advanced economies, particularly in knowledge-intensive sectors where skills can be sourced globally and deployed remotely (Kalleberg 2018). Even workers who remain formally employed are more likely to experience flexible schedules and nontraditional arrangements, raising significant challenges for employment law, tax systems, and social protection regimes designed around stable, long-term employment relationships (OECD 2019). Benefits such as health care coverage, pensions, and disability insurance often fail to align with fragmented work trajectories, increasing economic insecurity and inequality (Autor 2019).

At the same time, technological innovation is transforming the very concept of the workplace. Unlike traditional models centered on fixed physical locations, many contemporary forms of work are no longer tied to a specific site. While manufacturing and certain service roles still require physical presence, a growing share of professional and knowledge-based work can be performed remotely (OECD 2019). Distance work expands access to global labor markets and offers greater flexibility for workers balancing employment with caregiving responsibilities or other constraints (Barley et al. 2017).

As physical location becomes less central, geographic proximity may gradually lose some of its traditional importance in economic activity. This shift is visible in the emergence of technology clusters outside central metropolitan cores and in smaller cities that combine lower costs with strong educational and innovation ecosystems (Davis 2016). These developments challenge long-standing assumptions about cities as the dominant hubs of economic activity, even as new forms of spatial concentration continue to emerge.

However, greater organizational flexibility does not necessarily translate into greater worker autonomy. Many firms increasingly rely on data-driven technologies to monitor, evaluate, and manage workers, including those operating remotely. Algorithmic management systems and workforce analytics enable employers to exert unprecedented precision over dispersed labor forces (Zuboff 2019). Recruitment and evaluation practices are also evolving, as employers use digital traces and online platforms to assess skills beyond traditional credentials (Autor 2019). While these tools may improve efficiency, they raise serious ethical concerns regarding privacy, surveillance, transparency, and discrimination, underscoring the need for updated regulatory and ethical frameworks (Zuboff 2019).

Growing Diversity of the Workforce

The composition of the workforce in Western economies has changed markedly over the past several decades, with diversity emerging as a defining feature of contemporary labor markets. In the United States and much of Europe, this transformation reflects not only demographic change but also more profound economic, cultural, and institutional shifts linked to globalization, migration, educational expansion, and evolving social norms. Diversity today extends well beyond race and gender to include age, migration background, education, identity, lifestyle, and cognitive orientation. As a result, workplaces have become more pluralistic, complex, and reflective of broader societal change.

Immigration has been one of the most potent drivers of workforce diversity. Western economies have long relied on migrant labor to address shortages in sectors such as agriculture, construction, health care, hospitality, transportation, and information technology. In Europe, population aging and low fertility have increased dependence on migrants to sustain economic output and finance welfare systems (OECD 2023). In the United States, immigration has played an even more visible role. Although immigration rates relative to population were higher in the early 20th century, the absolute number of foreign-born workers today is historically unprecedented. By 2024, foreign-born individuals accounted for roughly one-fifth of the United States' civilian labor force, reflecting steady growth over the past decade (U.S. Bureau of Labor Statistics 2024).

The ethnic and racial composition of the workforce has shifted accordingly. Hispanic and Asian workers represent a growing share of the labor force and are among the fastest-expanding demographic groups in the United States. Higher fertility rates among Hispanic populations combined with continued immigration suggest that much of the future growth of the American workforce will come from socioethnic minority groups (Pew Research Center 2024). These changes are reshaping organizational cultures and compelling employers to adapt recruitment, management, and communication practices to increasingly diverse teams.

Gender diversity has also advanced substantially. Women now make up close to half of the labor force in most Western economies, and their representation continues to rise in professional, technical, and managerial occupations. In the United States, women surpass men in educational attainment, a trend with significant implications for occupational structure and career trajectories (National Center for Education Statistics 2023). Labor force participation patterns are shifting as well, with female participation increasing and male participation gradually declining. Despite persistent wage gaps, unequal access to leadership positions, and the continued burden of unpaid care work, gender diversity has become a structural and enduring feature of modern labor markets rather than a transitional phenomenon (International Labour Organization 2023).

Age diversity is another increasingly important dimension of workforce change. Rising life expectancy, delayed retirement, and financial pressures have encouraged older adults to remain economically active for longer. At the same time, younger generations are entering the labor market with distinct expectations regarding flexibility, work–life balance, and organizational values. Many workplaces now include three or even four generations working side by side, creating opportunities for mentoring, knowledge transfer, and innovation, while also posing challenges related to communication styles, technological adoption, and organizational cohesion (OECD 2023).

Educational and cognitive diversity have expanded in parallel with these demographic shifts. Knowledge-intensive sectors demand advanced analytical and technical skills. At the same time, the growth of service work, platform-mediated labor, and the gig economy has widened the range of educational backgrounds represented in the workforce. Employees may bring formal scientific training, vocational expertise, or experience-based knowledge acquired outside traditional academic institutions. This diversity of skills and perspectives can enhance organizational problem-solving and adaptability, but it also requires more flexible management practices and inclusive forms of coordination (Autor 2019).

Cultural and identity-based diversity has grown as well, particularly among younger cohorts. Younger workers in Europe and the United

States are more racially and ethnically diverse than previous generations. They are more open in expressing differences related to gender identity, sexual orientation, religion, and lifestyle. Workplaces increasingly serve as arenas where questions of inclusion, recognition, and belonging are negotiated. Many organizations now view diversity as a strategic asset associated with creativity, innovation, and global competitiveness, leading to the widespread adoption of diversity and inclusion initiatives. However, evidence suggests that outcomes vary widely, ranging from meaningful institutional change to largely symbolic compliance (Dobbin and Kalev 2016).

At the societal level, growing workforce diversity mirrors broader demographic and cultural transformations across Western societies. The United States, long shaped by immigration, remains at the forefront of this shift, while Western Europe is moving in a similar direction as labor shortages and demographic aging intensify pressure for more inclusive labor-market integration. Looking ahead, the workforce in advanced economies is expected to grow older, become more feminine, and become more ethnically diverse. These trends are closely linked to global migration, educational expansion, and changing social norms, making diversity a defining and enduring characteristic of 21st-century labor markets.

The Effects of Automation and AI

While technological change has always altered labor markets, contemporary advances differ in that AI systems increasingly perform not only physical and routine tasks but also cognitive, analytical, and decision-making functions. As a result, automation is reshaping job structures, skill requirements, organizational practices, and the broader social meaning of work across advanced and emerging economies.

One of the most visible effects of automation and AI is the displacement of routine work. Early waves of automation primarily affected manufacturing by replacing repetitive manual tasks with machines and industrial robots. Today, AI systems extend automation into sectors once considered resistant to mechanization. Algorithms can review legal documents, draft financial reports, interpret medical images, optimize logistics networks, and analyze large datasets faster and more consistently than human workers. This expansion of automation into professional services, finance, health care, education, and transportation reflects a shift from task automation based on physical repetition to automation based on pattern recognition and data processing (Autor et al. 2003). As tasks are increasingly decomposed into components that can or cannot be automated, job roles across industries are being restructured rather than eliminated wholesale.

This process contributes to growing labor market polarization. High-skilled, high-wage occupations that rely on creativity, complex problem-solving, strategic thinking, and interpersonal interaction continue to expand. At the lower end of the labor market, many jobs requiring physical presence, manual dexterity, or direct personal service remain relatively resistant to automation. In contrast, middle skill occupations characterized by routine cognitive or administrative tasks, such as clerical work, bookkeeping, and specific production roles, are particularly vulnerable. The result is an hourglass-shaped labor market, with growth concentrated at the top and bottom and contraction in the middle (Autor 2019). Workers displaced from routine occupations often face significant barriers to reemployment, as transitions into emerging roles typically require new skills and credentials.

Automation and AI also reshape the skills required for employability. Demand is rising for technical competencies such as data analysis, programming, machine learning, and systems integration. At the same time, employers increasingly value skills that remain difficult to automate, including communication, emotional intelligence, collaboration, ethical judgment, and adaptability. The future workforce must therefore combine technological literacy with distinctly human capabilities. This shift places growing pressure on education systems to prepare students for occupations that may not yet exist and on workers to engage in continuous learning throughout their careers (World Economic Forum 2023). As responsibility for skill development increasingly shifts from employers to individuals, inequalities may widen between those with access to education and training and those without.

Beyond individual workers, automation and AI are transforming the organization of work itself. Digital technologies enable remote work, virtual collaboration, and the coordination of geographically dispersed teams, accelerating trends toward flexible, location-independent employment. Firms can source talent globally, intensifying competition among workers while expanding opportunities for highly skilled professionals. At the same time, organizations increasingly rely on algorithmic management systems to allocate tasks, monitor performance, and evaluate productivity. While such systems can enhance efficiency and consistency, they also introduce new forms of digital surveillance that may reduce worker autonomy and intensify work demands (OECD 2019). Concerns about transparency, privacy, and algorithmic bias have become central to debates about the future of work.

Automation also alters the distribution of power within organizations and labor markets. Highly automated firms can scale operations without proportional increases in employment, relying on smaller core workforces supported by contractors, freelancers, and platform-based workers. As a result, traditional long-term employment relationships weaken, and job stability declines. The growth of the gig economy illustrates this trend, with platform-mediated work expanding in transportation, delivery, home services, and digital microtasks. AI systems play a central role by matching supply and demand, setting prices, and ranking workers, often through opaque processes that workers cannot easily contest (Srnicek 2017). This shift not only increases labor flexibility for firms but also exposes workers to greater precarity, income volatility, and reduced access to benefits.

Despite these disruptive effects, automation and AI also generate new forms of value and employment. They give rise to expanding industries centered on robotics, software development, cybersecurity, data science, and system integration. These sectors demand highly skilled labor and often offer relatively high wages. Moreover, automation can raise productivity, lower costs, and expand economic capacity, potentially increasing demand for goods and services and creating new jobs over time. Historical experience suggests that while technology displaces some jobs, it can also develop others through indirect and complementary effects (Acemoglu and Restrepo 2020). The challenge lies in the timing and distribution of these effects, as job creation often lags behind displacement and requires different skills.

The broader social implications of automation and AI are equally profound. Work has traditionally provided not only income but also identity, social status, and a sense of purpose. As machines assume a greater share of productive activity, societies may need to reconsider the centrality of paid employment in social life. Policy debates around universal basic income, shorter workweeks, job guarantees, and new forms of social protection reflect attempts to respond to the economic and moral consequences of technological change. Without effective institutional adaptation, automation risks deepening inequality, weakening social mobility, and exacerbating divides between those who benefit from technological progress and those who are displaced by it (International Labour Organization 2023).

Skills-Based Hiring

Skills-based hiring represents a significant shift in how organizations define talent and make recruitment decisions. Instead of relying primarily on formal credentials such as college degrees, institutional prestige, or prior job titles, skills-based hiring emphasizes what candidates can actually do. It focuses on demonstrable hard and soft skills, such as coding ability, analytical reasoning, communication, problem-solving, and adaptability. Indeed, it defines skills-based hiring as prioritizing skills, transferable experience, and potential to succeed in a role over formal educational attainment alone (Dahl Consulting Group 2025). This approach challenges decades of credential-centric hiring practices that gradually raised educational requirements for jobs that had not historically demanded them, a phenomenon widely described as degree inflation (Sigelman et al. 2024).

Several structural forces are driving renewed interest in skills-based hiring. First, persistent labor shortages in key sectors such as AI, cybersecurity, advanced manufacturing, and sustainability have made traditional credential filters increasingly impractical. Employers facing unfilled roles are discovering that formal degrees are often poor proxies for job readiness. Second, rapid technological change has shortened the shelf life of academic knowledge, particularly in technology-intensive fields. Skills acquired through practice, short-term training, or industry experience often prove more relevant than degrees earned years earlier. Third, equity and diversity considerations have gained prominence, especially in the

United States, where roughly two-thirds of adults over the age of 25 do not hold a bachelor's degree (Brookings Institution 2025). Degree-based hiring can systematically exclude large segments of the population, including racial minorities, immigrants, and workers from lower-income backgrounds.

Reflecting these pressures, many corporations and public sector employers have pledged to eliminate degree requirements for large numbers of roles. Between 2014 and 2023, the number of job postings that removed degree requirements nearly quadrupled, with the most significant surge occurring in 2022. On the surface, this suggests a major transformation in hiring norms. In practice, however, changes in job advertisements have not always translated into equally dramatic changes in hiring outcomes.

Empirical evidence indicates that the impact of skills-based hiring on actual employment patterns has so far been modest. An analysis of more than 11,000 roles at large United States firms found that removing degree requirements increased the share of nondegreed hires by only 3.5 percentage points. While nearly two-thirds of employers report using skills-based hiring for entry-level roles, often through competency-based job descriptions, structured interviews, and assessment tools, many organizations continue to hire similar proportions of degree holders as before (National Association of Colleges and Employers 2024). In this sense, the rhetoric surrounding skills-based hiring has frequently outpaced its implementation.

Research suggests that employers adopting skills-based hiring fall into three broad categories (Sigelman et al. 2024). The first group, representing about 37 percent of firms, made substantial changes and significantly increased hiring of nondegreed workers, on average by nearly 20 percent. Companies such as Walmart, Apple, General Motors, Target, ExxonMobil, Yelp, and several government agencies illustrate this approach. These organizations not only revised job postings but also redesigned assessments, training pipelines, and promotion pathways, leading to measurable improvements in workforce diversity and employee retention. The second group, accounting for roughly 45 percent of firms, formally removed degree requirements but saw little change in hiring outcomes. Firms such as Amazon, Oracle, Bank of America, and Lockheed

Martin exemplify this category, in which credentials continue to serve as informal screening devices. The third group, about 18 percent of firms, initially increased nondegreed hiring but later reverted to earlier practices when institutional support weakened. Nike, Uber, HSBC, and Delta Air Lines demonstrate how skills-based hiring can lose momentum when it is not embedded in core human resource systems.

When implemented with commitment, skills-based hiring produces meaningful benefits for both employers and workers. Employers gain access to larger and more diverse talent pools, reducing recruitment bottlenecks and improving organizational performance. Evidence shows that nondegreed workers hired into roles that previously required degrees have two-year retention rates roughly 10 percentage points higher than their degree-holding peers, lowering turnover and training costs. Workers also benefit through greater upward mobility. Nondegreed employees entering degree-restricted roles formerly earn, on average, 25 percent more annually, equivalent to about 12,400 dollars in additional wages. Some firms, such as PwC Australia, have actively embraced this logic by emphasizing human skills like emotional intelligence and critical thinking, recruiting across diverse disciplines, and integrating microcredentials into their talent pipelines (PwC Australia 2024).

Not all occupations are equally suited to skills-based hiring. Professions such as medicine, law, and engineering will continue to require formal degrees due to regulatory, ethical, and safety considerations. At the other extreme, removing degree requirements from low-skilled service jobs yields limited benefits. The most significant potential lies in middle-skills occupations, where degreed and nondegreed workers already work side by side. Roles such as construction managers, web developers, IT support specialists, production clerks, distribution managers, and first-line supervisors in food service and sales are particularly promising. Fully embracing skills-based hiring in these areas could create an estimated 250,000 additional opportunities each year.

Wellness Focus at Work

Over much of the 20th century, employment benefits were defined narrowly around wages, pensions, and access to health care. In recent decades, however, organizations have increasingly adopted a broader and more holistic understanding of employee well-being. This shift reflects growing recognition that productivity, engagement, and organizational sustainability depend not only on financial compensation but also on workers' physical, mental, financial, and social health. Workplace wellness has therefore moved from a peripheral benefit to a central component of contemporary employment relations (Grawitch and Ballard 2016).

Modern wellness frameworks typically encompass four interrelated domains. Physical wellness includes preventive health care, ergonomic workplace design, and initiatives that encourage movement and healthy lifestyles. Mental and emotional wellness focuses on stress reduction, access to counseling services, burnout prevention, and the normalization of mental health discussions in organizational culture. Financial wellness addresses issues such as retirement planning, debt management, and financial literacy, acknowledging that economic insecurity directly affects job performance and psychological well-being. Social and cultural wellness emphasizes inclusion, belonging, and respectful workplace relationships, recognizing that employees thrive when they feel valued and connected (Grawitch and Ballard 2016). Together, these dimensions reflect a shift from reactive health care benefits toward proactive well-being strategies.

Several structural forces explain why wellness has become a central concern in labor and employment policy. Generational change plays a significant role. Younger cohorts, particularly Millennials and Generation Z, place greater emphasis on balance, meaning, and psychological health in their working lives. According to Deloitte's Global Human Capital Trends report, well-being consistently ranks among the top factors influencing employer choice and employee retention for these groups (Deloitte 2023). This generational shift challenges organizations to compete not only on pay but also on the quality of work–life.

The COVID-19 pandemic further accelerated the wellness agenda. The crisis intensified stress, anxiety, and burnout while blurring boundaries between professional and personal life. Although remote and hybrid work models increased flexibility, they also introduced new risks of isolation, constant availability, and digital exhaustion. In response, many employers came to view wellness as an organizational responsibility rather than an individual concern, with direct implications for performance, resilience, and employer reputation (Kniffin et al. 2021). Tight labor markets have reinforced this perspective, as firms increasingly rely on wellness offerings to attract and retain scarce talent.

The economic rationale for investing in wellness is also compelling. The Global Wellness Institute estimates that stress-related absenteeism, presenteeism, and disengagement cost organizations trillions of dollars annually, making poor well-being a significant drag on productivity and growth (Global Wellness Institute 2021). As a result, benefits packages now extend well beyond traditional health care coverage. Many organizations offer counseling services, wellness stipends, mindfulness and resilience training, and flexible work arrangements, such as hybrid schedules or compressed workweeks, to support work–life balance (Gartner 2023). Digital wellness platforms, including telehealth services and mental health applications, have become widespread, particularly in large organizations. Structural changes are also evident in the creation of roles such as the chief wellness officer, signaling that well-being has become a strategic priority rather than a human resources add-on.

Large corporations illustrate how wellness has been institutionalized. Google has long integrated on-site health services and mindfulness programs into its organizational model. Deloitte has expanded access to mental health resources across its workforce, while Unilever's Lamplighter Program provides holistic well-being support to employees worldwide (Unilever 2021). Evidence suggests that such initiatives generate tangible benefits. Employees report improved health, reduced stress, and higher job satisfaction, while employers experience lower turnover, reduced absenteeism, and higher engagement. Organizations that embed wellness into their culture also benefit from stronger employer branding, enhancing their ability to recruit and retain skilled workers (Grawitch and Ballard 2016).

Despite these advantages, workplace wellness initiatives face essential criticisms. Many programs risk becoming superficial, focusing on symbolic perks such as fitness memberships or mobile applications while ignoring deeper structural issues, including excessive workloads, job insecurity, and poor management practices. Access to comprehensive wellness programs is uneven, with large corporations far more likely to invest than small- and medium-sized enterprises. Moreover, precarious and gig workers, who are often most exposed to stress and insecurity, are typically excluded from organizational wellness initiatives (Wood et al. 2019). Measuring outcomes presents additional challenges, as it is subjective and shaped by cultural and individual differences.

Nevertheless, the rise of workplace wellness signals a more profound transformation in the employment relationship. Work is increasingly organized around knowledge, creativity, and emotional labor, making human well-being a core productive resource. As a result, employment is shifting from a purely transactional exchange of labor for wages toward a more relational model in which well-being is embedded in the labor contract. Policy developments reinforce this shift. The European Union's integration of psychosocial risk management into occupational health and safety frameworks suggests that wellness is becoming a structural expectation rather than a voluntary corporate initiative (European Agency for Safety and Health at Work 2021). Thus, workplace wellness is not only a moral concern but a practical necessity for sustaining productivity, innovation, and long-term organizational performance.

References

Acemoglu, D., and Restrepo, P. 2020. "Robots and Jobs." *Journal of Political Economy* 128, no. 6, pp. 2188–2244. https://doi.org/10.1086/705716

Autor, D.H. 2019. "Work of the Past, Work of the Future." *AEA Papers and Proceedings* 109, pp. 1–32. https://doi.org/10.1257/pandp.20191110

Autor, D.H., Levy, F., and Murnane, R.J. 2003. "The Skill Content of Recent Technological Change: An Empirical Exploration." *Quarterly Journal of Economics* 118, no. 4, pp. 1279–1333. https://doi.org/10.1162/003355303322552801

Barley, S.R., Bechky, B.A., and Milliken, F.J. 2017. "The Changing Nature of Work." *Academy of Management Discoveries* 3, no. 2, pp. 111–115. https://doi.org/10.5465/amd.2017.0034

Barro, R.J., and Lee, J.-W. 2015. *Education Matters: Global Schooling Gains from the 19th to the 21st Century*. Oxford University Press.

Brookings Institution. 2025. "There is More to Skills-based Hiring than just Removing Degree Requirements." https://www.brookings.edu/articles/theres-more-to-skills-based-hiring-than-just-removing-degree-requirements/

Chetty, R., Friedman, J.N., Saez, E., Turner, N., and Yagan, D. 2017. "Mobility Report Cards: The Role of Colleges in Intergenerational Mobility." National Bureau of Economic Research Working Paper No. 23618. https://doi.org/10.3386/w23618

Dahl Consulting Group. 2025, August 12. "What is Skills-Based Hiring, and How does it Work?" https://www.dahlconsulting.com/2025/08/12/what-is-skills-based-hiring-and-how-does-it-work/

Davis, G.F. 2016. *The Vanishing American Corporation*. Berrett-Koehler Publishers.

Day, J.C., and Bauman, K. 2000. *Have We Reached the Top? Educational Attainment Projections of the U.S. Population*. U.S. Census Bureau, Population Division.

Deloitte. 2023. *2023 Global Human Capital Trends*. Deloitte Insights. https://www2.deloitte.com/insights

Dobbin, F., and Kalev, A. 2016. "Why Diversity Programs Fail." *Harvard Business Review* 94, no. 7, pp. 52–60.

Dubina, K.S., Ice, L., Kim, J.-L., and Rieley, M. 2021, October. "Projections Overview and Highlights, 2020–30." Monthly Labor Review. U.S. Bureau of Labor Statistics. https://www.bls.gov/opub/mlr/

European Agency for Safety and Health at Work. 2021. "Work-Related Stress and Psychosocial Risks: Trends and Policy Developments in Europe." https://osha.europa.eu

Gartner. 2023. "Future of Work Trends for 2023." Gartner Research. https://www.gartner.com

Global Wellness Institute. 2021. "The Global Workplace Wellness Economy." https://globalwellnessinstitute.org

Goldin, C., and Katz, L.F. 2008. *The Race between Education and Technology*. Harvard University Press.

Grawitch, M.J., and Ballard, D.W. 2016. *The Psychologically Healthy Workplace: Building a Win–Win Environment for Organizations and Employees*. American Psychological Association.

Gordon, R.J. 2016. *The Rise and Fall of American Growth: The U.S. Standard of Living since the Civil War*. Princeton University Press.

Haskel, J., and Westlake, S. 2018. *Capitalism without Capital: The Rise of the Intangible Economy*. Princeton University Press. https://doi.org/10.2307/j.ctvc77f5j

Hunt, V., Layton, D., and Prince, S. 2015. *Diversity Matters*. McKinsey & Company.

Ilmarinen, J. 2019. *Work Ability: A Comprehensive Guide*. Finnish Institute of Occupational Health.

International Labour Organization. 2023. *Global Employment Trends*. ILO. https://www.ilo.org

Kalleberg, A.L. 2018. *Precarious Lives: Job Insecurity and Well-Being in Affluent Democracies*. Polity Press.

Karoly, L.A., and Panis, C.W.A. 2004. *The 21st Century at Work: Forces Shaping the Future Workforce and Workplace in the United States*. RAND Corporation.

Kniffin, K.M., Narayanan, J., Anseel, F., Antonakis, J., Ashford, S.P., Bakker, A.B., Bamberger, P., Bapuji, H., Bhave, D.P., Choi, V.K., Creary, S.J., Demerouti, E., Flynn, F.J., Gelfand, M.J., Greer, L.L., Johns, G., Kesebir, S., Klein, P.G., Lee, S.Y., and Van Vugt, M. 2021. "COVID-19 and the Workplace: Implications, Issues, and Insights for Future Research and Action." *American Psychologist* 76, no. 1, pp. 63–77. https://doi.org/10.1037/amp0000716

Lam, D. 2011. "How the World Survived the Population Bomb: Lessons from 50 Years of Extraordinary Demographic History." *Demography* 48, no. 4, pp. 1231–1262. https://doi.org/10.1007/s13524-011-0044-6

National Association of Colleges and Employers. 2024. "Nearly Two-Thirds of Employers Use Skills-based Hiring Practices for New Entry-Level Hires." https://www.naceweb.org/talent-acquisition/trends-and-predictions/nearly-two-thirds-of-employers-use-skills-based-hiring-practices-for-new-entry-level-hires

National Center for Education Statistics. 2023. *Digest of Education Statistics*. U.S. Department of Education. https://nces.ed.gov

Ng, T.W.H., and Feldman, D.C. 2015. "The Moderating Effects of Age in the Relationships of Job Autonomy to Work Outcomes." *Work, Aging and Retirement* 1, no. 1, pp. 64–78. https://doi.org/10.1093/workar/wau003

OECD. 2001. *Education at a Glance 2001*. Organisation for Economic Co-operation and Development.

OECD. 2019. *OECD Employment Outlook 2019: The Future of Work*. OECD Publishing. https://doi.org/10.1787/9ee00155-en

OECD. 2019. *The Future of Work*. OECD Publishing. https://doi.org/10.1787/9ee00155-en

OECD. 2021. *Preventing Ageing Unequally*. OECD Publishing. https://doi.org/10.1787/97d5a9a6-en

OECD. 2022. *Education at a Glance 2022*. OECD Publishing. https://doi.org/10.1787/3197152b-en

OECD. 2023. *International Migration Outlook 2023*. OECD Publishing. https://doi.org/10.1787/b0f40584-en

Pew Research Center. 2023. *U.S. Population Aging and Demographic Change*. Pew Research Center. https://www.pewresearch.org

Pew Research Center. 2024. *The Changing Demographics of the U.S. Workforce*. Pew Research Center. https://www.pewresearch.org

PwC Australia. 2024. *Human Skills and the Future Workforce*. https://www.theaustralian.com.au/

Sigelman, M., Fuller, J., and Martin, A. 2024, February. *Skills-based Hiring: The Long Road from Pronouncements to Practice*. Burning Glass Institute.

Srnicek, N. 2017. *Platform Capitalism*. Polity Press.

Unilever. 2021. "Lamplighter Programme: Empowering Healthy Lifestyles." https://www.unilever.com

United Nations. 2013. *World Population Ageing 2013*. Department of Economic and Social Affairs, Population Division.

United Nations. 2017. *World Urbanization Prospects: The 2017 Revision*. Department of Economic and Social Affairs, Population Division.

United Nations. 2019. *World Population Prospects 2019*. United Nations Department of Economic and Social Affairs.

U.S. Bureau of Labor Statistics. 2024. *Foreign-Born Workers in the U.S. Labor Force*. U.S. Department of Labor. https://www.bls.gov

Wang, F. 2020. "China's Population Destiny: The Looming Crisis." *The China Quarterly* 244, pp. 995–1015. https://doi.org/10.1017/S0305741020000631

Wood, A.J., Graham, M., Lehdonvirta, V., and Hjorth, I. 2019. "Good Gig, Bad Gig: Autonomy and Algorithmic Control in the Global Gig Economy." *Work, Employment and Society* 33, no. 1, pp. 56–75. https://doi.org/10.1177/0950017018785616

World Economic Forum. 2016. *The Future of Jobs: Employment, Skills and Workforce Strategy for the Fourth Industrial Revolution*. World Economic Forum.

World Economic Forum. 2023. *The Future of Jobs Report 2023*. World Economic Forum.

Zuboff, S. 2019. *The Age of Surveillance Capitalism: The Fight for a Human Future at the New Frontier of Power*. PublicAffairs.

CHAPTER 7

The Transformations of Global Consumption

Globalization and Cultural Hybridization

In a highly interconnected environment defined by digital technologies, international trade, and transnational media flows, brands no longer operate within stable cultural or geographic boundaries. Instead, they function in markets where meanings, aesthetics, and identities circulate rapidly, producing hybrid cultural forms that combine global influences with local traditions. This shift reflects a move away from the simple international distribution of products toward the circulation of symbols, lifestyles, narratives, and identities (Tomlinson 1999). Global brands are therefore not only economic actors but also cultural forces that help shape social meanings and consumer identities (Tomlinson 1999).

One important implication of this transformation is that global expansion can no longer depend on uniform standardization. Earlier phases of globalization often resembled a one-directional diffusion of American consumer culture through brands such as Coca-Cola or McDonald's. Contemporary globalization, by contrast, demands sensitivity to local contexts. Robertson's concept of glocalization emphasizes the interaction between global integration and local adaptation and has become central to modern marketing strategy (Robertson 1995). Multinational firms increasingly modify products, messages, and brand expressions to align with local tastes, values, and everyday practices (Robertson 1995). Examples such as McDonald's offering regionally adapted menu items in India or KFC tailoring its offerings in China, illustrate how firms negotiate cultural meanings to appear both globally recognizable and locally relevant. These adjustments are not merely operational decisions but symbolic actions that embed brands within local cultural frameworks and strengthen social legitimacy (Figure 7.1).

Figure 7.1 Glocalization or cultural hybridization in McDonald's products

At the same time, the role of brands has evolved in ways that intensify their cultural significance. Brands now operate as systems through which meaning is transferred (McCracken 1986). They carry cultural values, aspirations, and identities from the broader social world into consumer experience (McCracken 1986). Companies such as Apple, Nike, and Coca-Cola do not simply sell products; they provide symbolic worlds that allow consumers to express individuality, status, and a sense of belonging. These symbolic systems remain effective because they are flexible and open to reinterpretation across contexts. Brands gain iconic status when they construct narratives that consumers in different societies can adapt to their own circumstances and identity projects (Holt 2004).

Digital communication technologies have further intensified this symbolic flexibility. Social media platforms such as TikTok, YouTube, and Instagram enable consumers to shape brand meanings rather than passively receive them. This approach aligns with the notion that value creation increasingly occurs through cocreation, as consumers help construct the symbolic and experiential dimensions of brands (Prahalad and Ramaswamy 2004). Cova and Cova describe this process as tribal marketing, in which communities of interest form around shared passions such as fashion, music, gaming, or environmental activism (Cova and Cova 2002). These digitally connected groups develop their own rituals, norms, and symbols and often influence brand direction more rapidly than corporate planning processes (Cova and Lusch 2002).

Youth culture plays a particularly influential role in this dynamic. Young consumers engage with culture through what Appadurai describes as mediascapes, global symbolic environments shaped by mass media and digital platforms (Appadurai 1996). Adolescents and young adults in cities such as London, Lagos, and Seoul often share similar visual styles, musical preferences, and online references, producing forms of cultural convergence that transcend national boundaries (Appadurai 1996). This generation expects brands to demonstrate inclusivity, cultural openness, and social awareness, while reacting negatively to rigid or culturally insensitive messaging. For marketers, this group represents both strong engagement and heightened scrutiny, as authenticity and cultural respect are closely monitored (Appadurai 1996).

Hybrid cultural industries illustrate the creative possibilities of globalization. The global success of Korean popular music offers a clear example. Its appeal lies in the combination of Western pop structures, Korean visual and performance traditions, multilingual expression, and digitally mediated fan communities. For firms operating globally, hybridization suggests that innovation increasingly depends on collaboration with local creators, experimentation across cultural boundaries, and respect for regional artistic practices. Hybridization thus becomes not only a cultural outcome but also a source of competitive advantage (Yeganeh 2019).

At the same time, hybridization raises ethical concerns. The circulation of cultural symbols can obscure power imbalances within global markets. Although cultural exchange often appears reciprocal, branding infrastructures remain dominated by firms based in advanced economies. Scholars caution that hybridization can conceal cultural appropriation, where elements from marginalized cultures are extracted without recognition, compensation, or sensitivity to historical context (Said 1993; Kraidy 2005). In an environment where criticism spreads quickly online, brands face reputational risks if they engage with cultural material irresponsibly. Ethical glocalization, therefore, requires transparency, collaboration with local communities, and awareness of cultural histories

(Kraidy 2005). At a deeper level, globalization and hybridization reshape consumer identity itself. Consumers draw on diverse cultural symbols to express who they are and who they wish to become (Bauman 2000). Brands function as symbolic resources within this process of identity construction. Marketing today is therefore less concerned with persuasion alone and more focused on enabling consumers to enact identities through the symbolic worlds that brands offer.

Digitalization, Data, and Platform Dominance

The digital revolution has reshaped the logic of marketing, shifting it from persuasion to prediction. In this environment, data has become the primary source of value, algorithms determine visibility, and platforms serve as the main channels of exchange. Marketing no longer relies mainly on creativity or intuition. Instead, it operates within a data-driven system in which every search, click, and purchase is recorded, analyzed, and converted into economic value. As digital technologies and dominant platforms have expanded, a new financial model has emerged in which consumer behavior is continuously observed, anticipated, and influenced through computational systems. Marketing is now inseparable from algorithms and platforms, as power and influence are exercised through data processing rather than human judgment (Srnicek 2017; Zuboff 2019).

This transformation began with the digitalization of commerce and communication. As consumers moved online, their everyday activities generated vast volumes of behavioral information, including search histories, social media interactions, location data, purchase records, and biometric signals. This information became a new form of capital. Firms such as Google, Meta, Amazon, and TikTok built their business strategies around collecting and analyzing user data, turning digital traces into insights about preferences and habits. Through advanced analytics, marketers could identify patterns of past behavior and estimate future actions. The capacity to predict human behavior itself became a marketable asset, marking a fundamental shift akin to that of capitalism.

Data-driven marketing has fundamentally altered the relationship between brands and consumers. During the mass media era, marketers relied on broad demographic categories and generalized assumptions. Today, algorithmic systems divide consumers into fine-grained segments based on interests, routines, emotional cues, and online behavior. Machine learning models use these signals to personalize recommendations, adjust prices, and deliver messages tailored to individuals. Streaming services suggest content based on viewing history, online retailers dynamically adjust prices, and social media feeds present content designed to maximize engagement. Thus, marketing has become a predictive discipline in which success depends more on statistical accuracy than creative intuition (Davenport and Harris 2017).

At the same time, marketing has become tightly bound to a small number of digital platforms. Attention and commercial exchange are concentrated within robust ecosystems operated by companies such as Meta, Google, Amazon, and TikTok. These firms do more than connect buyers and sellers. They control data flows, design the algorithms that regulate visibility, and determine the rules governing access to audiences. This system reflects what Srnicek (2017) describes as platform capitalism, an economic structure built around digital infrastructures that mediate interactions among users, producers, and advertisers. Network effects reinforce this dominance, as platforms grow more valuable and powerful as participation increases.

For marketers, platform dominance creates both opportunity and constraint. Platforms offer access to large audiences and advanced targeting tools, but they also impose opaque standards that brands cannot easily influence. Visibility depends on how content is ranked and recommended by algorithmic systems rather than on intrinsic quality alone. Algorithms now act as cultural intermediaries that organize attention and structure digital experience (Beer 2018).

The expansion of surveillance and predictive marketing also raises concerns about influence and manipulation. Continuous monitoring allows firms to infer desires, moods, and intentions, sometimes before consumers consciously recognize them. Subtle behavioral signals, such as scrolling patterns, viewing duration, and interaction speed, are used to estimate emotional states. This approach enables marketing strategies that deliver offers at moments of maximum susceptibility. The consumer experience is therefore carefully engineered, guiding choices in ways that appear spontaneous but are computationally optimized. As digital marketing increasingly designs environments that steer attention and emotion through data feedback loops, influence becomes embedded in the architecture of choice (Turow 2017).

Claims of personalization, however, often obscure more profound inequalities. Algorithmic systems are trained on historical data shaped by social bias, which can reproduce and amplify existing forms of exclusion. Research shows that targeted advertising may distribute employment opportunities, credit offers, or housing information unevenly across social groups. At the same time, the concentration of data and technical expertise within a small group of global corporations intensifies power asymmetries. This process has been described as data colonialism, in which human experience itself becomes a resource extracted and monetized by corporate actors (Couldry and Mejias 2019).

In an algorithmic marketplace, the boundary between choice and influence blurs. When systems predict preferences, they also shape them, narrowing the range of options to those aligned with commercial priorities. Consumers generate data through everyday activity while being continuously guided by predictive systems. Privacy and autonomy are redefined in contexts where invisible calculations influence decisions. What is presented as relevance often masks a more profound shift from spontaneity toward optimization.

Growing awareness of data extraction has prompted consumers and regulators to call for greater transparency and restraint. Policies such as the European Union's General Data Protection Regulation represent early efforts to limit unchecked data exploitation (European Union 2016). Some firms are experimenting with practices that emphasize trust, reduced tracking, and more transparent data governance. The future of digital marketing will depend on how societies balance efficiency with ethics and innovation with responsibility.

Personalization, Participation, and Cocreation

The digital revolution has transformed the relationship between brands and consumers by dismantling the one-way communication model that defined marketing in the industrial and mass media era. In the past, firms produced messages and consumers received them with limited opportunity for response or influence. Today, this distinction has eroded as consumers actively participate in shaping how brands are perceived, experienced, and even designed through digital technologies and social media platforms. Marketing has therefore evolved into an interactive and adaptive process in which consumers function simultaneously as audiences and contributors, fundamentally altering how value and meaning are created in the digital economy (Prahalad and Ramaswamy 2004).

A central feature of this transformation is personalization, which has replaced mass marketing with individualized engagement. Twentieth-century marketing emphasized standardized messages distributed to broad audiences through television, radio, and print media, prioritizing reach over relevance. Advances in data analytics, AI, and algorithmic targeting now allow firms to tailor messages, products, and experiences to individual preferences and behaviors. Digital traces, such as search histories, purchase patterns, clicks, and biometric indicators, enable marketers to build detailed consumer profiles and adjust communication in real time. As a result, marketing increasingly resembles an ongoing exchange rather than a one-way broadcast, with messages continuously adapted to each user's context (Tuten and Solomon 2018).

This shift reflects a broader cultural change in consumer expectations. Individuals increasingly expect brands to recognize their uniqueness and respond accordingly. Streaming services curate content aligned with users' tastes and moods, online retailers dynamically adjust recommendations, and digital platforms create customized interfaces for each participant. These practices exemplify what Pine and Gilmore described as the experience economy, in which value emerges from personalized, emotionally resonant interactions rather than from standardized products alone (Pine and Gilmore 1999). Personalization thus functions not merely as a technical tool but as a means of forging symbolic and affective ties between brands and consumers.

Personalization is closely linked to a second transformation: the rise of participatory marketing. Social media platforms enable users to review products, remix brand messages, create content, and circulate interpretations across networks. Rather than being peripheral, this participation is now central to value creation, as firms and consumers jointly shape products, experiences, and meanings through ongoing interaction (Prahalad and Ramaswamy 2004).

Cocreation operates across a wide range of industries. In gaming, users develop modifications and virtual assets that enhance collective experience. In fashion and consumer goods, firms invite customers to customize designs through digital interfaces. In technology, open-source communities contribute knowledge and innovation that advance shared platforms. Advertising itself has become participatory, as campaigns rely on user involvement to circulate and reinterpret brand narratives. The success of personalized branding initiatives illustrates how inviting consumers into the creative process transforms the brand from a finished object into an open framework for participation and identity expression (Pine and Gilmore 1999).

A third dimension of this new marketing logic is the rise of influencer and creator economies, which have altered how authority and trust operate in digital culture. Traditional advertising relied on centralized figures such as celebrities or corporate spokespeople. Influencer culture, by contrast, is decentralized and relational, built on perceived authenticity, accessibility, and ongoing interaction with followers. Influencers serve as cultural intermediaries, translating brand messages into everyday language that resonates with specific communities (Abidin 2018).

This redistribution of influence has significant implications for marketing practice. Individuals with relatively small but dedicated followings can exert a strong influence over consumer decisions within niche communities. Brands increasingly collaborate with creators to embed themselves within social networks rather than simply delivering promotional messages. At the same time, platforms enable creators to monetize content directly, fostering new forms of entrepreneurial activity. In this environment, personal identity and commercial identity increasingly overlap, blurring the line between cultural expression and economic exchange (Abidin 2018).

Despite its participatory appearance, this system raises essential concerns about power and labor. Much of the value generated through participation is captured by platforms and firms rather than by users themselves. User-generated content, ratings, and interactions supply data that enhance algorithms and profitability, often without direct compensation. Influencers, while seemingly autonomous, remain dependent on platform algorithms and face income instability tied to changes in visibility and engagement metrics (Terranova 2000).

Even so, participatory marketing represents a significant redefinition of marketing's social role. Brands increasingly function as facilitators of community, creativity, and dialogue rather than as authorities that dictate meaning. Firms that succeed in this environment emphasize openness, responsiveness, and shared meaning, integrating user contributions into design and communication processes. These practices signal a shift from persuasion to facilitation, in which the primary task of marketing is to support collective meaning-making rather than impose messages from above (Prahalad and Ramaswamy 2004). From a managerial perspective, this transformation demands new capabilities. Organizations must develop the capacity to listen, engage, and collaborate with diverse publics, while designing systems that encourage creativity and reciprocity.

The Attention Economy and Cultural Competition

The rise of the attention economy is closely tied to the rapid expansion of content production. Digital technologies have dramatically lowered barriers to publishing and distribution, enabling individuals, firms, and institutions to participate in an ever-growing flow of communication (Jenkins 2006). While this democratization of expression has expanded visibility and participation, it has also produced a paradox. As information becomes abundant, meaning becomes harder to sustain. Human cognitive capacities for deep processing and sustained reflection are limited, and the volume of available content increasingly exceeds these limits (Carr 2010). Scholars describe this condition as content saturation, in which communication overwhelms comprehension and attention becomes the primary bottleneck in the circulation of meaning (Han 2017). Within such an environment, attention functions simultaneously as a reward and as a filtering mechanism that determines what becomes visible, relevant, and valuable (Davenport and Beck 2001).

Algorithmic systems intensify these dynamics by shaping how attention is allocated. Digital platforms rely on automated ranking, recommendation, and targeting systems that prioritize content that sustains engagement. Because emotional arousal tends to prolong attention, algorithms often favor content that elicits strong affective responses such as excitement, fear, outrage, or moral indignation (Zuboff 2019). As a result, digital media environments increasingly privilege immediacy and reaction over deliberation and reflection (Han 2017). This logic extends well beyond advertising into journalism and politics. News organizations now compete not only with one another but also with entertainment and user-generated content for visibility, frequently adopting the stylistic conventions of social media to survive in crowded attention markets (Wu 2016; McChesney 2013). Political communication similarly shifts toward performance and spectacle, prioritizing circulation and virality over sustained debate (Yeganeh 2019).

Within this competitive attention landscape, brands and creators rely heavily on emotion and spectacle to stand out. Messages must be intense, visually striking, or morally charged to cut through dense streams of content (Wu 2016). Debord's concept of the society of the spectacle remains highly relevant in this context, as social relations are increasingly mediated through images staged for visibility rather than substance (Debord 1967). Contemporary marketing campaigns frequently deploy moral narratives, controversy, or identity-based appeals to generate emotional attachment and public attention. The objective extends beyond selling products to producing affective bonds that tie audiences to brands through feeling, identification, and symbolic alignment (Arvidsson 2005; Banet-Weiser 2012).

However, this emotional emphasis carries high social and cultural costs. Algorithmic systems reward engagement regardless of tone, making conflict, fear, and polarization especially effective at sustaining attention (Zuboff 2019). As a result, digital platforms tend to amplify divisive content, since disagreement and outrage hold attention longer than consensus-oriented discourse (Roose 2021). The attention economy thus privileges emotional extremes and superficial interaction over nuance, coherence, and accuracy, reshaping norms of public communication (Han 2017; Wu 2016). Shareability often trumps truth or insight, contributing to declining trust in media and public discourse.

Algorithms play a central role in structuring this system. Unlike earlier media environments shaped by editorial judgment and institutional norms, contemporary platforms rely on automated systems to allocate visibility (Gillespie 2018). These systems prioritize engagement metrics over social value or fairness, producing self-reinforcing dynamics in which already visible content gains further exposure (Zuboff 2019).

The consequences of this competition for attention extend beyond marketing and media to individual cognition and cultural institutions. Continuous exposure to digital stimuli fragments concentration and weakens the capacity for sustained thought (Carr 2010). Notifications and updates demand constant responsiveness, leaving little space for rest, silence, or contemplation (Han 2017). Attention increasingly shifts from a marker of agency to a resource to be extracted and monetized (Zuboff 2019). Institutions such as education, journalism, and the arts, which depend on sustained attention, struggle within environments optimized for speed, visibility, and distraction (Yeganeh 2019).

Creator-Driven Markets and Hyper-Convenience Expectations

The growing dominance of creators and influencers signals a fundamental shift in who shapes consumer preferences in digital markets. Traditional advertising has steadily lost credibility amid a saturated environment of promotional messages, algorithmic targeting, and widespread consumer skepticism. Corporate claims delivered through mass media no longer command the same authority or trust they once did. Instead, consumers increasingly rely on recommendations from online creators who appear relatable, accessible, and embedded in everyday digital life. This shift is closely linked to the rise of parasocial relationships, in which audiences form emotional bonds with mediated personalities who feel familiar despite the absence of direct interaction. Influencers occupy a hybrid position between peer and celebrity, enabling them to shape tastes, norms, and purchasing decisions with unusual immediacy and intimacy.

This transformation has significant implications for marketing strategy. Influence is no longer centralized or broadcast from the top down through standardized campaigns. Instead, it is distributed across networks of niche communities organized around specific interests, identities, and algorithmically curated content streams. Influencers function as trusted intermediaries within these communities, translating products and brands into culturally resonant narratives. Influencers are microcelebrities who strategically self-brand to cultivate credibility and trust with targeted audiences (Khamis et al. 2017).

The rise of the creator economy also blurs the boundary between production and promotion. Influencers rarely present products as isolated advertisements; instead, they integrate them into the ongoing performance of their digital identities. Abidin (2016) conceptualizes this practice as ambient advertising, in which marketing is embedded within everyday online expression rather than framed as a distinct persuasive act. As a result, brands must adopt cocreative approaches that grant creators interpretive freedom instead of imposing rigid scripts. Although this reduces managerial control over messaging, it often generates cultural legitimacy and authenticity that traditional advertising struggles to achieve. A further implication of creator-driven markets is speed. Cultural trends now emerge, circulate, and disappear at unprecedented rates. A single short video can propel an obscure product into global visibility within hours, while a poorly judged collaboration can damage a brand's reputation just as quickly. Firms must therefore invest in continuous monitoring, rapid response mechanisms, and advanced social listening capabilities.

Alongside the rise of creators, a second powerful trend shaping digital marketing is the escalation of expectations for convenience and instant gratification. Digital platforms have conditioned consumers to expect effortless purchasing, rapid delivery, intuitive interfaces, and frictionless returns. Delays, complexity, or inconvenience are increasingly perceived as unacceptable. This expectation reflects a broader acceleration of social life driven by digital technologies, which compress time and intensify demands for immediacy across economic and cultural domains (Rosa 2013). At the infrastructural level, delivering convenience requires highly responsive logistics systems, including automated warehouses, predictive inventory management, and fast delivery networks. Firms such as Amazon have set new benchmarks for speed and ease, forcing competitors to prioritize responsiveness alongside cost efficiency. Chopra and Meindl (2016) demonstrate that contemporary supply chains increasingly emphasize flexibility and speed rather than cost minimization alone.

Convenience has thus become a core dimension of competitive strategy rather than a supplementary service feature. Convenience also extends across the entire customer experience. Consumers expect one-click purchasing, mobile-optimized design, personalized recommendations, and seamless customer support across channels. Even minor interruptions, such as slow-loading pages or complex checkout processes, can result in immediate abandonment. Research on omnichannel retailing shows that seamless integration across digital and physical touchpoints significantly enhances satisfaction, trust, and loyalty (Verhoef et al. 2015). At a psychological level, extreme convenience reshapes expectations and behavior. Instant service normalizes immediate reward and lowers tolerance for delay. Subscription models, auto-replenishment systems, and predictive recommendations anticipate consumer needs before they are consciously articulated. Such experiential innovations transform not only customer expectations but also the competitive logic of entire industries (Berry et al. 2002).

Creator-driven influence and hyperconvenience reinforce one another. Creators generate desire through personalized and culturally resonant narratives, while convenience infrastructures enable consumers to act on those impulses instantly. A product highlighted in a viral video becomes far more compelling when it can be purchased in seconds and delivered within hours. Influence stimulates demand, while convenience converts attention into action with unprecedented speed.

The Shortening Product Life Cycles

In the contemporary economy, innovation cycles have accelerated to the point that products often become obsolete almost as soon as they reach the market. The traditional product life cycle, once structured around clear stages of introduction, growth, maturity, and decline, has been dramatically compressed. Previously represented as a bell-shaped curve marked by gradual expansion and slow decline, it now resembles a sharp spike characterized by rapid ascent followed by an equally rapid fall. This shift reflects what Hartmut Rosa describes as social acceleration, a condition in which technological, economic, and cultural processes intensify time pressure across all domains of life.

The product life cycle remains a central concept in marketing theory, used to explain how sales and profitability evolve. In earlier periods, products such as automobiles, household appliances, and consumer electronics experienced long phases of maturity during which firms benefited from stable demand and predictable margins. That stability has largely disappeared. Digitalization, globalization, and intense competition have shortened life cycles across most industries. Products no longer decline slowly; they are displaced quickly as new alternatives emerge (Yeganeh 2019).

Two closely connected forces drive this compression. The first is investor pressure for continuous growth. In a financialized economy, firm valuation depends heavily on the perception of ongoing innovation. Companies are therefore incentivized to replace products rapidly rather than extend their longevity. The second force is consumer demand for constant novelty. Newness has become associated with progress, status, and relevance. Innovation now serves as a symbolic marker of vitality for both firms and consumers, creating a feedback loop in which accelerated production fuels accelerated expectations.

The technology sector provides the clearest illustration of this dynamic. The lifespan of personal computers has declined sharply, while smartphones, tablets, and wearable devices follow tightly scheduled release cycles. These products are rarely replaced because they fail to function. Instead, they are displaced because they lack the latest features or design cues. Obsolescence becomes symbolic rather than functional, and technological rather than functional. Each new generation renders the previous one undesirable, collapsing the period of maturity and hastening decline. Globalization intensifies this process by reducing the time required for innovations to spread. In earlier eras, adoption unfolded gradually and unevenly across regions. Today, digital communication, global supply chains, and coordinated marketing allow products to reach international markets almost simultaneously. As a result, saturation and decline also occur more quickly and more uniformly. Product life cycles are no longer staggered across regions; they are now synchronized globally (Figure 7.2).

For firms, this acceleration creates significant strategic pressure. Shorter life cycles reduce the time available to recover development costs

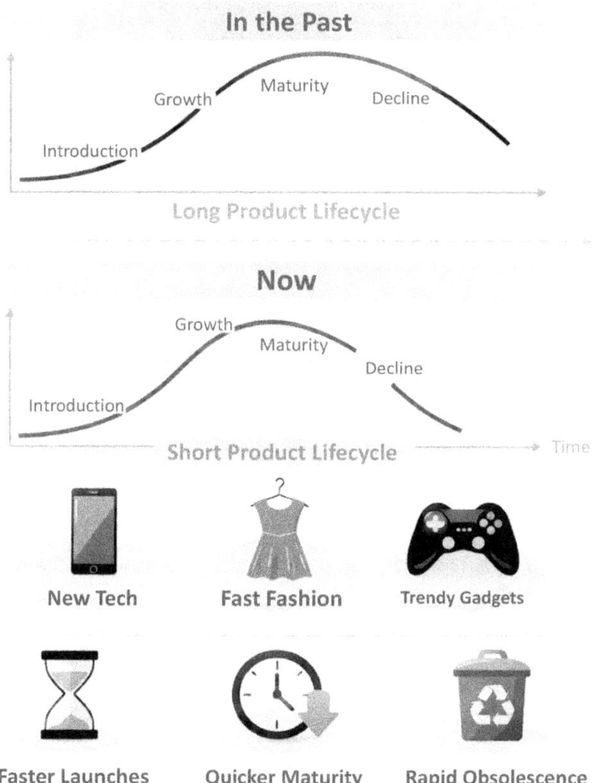

Figure 7.2 In the past decades, the product life cycles have shortened

or build durable brand relationships. Profit windows narrow, and firms must act aggressively from the moment of launch. Marketing efforts that once adapted gradually to life cycle stages are now compressed into a single phase. Products must be promoted aggressively and globally from the outset, as relevance can diminish within months.

Operational demands increase accordingly. Companies rely on agile production systems, flexible suppliers, and real-time data analytics to manage uncertainty. Inventory levels are kept low, and demand forecasting becomes continuous rather than periodic. This acceleration, however, produces several tensions. One concerns sustainability. Short product lifespans contribute to waste and resource depletion, particularly in the electronics industry. Market incentives favor disposability, even as public concern about environmental impact grows. Another tension lies in consumer experience. Ownership once signaled durability and continuity. Today, it often represents temporary relevance. Consumers feel pressure to replace functioning products to remain current, creating a cycle of dissatisfaction that weakens long-term attachment.

The rapid pace of replacement also reshapes marketing strategy. Firms focus on early adoption, emotional appeal, and immediate visibility rather than endurance. Global product launches are synchronized across markets and staged as major events to generate urgency and spectacle. The objective is speed rather than longevity, capturing attention and market share before competitors respond (Yeganeh 2019).

These dynamics tend to reinforce market inequality. Large firms with extensive resources can sustain continuous innovation and global promotion, while smaller competitors struggle to keep up. The ability to set the tempo of change becomes a source of power, concentrating advantage among dominant players and fostering oligopolistic tendencies. More broadly, the compression of the product life cycle reflects a transformation in the modern experience of time. Economic success increasingly depends on moving faster than others, innovating, and consuming ahead of the curve. Yet this pursuit of speed generates instability, exhaustion, and waste. The disappearance of the maturity phase mirrors a broader loss of equilibrium in contemporary life, where novelty is constant but permanence is rare. The shortened product life cycle thus captures both the vitality and the vulnerability of modern capitalism. It demonstrates extraordinary innovative capacity, while revealing deep dependence on continuous acceleration.

References

Abidin, C. 2016. "Aren't These Just Young, Rich Women doing Vain Things Online?" *Social Media + Society* 2, no. 2, pp. 1–17.

Abidin, C. 2018. *Internet Celebrity: Understanding Fame Online.* Emerald Publishing.

Appadurai, A. 1996. *Modernity at Large: Cultural Dimensions of Globalization.* University of Minnesota Press.

Bauman, Z. 2000. *Liquid Modernity.* Polity Press.

Beer, D. 2018. *The Data Gaze: Capitalism, Power and Perception*. Sage.

Berry, L.L., Carbone, L.P., and Haeckel, S.H. 2002. "Managing the Total Customer Experience." *MIT Sloan Management Review* 43, no. 3, pp. 85–89.

Bishop, S. 2020. "Algorithmic Labor and Visibility: How Platforms Govern the Creative Economy." *Social Media + Society* 6, no. 4, pp. 1–12.

Carr, N. 2011. *The Shallows: What the Internet is Doing to Our Brains*. W. W. Norton.

Chopra, S., and Meindl, P. 2016. *Supply Chain Management: Strategy, Planning, and Operation*. Pearson.

Couldry, N., and Mejias, U.A. 2019. *The Costs of Connection: How Data is Colonizing Human Life and Appropriating it for Capitalism*. Stanford University Press.

Cova, B., and Cova, V. 2002. "Tribal Marketing: The Tribalisation of Society and its Impact on Marketing Practice." *European Journal of Marketing* 36, no. 5/6, pp. 595–620.

Davenport, T.H., and Harris, J.G. 2017. *Competing on Analytics: The New Science of Winning*. Harvard Business Review Press.

Debord, G. 1967. *The Society of the Spectacle*. Zone Books.

Featherstone, M. 1995. *Undoing Culture: Globalization, Postmodernism and Identity*. Sage.

García Canclini, N. 1995. *Hybrid Cultures: Strategies for Entering and Leaving Modernity*. University of Minnesota Press.

Han, B.-C. 2017. *The Expulsion of the Other: Society, Perception, and Communication Today*. Polity Press.

Holt, D. 2004. *How Brands Become Icons*. Harvard Business School Press.

Jenkins, H. 2006. *Convergence Culture: Where Old and New Media Collide*. NYU Press.

Khamis, S., Ang, L., and Welling, R. 2017. "Self-Branding, 'Micro-Celebrity' and the Rise of Social Media Influencers." *Celebrity Studies* 8, no. 2, pp. 191–208.

Kraidy, M. 2005. *Hybridity, or the Cultural Logic of Globalization*. Temple University Press.

Levitt, T. 1965. "Exploit the Product Life Cycle." *Harvard Business Review* 43, no. 6, pp. 81–94.

McCracken, G. 1986. "Culture and Consumption." *Journal of Consumer Research* 13, no. 1, pp. 71–84.

Pine, B.J., and Gilmore, J.H. 1999. *The Experience Economy*. Harvard Business School Press.

Prahalad, C.K., and Ramaswamy, V. 2004. *The Future of Competition: Co-Creating Unique Value with Customers*. Harvard Business School Press.

Robertson, R. 1995. "Glocalization." In *Global Modernities*, eds. M. Featherstone, S. Lash, and R. Robertson, 25–44. Sage.

Roose, K. 2021. *The Chaos Machine: The Inside Story of How Social Media Rewired Our Minds and Our World.* HarperCollins.

Rosa, H. 2013. *Social Acceleration: A New Theory of Modernity.* Columbia University Press.

Said, E. 1993. *Culture and Imperialism.* Vintage.

Simon, H.A. 1971. "Designing Organizations for an Information-Rich World." In *Computers, Communication, and the Public Interest*, ed. M. Greenberger, 37–72. Johns Hopkins Press.

Srnicek, N. 2017. *Platform Capitalism.* Polity Press.

Terranova, T. 2000. "Free Labor: Producing Culture for the Digital Economy." *Social Text* 18, no. 2, pp. 33–58.

Toffler, A. 1980. *The Third Wave.* Bantam.

Tomlinson, J. 1999. *Globalization and Culture.* University of Chicago Press.

Tuten, T.L., and Solomon, M.R. 2018. *Social Media Marketing.* Sage.

Turow, J. 2017. *The Aisles have Eyes: How Retailers Track Your Shopping, Strip Your Privacy, and Define Your Power.* Yale University Press.

Verhoef, P.C., Kannan, P.K., and Inman, J. 2015. "From Multi-Channel to Omnichannel Retailing." *Journal of Retailing,*91, no. 2, pp. 174–181.

Wu, T. 2016. *The Attention Merchants: The Epic Scramble to Get Inside Our Heads.* Knopf.

Yeganeh, H. 2019. "An Analysis of Emerging Patterns of Consumption in the Age of Globalization and Digitalization." *FIIB Business Review* 8, no. 4, pp. 259–270.

Zuboff, S. 2019. *The Age of Surveillance Capitalism: The Fight for A Human Future at the New Frontier of Power.* PublicAffairs.

CHAPTER 8

Postbureaucratic Organizations in the Age of Platforms and Data

Platform-Based Organizational Models

In the digital age, the traditional firm, once defined by hierarchy, linear production, and internal control, has been reshaped by the rise of the platform-based organizational model. Companies such as Amazon, Uber, Airbnb, and Alibaba have transformed how economic value is created and coordinated by operating as intermediaries rather than conventional producers. These firms do not primarily manufacture goods or directly employ large workforces. Instead, they connect users, producers, and data flows within expansive digital ecosystems, relying on coordination rather than ownership as the basis of value creation. The idea of the firm as a platform represents a clear departure from the industrial model of organization. In classical economic theory, firms existed because they reduced transaction costs compared to market exchange, making internal coordination more efficient than relying on external contracts (Coase 1937). Digital technologies have significantly altered this logic. The Internet, mobile computing, and data analytics enable real-time coordination across global networks, weakening the traditional boundaries between firms and markets. As transaction costs decline, platforms emerge as hybrid institutions, part market and part organization, where value is generated through interaction rather than vertical integration (Parker et al. 2016).

At the core of the platform model is network intermediation. Rather than producing goods or services directly, platforms facilitate exchanges among users while capturing and processing the data generated by these interactions. The economic strength of this model lies in network effects, whereby a platform becomes more valuable as participation increases. Unlike traditional firms constrained by internal resources, platforms scale rapidly by leveraging external contributions rather than internal labor (Kenney and Zysman 2016).

This organizational architecture fundamentally alters the nature of management. In industrial firms, leadership focused on supervision, resource allocation, and efficiency through hierarchy. In platform organizations, management involves designing rules, incentives, and interfaces that govern interactions among largely autonomous participants. Leaders no longer issue instructions, but shape the conditions under which others interact and innovate. Platform leadership, therefore, resembles ecosystem governance, where success depends on enabling complementarities rather than enforcing compliance (Gawer 2021).

Effective ecosystem orchestration requires distinct managerial capabilities. Authority is less important than trust, transparency, and interoperability across diverse stakeholders. Platform leaders must balance the interests of users, producers, regulators, and investors while maintaining the system's coherence. Power in this context is exercised architecturally, through design decisions, data governance, and algorithmic rules rather than through direct supervision. Managing platforms thus requires an understanding of both technical systems and social dynamics, as leaders govern interactions rather than people themselves.

The platform model also redefines organizational boundaries. Employees and owned assets delineated traditional firms, whereas platform firms are defined by the ecosystems they enable. Many of today's most valuable companies create value by facilitating external innovation rather than internal production. The Apple App Store, for example, is not a product in itself but a marketplace that allows millions of developers to create complementary offerings. The platform supplies standards and infrastructure, while the ecosystem generates diversity and innovation. This structure not only enables extraordinary scalability but also creates vulnerability, as platform success depends on sustained cooperation among independent actors with divergent incentives (Jacobides et al. 2018).

Labor relations are also transformed under the platform model. Work within platform ecosystems is often organized through independent contracting rather than traditional employment. While this arrangement can increase flexibility and efficiency, it also raises concerns about insecurity, inequality, and algorithmic control. In the gig economy, management is embedded in digital systems that assign tasks, monitor performance, and automatically adjust incentives. Workers receive instructions not from supervisors but from algorithms that continuously process behavioral data. This form of governance reflects a broader shift toward data-driven control, in which power operates through surveillance and prediction rather than through direct authority (Srnicek 2017; Zuboff 2019).

The logic of platforms has spread beyond technology firms into sectors such as manufacturing, finance, and health care. Large corporations increasingly adopt platform strategies to connect suppliers, customers, and third-party developers within digital ecosystems. Industrial platforms such as GE's Predix, Siemens' MindSphere, and Salesforce's cloud ecosystem illustrate how value creation is becoming networked rather than linear. Leadership in these contexts requires systemic thinking, emphasizing interdependence, modular design, and openness rather than centralized control.

Despite their promise, platforms introduce deep tensions and contradictions. They often claim to democratize participation while concentrating power in a small number of global intermediaries. They promote decentralization but rely on highly centralized data infrastructures. They enable entrepreneurship yet capture disproportionate shares of value. As platform ecosystems expand, questions of governance, fairness, and accountability become increasingly pressing. Issues such as data ownership, value distribution, and algorithmic authority highlight the broader challenge of determining how much control should be delegated to digital systems in shaping economic and social life.

Toward a Postbureaucratic Organization and Leadership

Bureaucracy served as the dominant organizational logic of the industrial era. Rooted in Max Weber's model of rational legal authority, it relied on clear hierarchies, standardized procedures, and formal rules to ensure efficiency, predictability, and accountability. This structure functioned well in stable contexts where information moved slowly, and work could be divided into specialized routines (Yeganeh 2025). Managers planned and directed from above, employees executed predefined tasks, and consistency was maintained through adherence to established rules. As organizations entered the digital economy, however, the limitations of this model became increasingly apparent. Accelerating technological change, expanding data flows, and global interconnectedness rendered rigid hierarchies less effective. Procedures that once ensured order began to hinder innovation, responsiveness, and experimentation. In their place, postbureaucratic forms emerged, characterized by distributed authority, collaboration across boundaries, and adaptive learning processes (Heckscher and Donnellon 1994; Alvesson and Spicer 2012).

In postbureaucratic contexts, leadership cannot rely on traditional command-and-control mechanisms because authority is no longer confined to formal roles. Digital technologies flatten hierarchies and broaden access to information, enabling individuals at different levels to initiate action and collaborate directly. Knowledge circulates laterally rather than vertically, and coordination increasingly occurs through networks rather than chains of command. The leader's task, therefore, shifts from directing behavior to fostering clarity, alignment, and shared purpose within decentralized systems.

This transformation moves leadership away from task supervision toward the management of meaning. In conditions of uncertainty, people look to leaders less for precise instructions than for interpretive guidance that helps them understand complex situations and decide how to respond. Leaders influence action by framing events, constructing narratives, and highlighting priorities. Unlike bureaucratic managers, who rely on authority, procedures, and surveillance, postbureaucratic leaders work through communication, interpretation, and vision. Leadership thus becomes a social and linguistic process through which meaning, identity, and direction are continuously negotiated (Weick 1995; Cunliffe and Eriksen 2011).

Digital organizations illustrate this shift clearly. Platforms, networks, and hybrid teams operate across time zones, geographies, and organizational boundaries, often without stable hierarchies. A software engineer may collaborate directly with a designer located elsewhere, bypassing layers of management that once mediated such interactions. Agile practices rely on iterative cycles, feedback loops, and rotating leadership roles based on expertise rather than rank. In these environments, effective leadership requires emotional intelligence, relational competence, and the ability to create psychological safety. Leaders must cultivate trust across distance and diversity, ensuring that individuals remain informed, valued, and aligned despite working within fluid structures (Uhl Bien and Arena 2018).

As hierarchy weakens, influence replaces authority as the central resource of leadership. Mobilizing networks requires the ability to inspire, persuade, and connect rather than command. Leaders frame challenges in ways that invite engagement, articulate visions that resonate across cultural and disciplinary boundaries, and facilitate collaboration through dialogue. Leadership in such settings depends on adaptive capacity, understood as the ability to integrate multiple perspectives and respond creatively to emerging challenges. Rather than enforcing compliance, leaders orchestrate alignment among semiautonomous actors (Yeganeh 2025).

Communication becomes the primary mechanism of coordination in postbureaucratic organizations. With fewer formal rules and more permeable boundaries, shared understanding depends on ongoing interaction. Digital tools intensify this communicative environment by enabling constant connection while also multiplying voices and interpretations. Leaders must navigate this density of information and facilitate meaning without reverting to excessive control. This approach requires openness, transparency, and reflexivity, qualities associated with authentic leadership. Authentic leaders acknowledge uncertainty, invite dialogue, and cocreate understanding rather than presenting themselves as omniscient decision makers (Avolio and Gardner 2005).

At the same time, reduced hierarchy introduces new vulnerabilities. Without positional authority, leadership depends heavily on credibility, trust, and moral legitimacy. Consistency between words and actions becomes essential for sustaining influence. Distributed organizations also risk fragmentation if sensemaking is neglected. When individuals interpret events in isolation, coherence erodes. The leader's role is therefore not to eliminate ambiguity but to frame it constructively, transforming uncertainty into shared inquiry and difference into dialogue.

Figure 8.1 Irony, parody, and pastiche occupy an important place in Musk's communications

Source: Elon Musk's X account

This evolution reshapes the nature of power itself. In bureaucratic systems, power was positional and coercive. In postbureaucratic systems, it becomes relational and communicative. Power flows through networks of meaning rather than through formal authority. As Manuel Castells argues, power in the network society increasingly operates through control over communication flows and the capacity to shape attention, discourse, and interpretation (Castells 2010).

Organizations such as Spotify, Valve, and Haier illustrate these dynamics in practice. Spotify's team-based structure distributes leadership while maintaining shared principles and strategic coherence. Managers act primarily as coaches who enable problem-solving rather than issuing directives. These cases show how leadership can sustain alignment without suppressing autonomy, balancing freedom with focus.

Data-Driven and Algorithmic Management

For much of the 20th century, management was conceived as a craft grounded in analytical reasoning and human judgment. Effective managers were valued for their capacity to read markets, understand people, and recognize emerging opportunities, drawing heavily on tacit knowledge acquired through experience rather than formalized models or data systems (Mintzberg 2009; Polanyi 1966). Judgment under uncertainty was central to managerial authority, which rested on interpretive skill, situational awareness, and the ability to act decisively in ambiguous contexts. This conception of management began to erode as digital technologies expanded the scale and availability of organizational data. Over time, firms recognized that intuition alone could not compete with the speed, scope, and granularity of data generated by digital platforms, sensors, and enterprise systems. Large datasets enabled the detection of patterns and correlations beyond the reach of individual decision makers, enabling organizations to reduce uncertainty through forecasting, optimization, and prediction (Brynjolfsson and McElheran 2016; Davenport and Harris 2017).

This shift is not merely technological but epistemological, reflecting a more profound transformation in how organizations define knowledge, authority, and legitimacy. In traditional hierarchies, managerial authority was grounded in professional experience and judgment. Managers were expected to interpret incomplete information and make decisions under conditions of uncertainty (Mintzberg 2009). In data-driven organizations, by contrast, authority increasingly derives from statistical evidence, analytical models, and algorithmic outputs. Decision making becomes a process of translating reality into measurable variables and acting on the results produced by computational systems (Brynjolfsson and McElheran 2016; Davenport and Harris 2017).

The rise of algorithmic management makes these tensions particularly visible. Initially developed within digital platforms such as Uber, Amazon, and Deliveroo, algorithmic management refers to the use of automated systems to monitor, evaluate, and direct work (Srnicek 2017; Zuboff 2019). Algorithms assign tasks, schedule shifts, calculate compensation, and assess performance using continuous streams of behavioral data (Kellogg et al. 2020). These systems promise efficiency, consistency, and scalability. Unlike human managers, they do not tire, negotiate, or rely on subjective impressions (Davenport and Harris 2017). Over time, algorithmic management has expanded beyond platform labor into large organizations, where AI is increasingly used to screen job applicants, monitor productivity, and predict employee turnover (Kellogg et al. 2020).

In such environments, decision making becomes predictive rather than reactive. Machine learning systems analyze historical data to anticipate future outcomes, allowing organizations to intervene before problems emerge. In marketing, algorithms personalize content and pricing in real time. In finance, they assess credit risk and detect fraud. In human resources, they model engagement, performance, and attrition (O'Neil 2016; Zuboff 2019). Management increasingly takes the form of continuous experimentation, as feedback loops constantly refine organizational behavior. The organization itself begins to resemble a self-learning system, capable of adjusting its operations through data-driven insights.

Yet this transformation carries significant consequences. One is the erosion of human discretion. When algorithms define optimal outcomes, managers risk becoming executors of machine recommendations rather than interpreters of complex social realities (Zuboff 2019). The space for judgment, empathy, and co ntextual understanding narrows, even as decisions appear more objective and precise. Data systems do not simply describe behavior; they actively shape it by defining what counts as efficient, productive, or desirable. In doing so, they exercise a subtle form of control that is difficult to observe or contest (Srnicek 2017).

A second consequence is the illusion of objectivity. Algorithms are often treated as neutral, yet they reflect the assumptions embedded in their design and the biases present in their training data (O'Neil 2016). Historical datasets encode past decisions, including patterns of inequality and exclusion. When such data is used to guide future decisions, discrimination can be reproduced under the appearance of statistical impartiality (Zuboff 2019). Hiring algorithms may favor candidates who resemble past employees, while performance metrics may disadvantage forms of work that resist quantification (Kellogg et al. 2020). Many algorithmic systems operate as black boxes whose internal logic cannot be easily explained, even by their designers (Pasquale 2015). When automated systems deny loans, reject job applicants, or flag employees as underperforming, the reasoning may be mathematically valid yet ethically opaque. Beyond ethics, data-driven management reshapes organizational culture. Continuous measurement and optimization risk crowding out qualitative values such as trust, creativity, and care (Morozov 2013). What cannot be measured may be ignored, reinforcing a form of technological solutionism that assumes better data can resolve fundamentally social problems (Morozov 2013). In such contexts, management risks becoming mechanical, reducing human complexity to numerical indicators and probabilistic models (Zuboff 2019).

Networked and Fluid Organizational Boundaries

In the digital and globalized economy, the organizational boundaries that once clearly defined firms have become increasingly permeable. Structures traditionally built around hierarchy, ownership, and internal control are giving way to networked and fluid organizational forms in which firms operate as open systems linked to contractors, start-ups, suppliers, and online communities (Castells 2010). As a result, distinctions between employee and collaborator, producer and consumer, and firm and ecosystem are progressively dissolving (Iansiti and Levien 2004). This shift signals a fundamental reorganization of economic activity, moving from the firm as a closed hierarchy to the firm as a flexible node embedded within broader digital and social networks (Gulati et al. 2012).

The conception of the firm as a bounded entity has deep roots in industrial capitalism. Throughout much of the 20th century, corporations were vertically integrated, coordinating production, distribution, and labor within clearly demarcated organizational boundaries (Chandler 1977). Ronald Coase explained the existence of firms by arguing that internal coordination under managerial authority reduced transaction costs relative to market exchange (Coase 1937). This logic underpinned the rise of the bureaucratic corporation, a hierarchical structure designed to maximize stability, efficiency, and predictability (Weber 1978). As technological capabilities expanded and globalization intensified, however, the foundations of this model began to weaken. Digital networks, cloud computing, and data-driven platforms sharply reduced the costs of coordinating across organizational boundaries, making external collaboration increasingly efficient (Parker et al. 2016). Firms no longer need to own or directly control all the resources on which they depend, as they can increasingly connect, collaborate, and cocreate across networks of independent actors (Iansiti and Levien 2004).

This transformation is particularly evident in the rise of platform-based ecosystems. In these arrangements, firms function primarily as orchestrators rather than owners of production assets (Parker et al. 2016). Companies such as Apple, Amazon, and Google operate less as manufacturers and more as facilitators of value creation among users, developers, and partners (Kenney and Zysman 2016). Amazon Web Services, for example, provides digital infrastructure that enables thousands of firms to build, scale, and operate their businesses without owning physical assets or proprietary systems (Kenney and Zysman 2016). In such ecosystems, organizational boundaries extend far beyond legal or physical limits, and value emerges through interaction and interdependence rather than top-down instruction (Iansiti and Levien 2004). The shift toward networked organizations reflects a broader posthierarchical logic of coordination. Instead of rigid departmental structures and centralized authority, contemporary firms increasingly rely on modular architectures composed of semiautonomous units linked through shared objectives and digital interfaces (Gulati et al. 2012). Modularity enhances adaptability by allowing teams to form, dissolve, and reconfigure without destabilizing the organization as a whole (Schilling 2000). Authority becomes more distributed, and effectiveness depends less on positional power than on the capacity to integrate diverse contributions across organizational boundaries.

The expansion of the gig and freelance economy further reinforces organizational fluidity. Firms increasingly rely on independent contractors and external specialists rather than permanent employees, accessing skills through digital platforms that support project-based collaboration (Kässi and Lehdonvirta 2018). Platforms such as Upwork, Fiverr, and Toptal allow organizations to assemble temporary, globally distributed teams tailored to specific tasks (Kässi and Lehdonvirta 2018). While this model enhances flexibility and innovation, it also challenges traditional assumptions about employment, loyalty, and organizational identity. The firm increasingly resembles a network of relationships rather than a stable institutional structure (Srnicek 2017). Digital communities also play an increasingly important role in reshaping firm boundaries. Open-source initiatives such as Linux, Wikipedia, and GitHub illustrate how loosely coordinated networks can generate complex, high-quality outcomes without centralized control (Benkler 2006). Many organizations now incorporate such communities into their innovation processes through crowdsourcing initiatives, hackathons, and user-generated content (von Hippel 2005). In this context, customers become coproducers, contributing ideas, designs, and data that directly shape organizational offerings (von Hippel 2005). The firm no longer acts upon the market from above, but participates within it as one actor in a shared network of value creation (Benkler 2006).

Despite their advantages, networked and fluid organizational forms introduce significant challenges. The erosion of clear boundaries complicates issues of accountability, governance, and ownership. When production and decision making are distributed across multiple actors, assigning responsibility for outcomes becomes difficult, and intellectual property rights may be contested (Gawer and Phillips 2013). Dependence on digital platforms also creates vulnerabilities related to data ownership, cybersecurity, and asymmetric power relations within ecosystems dominated by a small number of global intermediaries (Srnicek 2017). From a managerial perspective, operating in such environments requires a redefinition of core competencies. Traditional management emphasized authority, oversight, and internal control, whereas networked organizations demand orchestration, trust building, and facilitation across boundaries (Gulati et al. 2012). Leaders must align diverse interests, maintain coherence without rigid hierarchy, and design conditions that enable collaboration among autonomous actors. The shift toward networked boundaries also reshapes organizational culture. In systems of distributed collaboration, culture must provide both identity and flexibility, allowing organizations to integrate external partners and communities while preserving a sense of shared purpose (Schein 2010). At the same time, networks can generate new hierarchies based on visibility, access to information, and algorithmic control, challenging the assumption that openness necessarily leads to equality (Barabási 2002).

Toward Employee Experience and Engagement in Organizations

In recent years, organizations have increasingly acknowledged that long-term success depends not only on customer satisfaction and financial performance but also on the quality of employee experience. This perspective reflects a departure from a transactional view of work in which employees were treated primarily as inputs in production. Instead, employees are now understood as stakeholders whose everyday experiences shape organizational culture, productivity, and innovation capacity.

Employee experience refers to the set of interactions an individual has with an organization throughout the employment life cycle, from recruitment and onboarding to daily work practices, career development, and even postemployment relationships. It includes tangible elements such as workplace design, digital tools, and formal policies, as well as intangible dimensions such as leadership quality, psychological safety, autonomy, and shared values. Closely related to employee experience is engagement, which describes the psychological commitment employees bring to their work and organization. Engaged employees display enthusiasm, discretionary effort, and alignment with organizational objectives, contributing beyond formal role requirements (Kahn 1990).

Several interrelated forces explain why employee experience and engagement have become central organizational concerns. One important driver is the rise of the intangible economy. As economic value increasingly derives from knowledge, innovation, and organizational culture, competitive advantage depends less on physical assets and more on human capital. In this context, employees are not interchangeable units of labor but distinct contributors of expertise and creativity, making it essential for organizations to design environments that support learning, collaboration, and innovation (Haskel and Westlake 2018).

Demographic change represents a second driver. The growing presence of Millennials and Generation Z in the workforce has reshaped expectations about work. These cohorts place greater emphasis on purpose, flexibility, personal development, and well-being than previous generations. Meaningful work, growth opportunities, and work–life integration are often prioritized over job security alone, requiring organizations to adapt their practices to attract, engage, and retain talent (PwC 2016).

A third factor is digitalization and the transformation of work arrangements. Digital technologies now mediate most aspects of employee experience, including communication, collaboration, performance management, and learning. The COVID-19 pandemic accelerated the adoption of remote and hybrid work, forcing organizations to reconsider how engagement and connection can be sustained in dispersed teams. As work becomes less tied to physical locations, employee experience increasingly depends on digital infrastructure, leadership practices, and intentional efforts to foster belonging (Carnevale and Hatak 2020).

Changing cultural values further reinforce this shift. Broader societal attention to DEI, and sustainability has reshaped employee expectations. Many employees seek workplaces that respect individual differences, promote fairness, and align with wider social and environmental values. Engagement increasingly depends on whether organizations are perceived as ethically responsible and socially responsive, rather than solely as economic entities (Shuck and Reio 2014).

As a result of these forces, investment in employee experience is no longer viewed as a peripheral human resources initiative. It has become a strategic priority. Research consistently shows that engaged employees are more productive, more innovative, and less likely to leave their organizations. Higher engagement is also associated with lower absenteeism, fewer safety incidents, and stronger financial performance, reinforcing the business case for sustained investment in employee experience (Gallup 2017).

From a strategic management perspective, employee experience is closely linked to customer experience. The service profit chain model demonstrates that employees who feel supported and engaged are more likely to deliver high-quality service, thereby strengthening customer satisfaction, loyalty, and revenue growth. Organizations are also recognizing the role of employee experience in shaping employer brand. In competitive labor markets, a reputation as an attractive workplace influences the ability to recruit and retain skilled employees. Firms such as Google, Salesforce, and Microsoft have invested heavily in creating work environments that combine high performance with employee well-being. These practices foster psychological commitment internally while signaling organizational values to prospective employees externally (Morgan 2017). The growing emphasis on employee experience has translated into concrete organizational practices.

Many employers are redesigning physical and virtual work environments to support collaboration, flexibility, and health through hybrid work arrangements, wellness initiatives, and digital collaboration tools (Steelcase 2021). Leadership development increasingly emphasizes coaching, empathy, and emotional intelligence rather than command-and-control, reflecting a more human-centered approach to management (Goleman 2011). Organizations are also moving toward continuous listening practices. Annual engagement surveys are being supplemented or replaced by real-time feedback systems, pulse surveys, and analytics tools that allow organizations to identify emerging issues and respond more quickly to employee needs (Gartner 2020). Career development has become more personalized, with greater emphasis on continuous learning, upskilling, and reskilling to support adaptability in fast-changing industries (World Economic Forum 2020).

References

Alvesson, M., and Spicer, A. 2012. "Critical Leadership Studies: The Case for Critical Performativity." *Human Relations 65*, no. 3, pp. 367–390.

Ancona, D., and Bresman, H. 2011. *X-Teams: How to Build Teams that Lead, Innovate, and Succeed.* Harvard Business Review Press.

Avolio, B.J., and Gardner, W.L. 2005. "Authentic Leadership Development: Getting to the Root of Positive Forms of Leadership." *The Leadership Quarterly 16*, no. 3, pp. 315–338.

Barabási, A.-L. 2002. *Linked: The New Science of Networks.* Perseus.

Benkler, Y. 2006. *The Wealth of Networks: How Social Production Transforms Markets and Freedom*. Yale University Press.

Brynjolfsson, E., and McElheran, K. 2016. "Data in Action: Data-Driven Decision Making in U.S. Manufacturing." *Academy of Management Perspectives 30*, no. 3, pp. 264–290.

Carnevale, J.B., and Hatak, I. 2020. "Employee Adjustment and Well-being in the Era of COVID-19: Implications for Human Resource Management." *Journal of Business Research 116*, pp. 183–187. https://doi.org/10.1016/j.jbusres.2020.05.037

Castells, M. 2010. *The Rise of the Network Society*. Wiley-Blackwell.

Chandler, A.D. 1977. *The Visible Hand: The Managerial Revolution in American Business*. Harvard University Press.

Coase, R.H. 1937. "The Nature of the Firm." *Economica 4*, no. 16, pp. 386–405.

Cunliffe, A.L., and Eriksen, M. 2011. "Relational Leadership." *Human Relations 64*, no. 11, pp. 1425–1449.

Davenport, T.H., and Harris, J.G. 2017. *Competing on Analytics: The New Science of Winning*. Harvard Business Review Press.

Deloitte. 2021. *2021 Global Human Capital Trends: The Social Enterprise in a World Disrupted*. Deloitte Insights.

Gallup. 2017. *State of the Global Workplace*. Gallup.

Gartner. 2020. *Future of Work Trends Post-COVID-19*. Gartner.

Gawer, A. 2021. Digital platforms' boundaries: The interplay of firm scope, platform sides, and digital interfaces. *Long Range Planning 54*, no. 5, p. 102045.

Gawer, A., and Phillips, N. 2013. "Institutional Work as Logics Shift: The Case of Intel's Transformation to Platform Leader." *Organization Studies 34*, no. 8, pp. 1035–1071.

Goleman, D. 2011. *Leadership: The Power of Emotional Intelligence*. More Than Sound.

Gulati, R., Puranam, P., and Tushman, M. 2012. "Meta-Organization Design: Rethinking Design in Interorganizational and Community Contexts." *Strategic Management Journal 33*, no. 6, pp. 571–586.

Haskel, J., and Westlake, S. 2018. *Capitalism without Capital: The Rise of the Intangible Economy*. Princeton University Press.

Heckscher, C., and Donnellon, A. (eds.). 1994. *The Post-Bureaucratic Organization: New Perspectives on Organizational Change*. Sage.

Heskett, J.L., Sasser, W.E., and Schlesinger, L.A. 1994. *The Service Profit Chain: How Leading Companies Link Profit and Growth to Loyalty, Satisfaction, and Value*. Free Press.

Iansiti, M., and Levien, R. 2004. *The Keystone Advantage: What the New Dynamics of Business Ecosystems Mean for Strategy, Innovation, and Sustainability*. Harvard Business School Press.

Jacobides, M.G., Cennamo, C., and Gawer, A. 2018. "Towards a Theory of Ecosystems." *Strategic Management Journal 39*, no. 8, pp. 2255–2276.

Kahn, W.A. 1990. "Psychological Conditions of Personal Engagement and Disengagement at Work." *Academy of Management Journal 33*, no. 4, pp. 692–724. https://doi.org/10.5465/256287

Kässi, O., and Lehdonvirta, V. 2018. "Online Labour Index: Measuring the Online Gig Economy for Policy and Research." *Technological Forecasting and Social Change 137*, pp. 241–248.

Kellogg, K.C., Valentine, M.A., and Christin, A. 2020. "Algorithms at Work: The New Contested Terrain of Control." *Academy of Management Annals 14*, no. 1, pp. 366–410.

Kenney, M., and Zysman, J. 2016. "The Rise of the Platform Economy." *Issues in Science and Technology 32*, no. 3, pp. 61–69.

Leonardi, P.M. 2014. "Social Media, Knowledge Sharing, and Innovation: Toward a Theory of Communication Visibility." *Information Systems Research 25*, no. 4, pp. 796–816.

Mintzberg, H. 2009. *Managing*. Berrett-Koehler Publishers.

Morgan, J. 2017. *The Employee Experience Advantage: How to Win the War for Talent by Giving Employees the Workspaces They Want, the Tools They Need, and a Culture They can Celebrate*. Wiley.

Morozov, E. 2013. *To Save Everything, Click Here: The Folly of Technological Solutionism*. PublicAffairs.

Nonaka, I., and Takeuchi, H. 1995. *The Knowledge-Creating Company*. Oxford University Press.

O'Neil, C. 2016. *Weapons of Math Destruction: How Big Data Increases Inequality and Threatens Democracy*. Crown.

Ostrom, E. 1990. *Governing the Commons: The Evolution of Institutions for Collective Action*. Cambridge University Press.

Parker, G.G., Van Alstyne, M.W., and Choudary, S.P. 2016. *Platform Revolution: How Networked Markets are Transforming the Economy—and How to Make Them Work for You*. W. W. Norton.

Pasquale, F. 2015. *The Black Box Society: The Secret Algorithms that Control Money and Information*. Harvard University Press.

Pfeffer, J., and Sutton, R.I. 2006. *Hard Facts, Dangerous Half-Truths, and Total Nonsense: Profiting from Evidence-Based Management*. Harvard Business School Press.

Polanyi, M. 1966. *The Tacit Dimension*. Doubleday.

PwC. 2016. *Millennials at Work: Reshaping the Workplace*. PricewaterhouseCoopers.

Schein, E.H. 2010. *Organizational Culture and Leadership*, 4th ed. Jossey-Bass.

Schilling, M.A. 2000. "Toward a General Modular Systems Theory and Its Application to Interfirm Product Modularity." *Academy of Management Review 25*, no. 2, pp. 312–334.

Shuck, B., and Reio, T.G. 2014. "Employee Engagement and Well-Being: A Moderation Model and Implications for Practice." *Journal of Leadership & Organizational Studies 21*, no. 1, pp. 43–58. https://doi.org/10.1177/1548051813494240

Simon, H.A. 1977. *The New Science of Management Decision*. Prentice-Hall.

Srnicek, N. 2017. *Platform Capitalism*. Polity Press.

Steelcase. 2021. *The Future of Work: Hybrid, Flexible, and Employee-Centered*. Steelcase Global Report.

Uhl-Bien, M., and Arena, M. 2018. "Leadership for Organizational Adaptability." *The Leadership Quarterly 29*, no. 1, pp. 89–104.

von Hippel, E. 2005. *Democratizing Innovation*. MIT Press.

Weber, M. 1978. *Economy and Society*, eds. G. Roth and C. Wittich. University of California Press.

Weick, K.E. 1995. *Sensemaking in Organizations*. Sage.

World Economic Forum. 2020. *The Future of Jobs Report 2020*. World Economic Forum.

Yeganeh, H. 2025. "Postmodern Culture in Action: An Analysis of Elon Musk's Management and Leadership Style." *International Journal of Sociology and Social Policy*, pp. 1–20.

Zuboff, S. 2019. *The Age of Surveillance Capitalism: The Fight for a Human Future at the New Frontier of Power*. PublicAffairs.

PART 3

Digitalization, Finance, and Investment

CHAPTER 9

The Digital Economy as a System of Control and Extraction

Data, Platforms, and the Digital Economy

Value creation today is rooted in the generation, circulation, and exploitation of digital information, transforming how firms compete, how markets function, and how individuals interact with economic systems (Kitchin 2014). This transformation is not merely technological but structural, reshaping social relations, organizational boundaries, and forms of governance. Four developments in particular illustrate this shift: the rise of big data and predictive analytics, the platformization of business, the emergence of digital twins, and the expansion of subscription and "as-a-Service" models.

Big data and predictive analytics have become central to economic decision making. The proliferation of digital interactions, sensors, and connected devices has generated vast datasets that can be analyzed to predict behavior, optimize processes, and manage risk (Kitchin 2014). Advances in machine learning and computational capacity allow organizations to extract insights from these datasets at unprecedented speed and scale. Retailers use predictive models to personalize recommendations and manage supply chains, health care systems analyze patient data to detect disease earlier, and financial institutions deploy algorithms to assess creditworthiness and detect fraud in real time. Because algorithms rely on historical data, they often reproduce existing biases embedded in past social and economic structures. Predictive policing systems, for example, have been shown to disproportionately target marginalized communities, while algorithmic credit scoring can reinforce inequalities in access to finance (Angwin et al. 2016).

A second defining feature of the digital economy is the platformization of business. Platforms function as intermediaries that facilitate interactions between producers and consumers, extracting value by controlling access, data, and network effects (Parker et al. 2016). Digital platforms dominate sectors ranging from commerce and media to transportation and finance, benefiting from "winner-takes-all" dynamics that entrench incumbents and raise barriers to entry. The more users a platform attracts, the more valuable it becomes, creating self-reinforcing cycles of growth and concentration. App ecosystems, online marketplaces, and integrated "super apps" exemplify how platforms restructure markets and embed themselves into everyday life (Cusumano et al. 2019).

Platforms increasingly shape consumption patterns, social communication, and political discourse by controlling visibility, access, and rules of participation. At the same time, they blur the boundaries between private enterprise and public governance, as platform owners effectively regulate digital spaces without democratic oversight (Van Dijck et al. 2018). In response to growing concerns about monopolistic power and systemic risk, regulators have begun to intervene to promote competition and transparency, as illustrated by recent digital market regulations in the European Union. Platforms thus represent both engines of innovation and sources of structural vulnerability within the digital economy.

Digital twins constitute a third significant development. A digital twin is a virtual replica of a physical object, process, or system that updates in real time through data from sensors and connected devices. Digital twins allow organizations to simulate scenarios, test interventions, and optimize outcomes before acting in the physical world (Tao et al. 2018). In manufacturing and aviation, digital replicas of machinery enable predictive maintenance and faster innovation. At the same time, urban planners use digital twins of cities to model traffic flows, energy use, and environmental impacts.

The societal potential of digital twins extends beyond industry. In health care, digital replicas of organs or patients could enable personalized treatment and virtual testing of therapies. In environmental management, digital twins of ecosystems may support climate modeling and policy design. However, these applications also raise ethical and governance challenges, particularly concerning data ownership, privacy, and the replication of human systems (Fuller et al. 2020).

A fourth defining trend is the spread of subscription and "as-a-Service" business models. Originally associated with software, these models now extend to infrastructure, platforms, hardware, and consumer services. Rather than owning products outright, users pay recurring fees to access them. For firms, subscriptions generate predictable revenues, strengthen customer lock-in, and enable continuous data collection. At the same time, for consumers and enterprises, they reduce upfront costs and enhance flexibility (Cusumano et al. 2019). At the same time, these models raise concerns about dependence on corporate providers, erosion of ownership rights, and long-term sustainability.

Big data analytics, platformization, digital twins, and subscription models illustrate the transformation of capitalism into a data-driven, platform-based, and service-oriented system. These developments promise efficiency, innovation, and improved services, but they also risk reinforcing inequality, concentrating power, and eroding privacy.

Artificial Scarcity Capitalism

In the traditional economy, value has been grounded in scarcity. Land is finite, labor is constrained, and capital requires time and effort to accumulate and deploy, forming the basis of prices, ownership, and exchange. The digital economy, by contrast, operates under fundamentally different conditions. Once created, digital artifacts such as software, music, or images can be reproduced endlessly at negligible cost. These goods are nonrival: one person's use does not diminish another's (Varian 2019). In principle, this suggests a world of abundance in which the classical foundations of economic value lose their force. Yet the experience of the past decade points in the opposite direction. Some of the most successful digital business models are not built on openness and abundance, but on the deliberate restriction of access. By enclosing and tokenizing digital goods, firms transform what is potentially infinite into something scarce, thereby generating economic rents (Brekke and Fischer 2021).

This logic can be described as artificial scarcity capitalism (ASC). This emerging pattern is increasingly central to the digital economy. ASC captures the way value is engineered in domains that would otherwise resist scarcity. Bitcoin, with its hard-coded supply cap, virtual land in metaverse platforms, nonfungible tokens (NFTs) in digital art markets, and rare in-game items in online gaming, all follow this logic (Brekke and Fischer 2021). Although these phenomena appear diverse, they share a common strategy: scarcity is not discovered but designed. Together, they mark a shift in how digital business models create, capture, and legitimize value (O'Dwyer 2023).

At the core of ASC is the deliberate construction of digital scarcity. As Brekke and Fischer define it, digital scarcity is a "credibly maintained limitation, imposed through software, of digital information, goods or services that may be accessed and used entirely digitally" (Brekke and Fischer 2021). Because digital goods are inherently reproducible, scarcity must be imposed rather than assumed. ASC achieves this by embedding limits through technical protocols, legal arrangements, governance structures, and social recognition, thereby reorganizing digital abundance into assets that can be owned, traded, and priced (Srnicek 2017).

The mechanisms through which ASC operates are distinct but tightly connected. Protocol-limited supply provides the most straightforward example. Bitcoin's maximum supply of 21 million coins is hard-coded into its protocol, and the credibility of this constraint underpins its value (Narayanan et al. 2016). Scarcity here emerges not from material limits but from the perceived difficulty of altering the protocol itself. Tokenization represents a second mechanism. While a digital image or song can be copied endlessly, the token that certifies authenticity or ownership is scarce, shifting value from content to ownership claims (Dowling 2022). Governance and access control form a third mechanism. Metaverse platforms divide infinite digital environments into discrete parcels that can only be traded by token holders, imposing scarcity through rules rather than geography (Figure 9.1). Intermediation further reinforces this logic, as platforms charge fees for minting, trading, or transferring digital assets, positioning themselves as gatekeepers of scarcity and as extractors of rents (Srnicek 2017). Finally, narratives of exclusivity give these arrangements symbolic force. Claims such as "limited edition," "prime location," or

Figure 9.1 The Metaverse is a fully immersive digital environment where physical boundaries dissolve. The Metaverse space is restricted by artificial scarcity.

"genesis token" transform technical limits into cultural signals of prestige, encouraging speculation and demand (Veblen 1899; O'Dwyer 2023).

Blockchain technology provides the infrastructure that makes these mechanisms credible. By ensuring immutability, transparency, and verifiability, blockchain systems reduce reliance on centralized trust (Narayanan et al. 2016). Yet their role extends beyond technical enforcement. Blockchain actively converts digital culture into tradable property, embedding scarcity into the architecture of digital exchange and accelerating the financialization of cultural production (O'Dwyer 2023).

The rise of ASC also exposes deep legal ambiguities. Ownership in digital environments remains far less clear than in traditional property regimes. Purchasing an NFT rarely grants copyright or full usage rights over the underlying work; in most cases, it transfers only the token itself (Dowling 2022). The assumption that rights naturally travel with tokens clashes with existing private law frameworks, particularly in civil law systems. Legal scholars argue that private law may need to adapt by extending tokenization to contractual or usufructuary rights. However, such reforms are slow and contested (Garcia-Teruel 2023). Ultimately, digital scarcity depends on institutional recognition by courts, platforms, and communities. Without this support, scarcity risks collapsing into little more than code (Brekke and Fischer 2021).

The effects of ASC are most visible in three domains. Bitcoin shows how protocol rules can transform digital ledger entries into money by enforcing scarcity through consensus (Narayanan et al. 2016). Metaverse platforms demonstrate how limitless virtual space can be enclosed and sold as scarce property (Castronova 2021). NFT-based digital art reveals how authenticity and uniqueness can be manufactured in a medium defined by perfect copyability, shifting attention from artistic content to ownership claims (Dowling 2022).

Despite its growing influence, ASC remains fragile and contested. It reflects a broader tension between digital openness and enclosure. While digital infrastructures are designed to facilitate sharing and replication, firms continually impose boundaries through technical and legal means (Bollier 2014). Because scarcity is engineered, its value rests heavily on collective belief. When narratives break down, markets can collapse, as illustrated by the sharp decline in NFT markets after 2021 (O'Dwyer 2023). ASC also exacerbates inequality by concentrating gains among early adopters, platform owners, and speculators, while excluding others (Piketty 2014). Its legitimacy depends on consensus, which hacks, protocol forks, or regulatory intervention can disrupt. Cultural resistance is also significant, with many technologists and artists rejecting enclosure in favor of open and commons-based models (Bollier 2014).

The emergence of ASC signals a new phase in digital business. Scarcity, long the foundation of economic value, is being reconstructed through code, law, and narrative. For firms, this opens new avenues for asset creation, speculation, and rent extraction. For regulators, it raises difficult questions about property, ownership, and consumer protection. For society, it intensifies inequality and challenges the moral foundations of digital capitalism.

Digital Tokenization

Tokenization refers to the conversion of ownership rights into digital tokens recorded on a blockchain (Schär 2021). Each token represents a claim, share, or unit of an underlying asset and can be transferred securely and transparently without relying on traditional intermediaries (Zetsche et al. 2019). Because blockchains operate through decentralized networks, these tokens can be exchanged across borders with minimal friction. Unlike conventional shares or paper deeds, tokenized ownership is programmable through smart contracts, divisible into tiny units, and tradable on a global scale by anyone with Internet access (Regner et al. 2019). For this reason, tokenization is not simply a technical innovation; it reshapes how ownership is defined, exchanged, and valued, with implications for finance, culture, and the logic of scarcity itself (World Economic Forum 2021).

One of the most prominent applications is the tokenization of real-world assets. Markets that have long been illiquid and exclusionary, such as real estate, can be digitized and opened to a broader pool of participants (Alberts and Mik 2022). A commercial building valued at $10 million, for example, can be represented by 1 million tokens, each corresponding to a small ownership stake. Rental income can then be distributed automatically through smart contracts in proportion to token holdings, lowering entry barriers for investors previously excluded from property markets (Alberts and Mik 2022). A similar logic applies to fine art, where high-value works can be fractionalized, enabling collective investment in cultural assets (Regner et al. 2019). While this resembles earlier forms of securitization, blockchain technology increases efficiency, transparency, and divisibility. The same approach can be applied to commodities such as gold, diamonds, or agricultural products, improving liquidity and facilitating fractional ownership. Even traditional financial instruments, including equities and bonds, can be issued as tokens, reducing settlement times and enabling continuous global trading (Schär 2021).

Beyond physical assets, tokenization has had its most visible effects in digital-native environments. Cryptocurrencies represent the earliest example: algorithmically scarce tokens designed to function as money without central issuers. Ethereum expanded this model by introducing programmable tokens, enabling decentralized finance and automated contractual relations. Stablecoins attempt to bridge digital and traditional finance by pegging token values to national currencies, facilitating faster payments with reduced volatility (Arner et al. 2017). NFTs operate differently. Each NFT represents a unique digital object, such as an artwork, a piece of music, or a virtual collectible. The value does not lie in the digital file itself, which remains freely reproducible, but in the blockchain record that certifies uniqueness and ownership (Dowling 2022). In this way, tokenization manufactures scarcity in a medium otherwise defined by abundance. Virtual worlds extend this logic further by tokenizing parcels of digital land. Although virtual space is unlimited, platforms impose fixed supplies, allowing scarcity to be monetized through design (Castronova 2021).

The appeal of tokenization lies in its promise to broaden participation and reshape ownership. Fractionalization allows small investors to enter markets that institutions and elites once dominated. Assets that were difficult to sell become tradable in secondary markets, improving liquidity. Smart contracts automate dividend payments, royalties, and compliance, reducing administrative costs and reliance on intermediaries. Because tokenized assets can move across jurisdictions with ease, they challenge the dominance of banks, exchanges, and clearing houses, contributing to the decentralization of global finance (World Economic Forum 2021).

At the same time, tokenization reveals more profound contradictions within digital capitalism. Much of its economic value depends on the deliberate construction of scarcity. The exact mechanisms that promise inclusion and efficiency also intensify the commodification of culture, creativity, and social meaning (O'Dwyer 2023). The NFT boom of 2021 and its subsequent collapse illustrate this tension. While new markets and communities emerged rapidly, prices proved highly volatile, revealing how fragile value can be when it rests on engineered exclusivity and speculative belief (Dowling 2022). Legal uncertainty compounds the problem. Owning a token does not necessarily confer enforceable rights over the underlying asset within existing legal systems (Zetsche et al. 2019). Despite the rhetoric of decentralization, many token ecosystems concentrate power and wealth among early adopters, developers, and platform operators, reproducing familiar inequalities.

Tokenization ultimately introduces a paradox at the heart of market logic. In traditional economies, prices emerge from the interaction of supply and demand under material constraints. Goods are scarce because production is costly and resources are limited. In digital environments, production is immaterial and marginal costs approach zero (Varian 2019).

Under these conditions, the natural foundations of scarcity weaken. Tokenization responds by re-creating scarcity through design rather than through production. Prices no longer reflect limits imposed by nature or labor but depend on artificial constraints, symbolic exclusivity, and speculative expectations (Brekke and Fischer 2021). This shift does not eliminate markets, but it transforms their underlying logic. Scarcity is no longer given; it is engineered.

Digital Infrastructure and Connectivity

In the 21st century, digital infrastructure has become as essential to economic and social life as roads, electricity, or clean water once were. Connectivity, computing power, and data-processing capacity now underpin innovation across nearly every sector, shaping how societies function, how firms compete, and how governments deliver services (OECD 2021). Digital infrastructure is no longer a background condition but a strategic asset that determines competitiveness and resilience. Four interrelated trends illustrate the scope of this transformation: the rollout of advanced mobile networks, the expansion of the Internet of Things (IoT), the consolidation and diversification of cloud computing, and the early but consequential progress in quantum computing.

The deployment of 5G networks marks a decisive shift in global connectivity. Unlike earlier generations of mobile technology, 5G offers ultralow latency, significantly higher data speeds, and the capacity to connect vast numbers of devices simultaneously (Ericsson 2023). These features enable applications that were previously impractical, including autonomous vehicles, remote medical procedures, and immersive augmented and virtual reality. For businesses, 5G supports real-time data collection and rapid decision making. Manufacturers can monitor machinery continuously to predict failures before they occur, logistics firms can track shipments with precision, and media companies can deliver interactive digital experiences. In the public sector, governments increasingly view 5G as the foundation for smart cities, where traffic systems, energy grids, and environmental monitoring operate in real time (OECD 2021).

The social consequences of this level of connectivity are substantial. Improved efficiency promises reduced congestion, lower emissions, and expanded access to services, particularly in health care and transportation. At the same time, advanced network deployment exposes persistent inequalities. High infrastructure costs risk widening digital divides between urban and rural areas and between wealthy and poorer regions. Security concerns further complicate adoption, as dependence on a limited number of global equipment suppliers raises geopolitical and cybersecurity vulnerabilities. Looking ahead, research on 6G networks points toward even more radical possibilities, including integration with AI at the network level and new forms of immersive communication (Samsung 2022). These developments will intensify debates around privacy, surveillance, and equitable access.

Closely linked to advances in connectivity is the rapid growth of the IoT. IoT refers to networks of physical objects embedded with sensors and software that enable continuous data collection and exchange (Roman et al. 2013). These devices range from household appliances and wearable health monitors to industrial machinery and agricultural equipment. The scale of expansion is striking, with projections suggesting tens of billions of connected devices worldwide by the end of the decade (Statista 2023). For firms, IoT enables new forms of efficiency and value creation. In manufacturing, industrial IoT systems reduce downtime through predictive maintenance. In agriculture, sensors optimize irrigation and fertilizer use, improving yields while conserving resources. Health care providers use remote monitoring to track patients outside hospitals, reducing costs and improving outcomes.

From a societal perspective, IoT offers tangible benefits. Smart homes can reduce energy consumption, connected vehicles improve road safety, and real-time monitoring of infrastructure, such as bridges or power grids, enhances resilience. Yet these benefits come with significant risks. Each connected device represents a potential security vulnerability, and large-scale breaches have already demonstrated how IoT systems can be exploited (Roman et al. 2013). Continuous data collection also raises concerns about surveillance and the erosion of personal privacy.

Suppose that connectivity forms the nervous system of the digital economy, and that cloud computing functions as its cognitive core. Cloud platforms provide scalable storage, processing power, and software services on demand, enabling organizations to operate without the heavy upfront investment in physical infrastructure (Gartner 2022). Cloud computing has become central to modern business, supporting remote work, digital collaboration, AI, and large-scale data analytics. Its rapid expansion reflects both cost efficiency and strategic dependence. Start-ups and small firms gain access to computational resources once reserved for large corporations. At the same time, established enterprises use cloud services to increase flexibility and speed.

A notable shift within this domain is the move toward multicloud and hybrid strategies. Rather than relying on a single provider, organizations distribute workloads across multiple platforms to reduce risk, avoid vendor lock-in, and comply with data sovereignty requirements. For society, cloud services expand access to digital tools in education, health care, and commerce, fostering innovation and inclusion. At the same time, the concentration of cloud infrastructure in the hands of a few providers raises concerns about competition and systemic vulnerability. A single outage can disrupt services across entire sectors. Environmental impact is another growing issue, as large data centers consume substantial energy, underscoring the need for efficiency improvements and renewable power sources (Mytton 2021).

The most speculative yet potentially transformative element of digital infrastructure is quantum computing. By exploiting the principles of quantum mechanics, quantum computers promise to solve problems that remain intractable for classical machines (Preskill 2018). Although still in an experimental stage, progress has been rapid, with major technology firms and specialized start-ups racing to achieve practical quantum advantage. For businesses, quantum computing could revolutionize optimization, financial modeling, and drug discovery by simulating complex systems with unprecedented accuracy.

The societal implications of quantum computing are equally far-reaching. Advances in materials science, climate modeling, and energy storage could address some of the most pressing global challenges. At the same time, quantum computing poses serious risks to existing cryptographic systems that underpin worldwide finance and digital security. Anticipating these threats, governments and corporations are investing in postquantum encryption to protect critical infrastructure (Chen et al. 2016). While widespread commercial use remains years away, continued progress suggests that quantum technologies will eventually redefine the limits of *computation*.

Immersive and Human-Centric Technologies

Technological progress in the 21st century is no longer driven solely by the increasing power of machines, but also by the evolving ways humans interact with them. A growing wave of immersive and human-centric technologies seeks to blur the boundaries between the digital and physical worlds, creating new forms of experience, communication, and productivity. At the core of this transformation are extended reality (XR) technologies, the emerging concept of the metaverse, and advances in human–machine interfaces (HMIs), including brain–computer connections, wearable devices, and haptic systems. Together, these innovations promise far-reaching impacts on education, training, health care, entertainment, and commerce, while simultaneously raising complex questions about ethics, equity, and human identity.

XR is one of the most visible expressions of this shift. XR functions as an umbrella term encompassing Virtual Reality (VR), Augmented Reality (AR), and Mixed Reality (MR), each integrating digital and physical environments to varying degrees. VR immerses users in fully virtual worlds, AR overlays digital elements onto the physical environment, and MR enables interactive combinations of real and virtual objects. These technologies are already finding practical applications across industries. In training and education, VR enables realistic simulations in fields such as aviation, health care, and manufacturing, allowing learners to practice complex tasks in safe, cost-effective environments while improving performance outcomes (Radianti et al. 2020). In organizational settings, XR supports remote collaboration through immersive virtual meeting spaces that enhance a sense of shared presence among distributed teams. In retail, AR applications allow consumers to preview furniture in their homes or try on clothing virtually, personalizing the shopping experience and reducing uncertainty. The entertainment sector has likewise been transformed through immersive storytelling and participatory environments that extend gaming, live performances, and cultural events.

From a societal perspective, XR offers both significant opportunities and notable risks. On the positive side, it can expand access to high-quality education through globally available simulations, support health care through VR-based therapies for pain management and mental health, and foster inclusion by enabling people with disabilities to engage in tailored virtual environments. At the same time, prolonged exposure to immersive systems may lead to physical discomfort, such as motion sickness, and intensify concerns about digital addiction. Unequal access to XR hardware and infrastructure further risks deepening existing social inequalities. High costs and technological barriers could turn XR into a luxury rather than a broadly empowering tool, making affordability and accessibility central policy concerns (Milgram and Kishino 1994).

Closely linked to XR is the development of the metaverse, often described as a persistent, shared, and immersive digital universe in which individuals interact with one another, virtual objects, and digital environments through avatars. Although still largely experimental, the metaverse has gained momentum as major technology firms invest heavily in platforms and infrastructure. Estimates suggest that it could generate trillions of dollars in economic value by 2030, with applications spanning e-commerce, work, education, and entertainment (McKinsey 2022). For businesses, the metaverse offers new markets and business models, including virtual economies enabled by blockchain technologies such as NFTs and cryptocurrencies. Digital goods ranging from avatar clothing to virtual real estate are already being traded. In contrast, "digital twins" allow consumers to experience products virtually before purchasing. Workplaces may evolve from video-based communication to immersive virtual offices, and education may increasingly rely on interactive, gamified virtual campuses.

Socially, the metaverse introduces new possibilities for identity formation and community building. Avatars allow individuals to experiment with self-representation beyond physical constraints, potentially fostering inclusivity and creative expression. Virtual communities may also strengthen cross-border connections and cultural exchange. However, these possibilities are accompanied by serious challenges. Participation depends on access to advanced devices, reliable connectivity, and digital literacy, which may exclude marginalized populations. Virtual economies are vulnerable to speculation and volatility, as illustrated by the fluctuations in NFT markets.

Alongside XR and the metaverse, advances in HMIs represent another critical frontier. HMIs aim to create seamless links between humans and machines, enhancing communication, productivity, and sensory experience. These technologies include brain–computer interfaces, wearable devices, and haptic feedback systems. BCIs translate neural signals into digital commands, enabling direct interaction between the brain and external devices. Experimental developments suggest promising applications for individuals with paralysis, such as controlling prosthetics or communicating without speech, with longer-term possibilities for cognitive enhancement remaining largely speculative (He et al. 2020). Wearable technologies, including smartwatches and health trackers, are already widespread, providing continuous biometric data for personal use and health care monitoring. In professional contexts, wearables can improve safety in hazardous environments and deliver real-time instructions. Haptic systems extend digital interaction by incorporating the sense of touch, allowing users to feel virtual objects through specialized gloves, suits, or controllers.

For businesses, HMIs expand innovation by integrating human capabilities more directly into digital systems. For society, they offer enhanced accessibility, improved health monitoring, and more effective learning environments. Nevertheless, these technologies raise profound ethical and security concerns. Brain–computer interfaces, in particular, challenge conventional notions of privacy and autonomy, as neural data could expose deeply personal information. Wearables and haptic systems also generate sensitive biometric data that employers, insurers, or governments may misuse.

References

Alberts, J., and Mik, E. 2022. "Tokenization of Real-World Assets and the Future of Financial Markets." *Journal of Financial Regulation and Compliance 30, no.* 4, pp. 512–528.

Angwin, J., Larson, J., Mattu, S., and Kirchner, L. 2016. *Machine Bias: There's Software used Across the Country to Predict Future Criminals. And It's Biased Against Blacks*. ProPublica.

Arner, D.W., Barberis, J., and Buckley, R.P. 2017. "FinTech, RegTech, and the Reconceptualization of Financial Regulation." *Northwestern Journal of International Law & Business 37, no.* 3, pp. 371–413.

Bollier, D. 2014. *Think like a Commoner: A Short Introduction to the Life of the Commons*. New Society Publishers.

Brekke, J.K., and Fischer, A. 2021. "What is Digital Scarcity?" *Internet Policy Review 10, no.* 2. https://doi.org/10.14763/2021.2.1552

Castronova, E. 2021. *Wildcat Currency: How the Virtual Money Revolution is Transforming the Economy*. Yale University Press.

Chen, L., Chen, L.K., Jordan, S., Liu, Y.-K., Moody, D., Peralta, R., … Smith-Tone, D. 2016. *Report on Post-Quantum Cryptography*. National Institute of Standards and Technology.

Cusumano, M.A., Gawer, A., and Yoffie, D.B. 2019. *The Business of Platforms: Strategy in the Age of Digital Competition, Innovation, and Power*. Harper Business.

Dowling, M. 2022. "Is Non-Fungible Token Pricing Driven by Cryptocurrencies?" *Finance Research Letters 44*, p. 102097. https://doi.org/10.1016/j.frl.2021.102097

Ericsson. 2023. *Ericsson Mobility Report: November 2023*. Ericsson.

Fuller, A., Fan, Z., Day, C., and Barlow, C. 2020. "Digital Twin: Enabling Technologies, Challenges and Open Research." *IEEE Access, 8*, pp. 108952–108971.

Gartner. 2022. *Forecast: Public Cloud Services, Worldwide, 2020–2026*. Gartner Research.

Garcia-Teruel, R. 2023. "Legal Challenges of Tokenized Property Rights." *Computer Law & Security Review 48*, p. 105741. https://doi.org/10.1016/j.clsr.2022.105741

He, B., Wu, D., and Wang, Y. 2020. "Brain–Computer Interfaces: The Frontiers of Human–Machine Integration." *Nature Reviews Neuroscience 21, no.* 9, pp. 509–525. https://doi.org/10.1038/s41583-020-0330-9

Kitchin, R. 2014. *The Data Revolution: Big Data, Open Data, Data Infrastructures and Their Consequences*. SAGE.

McKinsey & Company. 2022. *Value Creation in the Metaverse: The Real Business of the Virtual World*. McKinsey Global Institute.

Milgram, P., and Kishino, F. 1994. "A Taxonomy of Mixed Reality Visual Displays." *IEICE Transactions on Information and Systems, E77-D, no.* 12, pp. 1321–1329.

Mytton, D. 2021. "Data Centre Energy use and Environmental Impact." *Applied Energy 303*, pp. 117–118. https://doi.org/10.1016/j.apenergy.2021.117783

Narayanan, A., Bonneau, J., Felten, E., Miller, A., and Goldfeder, S. 2016. *Bitcoin and Cryptocurrency Technologies: A Comprehensive Introduction*. Princeton University Press.

O'Dwyer, R. 2023. *Blockchain and the Cultural Logic of Scarcity*. University of Westminster Press.

Organisation for Economic Co-operation and Development. 2021. *The Impact Of 5G Networks on Business, Society, and the Economy*. OECD Publishing.

Parker, G.G., Van Alstyne, M.W., and Choudary, S.P. 2016. *Platform Revolution: How Networked Markets are Transforming the Economy and How to Make Them Work for You*. W. W. Norton & Company.

Piketty, T. 2014. *Capital in the Twenty-First Century*. Harvard University Press.

Preskill, J. 2018. "Quantum Computing in the NISQ Era and Beyond." *Quantum 2*, p. 79. https://doi.org/10.22331/q-2018-08-06-79

Radianti, J., Majchrzak, T.A., Fromm, J., and Wohlgenannt, I. 2020. "A Systematic Review of Immersive Virtual Reality Applications for Higher Education: Design Elements, Lessons Learned, and Research Agenda." *Computers & Education 147*, p. 103778. https://doi.org/10.1016/j.compedu.2019.103778

Regner, F., Urbach, N., and Schweizer, A. 2019. "NFTs in Practice: Non-Fungible Tokens as Core Component of a Blockchain-Based Event Ticketing Application." *Proceedings of the 40th International Conference on Information Systems (ICIS)*.

Roman, R., Zhou, J., and Lopez, J. 2013. "On the Security of Wireless Sensor Networks." *Computer Communications 36, no.* 12, pp. 1341–1355.

Samsung. 2022. *6G: The Next Hyper-Connected Experience for All*. Samsung Research White Paper.

Schär, F. 2021. "Decentralized Finance: On Blockchain- and Smart Contract-based Financial Markets." *Federal Reserve Bank of St. Louis Review 103, no.* 2, pp. 153–174. https://doi.org/10.20955/r.103.153-174

Srnicek, N. 2017. *Platform Capitalism*. Polity Press.

Statista. 2023. *Internet of Things (IoT) Connected Devices Installed Base Worldwide from 2019 to 2030*. Statista Research Department.

Tao, F., Zhang, H., Liu, A., and Nee, A.Y.C. 2018. "Digital Twin in Industry: State-of-the-Art." *IEEE Transactions on Industrial Informatics 15, no.* 4, pp. 2405–2415.

Van Dijck, J., Poell, T., and de Waal, M. 2018. *The Platform Society: Public Values in a Connective World*. Oxford University Press.

Varian, H.R. 2019. "Artificial Scarcity." In *Innovation Policy and the Economy*, eds. J. Lerner and S. Stern, vol. 19, 191–219. University of Chicago Press.

Veblen, T. 1899. *The Theory of the Leisure Class*. Macmillan.

World Economic Forum. 2021. *Global Standards Mapping Initiative: An Overview of Blockchain Technical Standards*. World Economic Forum.

Zetsche, D.A., Buckley, R.P., and Arner, D.W. 2019. "The Distributed Ledger Technology Revolution and Digital Finance." *Journal of International Economic Law 22, no.* 1, pp. 1–34.

CHAPTER 10

The Tyranny of Finance

The Financialization of Society

Over the past few decades, finance has changed its place in the economy. It once operated mainly in the background, channeling savings into investment, spreading risk, and maintaining payment systems, but it has increasingly moved to the center of economic and social life (Epstein 2005). Financial markets, institutions, and incentives now shape corporate strategy, public policy, and household security, a shift commonly described as financialization (Epstein 2005). While this transformation began in the late 20th century, digital technologies and the rise of intangible value have significantly intensified it, allowing finance to operate with growing autonomy from productive activity (Arner et al. 2016).

In its traditional role, finance supported production by allocating capital, managing uncertainty, and facilitating exchange. Financialization altered this relationship by turning finance itself into a primary source of profit generation rather than a service to the real economy (Epstein 2005). The expansion of derivatives and securitization illustrates this shift, as instruments designed to hedge risk increasingly became vehicles for speculation. Securitization further transformed loans into layered and opaque financial products, enabling returns to be generated through trading claims rather than through investment in productive capacity. As a result, financial activity could expand even when wages stagnated or real investment slowed, deepening the separation between finance and production (Krippner 2005).

The growing power of financial intermediaries reinforced this autonomy. Investment banks, hedge funds, and private equity firms expanded across borders and sectors, accumulating influence over corporate governance and policy decisions (Krippner 2005). These actors do not merely intermediate capital flows; they shape markets and managerial behavior by embedding financial priorities such as shareholder value, short-term performance, and market signaling into nonfinancial firms (Krippner 2005). Compensation structures tied to stock prices and pressures for rapid returns further institutionalize financial logics within everyday business decision making.

Digitalization has accelerated these dynamics by reshaping how finance operates. Algorithmic and high-frequency trading systems execute transactions at machine speed, responding to signals and exploiting minute price movements in fractions of a second (Arner et al. 2016). While such technologies can improve liquidity, they also encourage speculative strategies and heighten volatility by rewarding speed over long-term judgment. Digitization thus produces a financial environment increasingly driven by instantaneous valuation and data flows, rather than by sustained engagement with productive outcomes (Arner et al. 2016).

The rise of the intangible economy has further strengthened this speculative orientation. In advanced economies, intangible assets such as data, intellectual property, software, and brand value now account for the majority of corporate worth (Haskel and Westlake 2018). Because these assets derive much of their value from expectations about future performance, valuation becomes highly sensitive to narratives and sentiment. This dynamic amplifies boom-and-bust cycles, as optimism drives prices upward while shifts in belief trigger abrupt sell-offs. The dot-com bubble of the late 1990s and the more recent rise and collapse of firms such as WeWork demonstrate how intangible-heavy valuations can inflate rapidly and unravel just as quickly (Haskel and Westlake 2018).

Financialization has also become embedded in everyday life. Households are increasingly exposed to financial markets through mortgages, pensions, student loans, and consumer credit, tying personal security to market fluctuations (Davis and Kim 2015). Digital platforms intensify this exposure by lowering barriers to participation and amplifying speculative behavior. The GameStop episode of 2021 showed how online communities, algorithmic amplification, and commission-free trading could drive dramatic price swings disconnected from underlying fundamentals. Cryptocurrency markets reflect an even more extreme version of this pattern, with valuations often driven by collective belief and momentum rather than stable economic anchors (Davis and Kim 2015).

The broader consequences of these trends are significant. Financialization in the digital age promotes short-termism, as firms prioritize quarterly earnings, shareholder payouts, and financial engineering over long-term investment in innovation, skills, and infrastructure. Stock buybacks and cost-cutting frequently take precedence over productive expansion, reinforcing a speculative orientation. At the same time, the dominance of financial and intangible assets exacerbates inequality, as those with access to capital benefit disproportionately from rising valuations while others face growing precarity (Haskel and Westlake 2018).

The fragility of this system is evident in recurring crises. The global financial crisis of 2008 exposed the risks of an economy built on complex and opaque financial instruments whose systemic implications were poorly understood. Although regulatory reforms followed, the rapid expansion of digital finance, cryptocurrencies, and decentralized financial systems continues to outpace oversight. Regulatory frameworks remain largely national, while capital and digital assets circulate globally, creating gaps that speculative finance can exploit (Palan 2013). Without effective mechanisms to restrain excess and reanchor finance to productive and social goals, economies remain vulnerable to repeated cycles of instability.

The Financial Markets Paradox

The rise of the digital economy has brought with it profound structural changes to global capitalism, not least the growing centrality of financial markets. Financial markets are often celebrated as the epitome of efficiency within the market paradigm. They function globally, operate around the clock, integrate vast numbers of participants, and provide extensive information at declining transaction costs. From this perspective, financial markets appear to embody the ideals of a perfect market: transparency, liquidity, and accessibility. Yet, despite these apparent advantages, financial markets have become the subject of widespread dissatisfaction among policymakers, regulators, scholars, and even practitioners. This contradiction, known as the "Financial Markets Paradox," highlights the tension between the theoretical promises of financial markets and their practical consequences.

At its core, the paradox arises because financial markets, while efficient in information processing and cost reduction, simultaneously create instability, distort policy priorities, and undermine long-term economic development.

The first element of the paradox concerns the disproportionate power that financial markets wield over governments, corporations, and societies. Rather than merely serving as neutral facilitators of capital allocation, markets increasingly influence policy decisions, sometimes creating what critics describe as the "dictatorship of financial markets." As Strange (1996) argued, the growing autonomy of finance allows it to discipline states by rewarding or punishing fiscal and monetary choices through currency markets, bond spreads, or credit ratings. For example, during the 2022 bond market turmoil in the United Kingdom, markets reacted sharply to the government's proposed unfunded tax cuts, forcing a policy reversal and the resignation of Prime Minister Liz Truss. This episode illustrates how market sentiment can override democratic processes, privileging short-term investor confidence over long-term economic strategy (Tooze 2022).

Second, financial markets are marked by volatility that far exceeds the underlying fluctuations of the real economy. Foreign exchange, equities, and interest rates are all prone to persistent, contagious swings driven by speculation, herd behavior, or sudden shifts in expectations. The 2008 global financial crisis remains the starkest reminder of this volatility, but more recent episodes continue to highlight the problem. The GameStop short squeeze in early 2021 demonstrated how digital platforms could fuel massive price swings disconnected from fundamentals, with retail investors collectively pushing up stock prices in defiance of institutional short sellers (Gorton and Zentefis 2022). Likewise, the collapse of major cryptocurrency exchanges like FTX in 2022 revealed how speculative bubbles in digital assets can suddenly implode, wiping out billions in value and destabilizing investors worldwide. These events underscore how digital finance, far from ensuring stability, often amplifies systemic risks.

The third dimension of the paradox lies in the misleading signals that financial markets send about economic value and performance. In principle, prices in financial markets should reflect underlying fundamentals such as productivity, innovation, or long-term profitability. In practice, markets often prioritize short-term financial metrics and speculative trends. Krippner (2005) observes that financialization has reoriented corporate behavior toward shareholder value maximization, encouraging practices such as stock buybacks and financial engineering at the expense of productive investment. Similarly, the inflated valuations of firms such as WeWork or tech start-ups with limited tangible output demonstrate how markets frequently deviate from real economic fundamentals. By privileging speculative growth narratives, financial markets distort resource allocation and reinforce economic inequality (Davis and Kim 2015).

Together, these three dynamics encapsulate the Financial Markets Paradox: the very institutions celebrated for their efficiency are simultaneously criticized for their destabilizing power, volatility, and short-termism. The paradox reflects broader structural transformations in the digital or intangible economy, where value is increasingly tied to expectations, information flows, and speculative capital rather than tangible production. As Haskel and Westlake (2018) note, intangible assets—such as data, intellectual property, and brand equity—dominate corporate valuations, making financial markets even more central to the pricing and circulation of future-oriented value. This shift deepens the disconnect between financial signals and productive realities, reinforcing the contradictions that fuel dissatisfaction with finance. On one hand, financial markets remain indispensable to the functioning of global capitalism, enabling capital allocation, risk sharing, and liquidity provision. On the other hand, their outsized influence, instability, and distortions present challenges for economic governance and social well-being. Regulators face the daunting task of mitigating volatility and speculative excess while preserving the efficiency benefits of financial markets.

Growth of Asset-Based Inequality

Assets rather than wages increasingly drive the contemporary economy. This shift marks a structural transformation in how wealth is generated, accumulated, and distributed. Asset-based inequality refers to disparities in ownership of financial, physical, and intangible assets that appreciate over time—such as stocks, bonds, real estate, intellectual property, and digital platforms. As returns on capital outpace labor income growth, the gap between asset owners and nonowners widens. This trend has become one of the most consequential dynamics shaping social stratification in the 21st century (Piketty 2014; Stiglitz 2012). It is not merely a distributional issue but a reflection of deep changes in the architecture of capitalism, driven by financialization, digitalization, global markets, and the rise of intangible value (Haskel and Westlake 2018).

Several factors explain the acceleration of asset-based inequality. The most prominent is the long-term decoupling of productivity and wages. While productivity has increased steadily in many advanced economies since the 1980s, real wages have remained largely stagnant (OECD 2020). The benefits of technological innovation, efficiency gains, and globalization have flowed predominantly to capital rather than labor. As Piketty (2014) famously argued, when the rate of return on capital exceeds the rate of economic growth, wealth concentrates in the hands of those who already possess assets. This mechanism reinforces itself across generations, as wealth accumulates faster than income and becomes increasingly detached from productive work.

A second driver is the expansion of financial markets and the deepening of financialization. Over the past four decades, households and firms have become more embedded in financial systems, not only as borrowers but also as investors (Epstein 2018). The rising influence of institutional investors, private equity, venture capital, and hedge funds has elevated the role of financial engineering in wealth creation. Yet participation in these financial markets remains highly unequal. In the United States, for example, the top 10 percent of households own more than 80 percent of all stocks by value (Federal Reserve 2023). This asymmetry means that periods of market growth disproportionately benefit those who already hold substantial portfolios, while those dependent on wages see little improvement in their economic position (Saez and Zucman 2019).

Housing markets have further amplified asset inequality. Real estate has transitioned from a basic need to a primary vehicle for wealth accumulation. Urbanization, limited housing supply, and global investment flows have pushed property prices beyond the reach of many younger and middle-income households (UN-Habitat 2020). As a result, homeownership rates have declined in numerous advanced economies, particularly among younger generations. Those who enter the property market early benefit from rising values and accumulate equity that can be leveraged for further investment. Those who are excluded face escalating rents and diminished opportunities to build wealth. The divergence between owners and renters, therefore, contributes to an entrenched divide in life chances, mobility, and security (Aalbers 2016).

The rise of intangible assets—data, software, algorithms, brands, patents, and network effects—adds a new layer to asset-based inequality. Intangibles generate high returns but are controlled by a concentrated set of corporations and investors. Companies whose value derives largely from intangible assets, such as technology firms and digital platforms, often scale globally with minimal labor input (Brynjolfsson and McAfee 2014). The profits they generate accrue to shareholders rather than workers, reinforcing the imbalance between capital and labor. This dynamic also reshapes corporate power. Firms with strong intangible asset portfolios enjoy market dominance, pricing power, and strategic influence, all of which contribute to the concentration of wealth among their owners (Zuboff 2019; Haskel and Westlake 2018).

Intergenerational effects exacerbate these patterns. Wealth, once accumulated, reproduces itself. Inheritances, trusts, family networks, and unequal starting points create durable advantages for younger generations of asset holders (Pfeffer 2018). By contrast, individuals born into families with limited or no assets must rely solely on labor income, which rarely grows at the same pace as capital income. The rising costs of education, health care, and housing place additional burdens on those without inherited wealth, making upward mobility more difficult (OECD 2018).

The consequences of asset-based inequality extend beyond economic disparities. They reshape social relations, political dynamics, and cultural expectations. Economically, unequal asset ownership leads to uneven exposure to risk and volatility. Households with diversified portfolios can weather downturns; those dependent on wages face instability and insecurity. Politically, asset concentration enhances the influence of wealthy individuals, corporations, and financial actors. Their ability to shape policies—taxation, regulation, labor markets, and housing—often reinforces structures that protect capital returns at the expense of broader social welfare (Hacker and Pierson 2010). Culturally, societies become divided between those who experience the economy through the lens of capital appreciation and those for whom economic life remains precarious. This divide influences attitudes toward work, opportunity, social mobility, and fairness.

The growth of asset-based inequality reflects the underlying logic of contemporary capitalism: wealth increasingly arises not from labor but from ownership, valuation, and control of appreciating assets. As this structure deepens, societies confront a widening chasm between those who own the future and those who merely work within it. The challenge ahead lies in designing institutions and policies that rebalance these foundations and ensure that asset ownership does not become the exclusive privilege of a shrinking elite.

Dominance of Institutional Investors

Institutional investors have emerged as the most powerful actors in contemporary capitalism. Pension funds, mutual funds, insurance companies, sovereign wealth funds, hedge funds, and private equity firms now dominate global financial markets, reshaping corporate governance, market dynamics, and the distribution of economic power. Over the past four decades, their expanding control over financial assets has transformed the relationships between firms, shareholders, workers, and states. This shift reflects broader trends associated with financialization, demographic change, technological innovation, and the rise of globally integrated markets centered on intangible assets.

The growth of institutional investors is closely tied to structural changes in savings and retirement systems. Beginning in the 1980s, many advanced economies moved away from defined-benefit pension schemes toward defined-contribution plans. This transition shifted investment risk from employers to individuals while directing vast pools of household savings into financial markets through pension funds and asset managers. Deregulation of capital markets and the expansion of private retirement savings further accelerated this process, positioning institutional investors as the primary intermediaries between households and financial markets (Clark and Monk 2017). Today, institutional investors hold a dominant share of global equity and bond markets. In the United States, they own roughly 80 percent of publicly traded equities, underscoring the degree to which ownership has become concentrated in institutional hands (Coffee 2020).

This concentration of ownership translates directly into influence over corporate decision making. Institutional investors shape governance through proxy voting, board engagement, shareholder proposals, and ongoing dialogue with management. Traditional models of corporate governance assumed dispersed ownership and limited coordination among shareholders. In contrast, the rise of large institutional blockholders has produced a more centralized ownership structure. A small group of asset managers, most notably the so-called "Big Three" index fund providers—BlackRock, Vanguard, and State Street now exercise voting power across thousands of firms simultaneously (Fichtner et al. 2017). Their stewardship practices affect executive compensation, mergers and acquisitions, capital allocation, and corporate policies on ESG issues.

A defining feature of this new landscape is the rapid expansion of passive investing. Index funds and exchange-traded funds track market indices rather than actively selecting securities, offering low fees and broad diversification. As a result, passive strategies have grown faster than traditional active management, and passive funds now hold more U.S. equity assets than active funds (S&P Dow Jones Indices 2023). This shift has important implications. Large index fund managers automatically become major shareholders in most publicly listed companies, regardless of the performance of individual firms. Such widespread ownership gives rise to "common ownership," in which the same investors hold significant stakes in competing firms, potentially influencing competition, pricing behavior, and market outcomes (Azar et al. 2018).

Institutional dominance also shapes firm behavior from within. Pressure to meet shareholder expectations often leads companies to prioritize financial indicators such as earnings per share, share price appreciation, and short-term profitability. Practices such as stock buybacks, cost-cutting, and financial restructuring have become central tools for boosting shareholder returns, sometimes at the expense of long-term investment in labor, research, or productive capacity (Lazonick 2014). Activist hedge funds reinforce these dynamics by targeting firms that they deem underperforming and pushing for rapid changes designed to unlock short-term value. Supporters view this activism as a mechanism of managerial discipline, while critics argue that it entrenches short-termism and increases economic fragility.

At the same time, institutional investors play a crucial role in the expansion of firms built on intangible assets. Technology companies, digital platforms, and intellectual property–intensive enterprises rely heavily on institutional capital to scale and compete globally. Venture capital and private equity are central to this process, shaping the direction of innovation and the structure of emerging industries. Private equity firms, in particular, control extensive portfolios and employ strategies such as leveraged buyouts and aggressive restructuring. These practices can not only boost efficiency and profitability but also have far-reaching consequences for employment conditions, labor bargaining power, and income distribution (Appelbaum and Batt 2014).

The influence of institutional investors extends beyond markets into the political sphere. Through lobbying, regulatory engagement, and participation in policy debates, they shape financial regulation, taxation, and disclosure standards. Sovereign wealth funds introduce an additional geopolitical dimension, as states deploy large pools of capital to diversify national wealth, secure strategic interests, and exert influence in global markets (Truman 2019). This intertwining of finance, politics, and corporate governance highlights how institutional power increasingly blurs the boundary between private economic authority and public decision making.

The rise of institutional investors, however, is marked by deep tensions. On one hand, their scale and long-term investment horizons, particularly in pension and index funds, can support stability and responsible governance. Many large institutions now promote ESG integration, climate disclosure, and diversity initiatives, arguing that these practices enhance long-term value and reduce systemic risk (Eccles and Klimenko 2019). On the other hand, institutional dominance reinforces wealth concentration. The benefits of asset appreciation accrue primarily to households with substantial retirement savings or financial wealth, while those without access to financial assets remain largely excluded. This dynamic contributes to persistent inequalities in wealth, opportunity, and political influence.

A further concern lies in the concentration of power itself. A small group of asset managers collectively holds voting authority over a significant share of global corporations, raising questions about accountability, competition, and democratic oversight. These institutions are not elected, yet their decisions shape corporate behavior, labor outcomes, and even public policy. As Braun (2022) argues, the growing role of institutional investors challenges conventional understandings of economic governance and blurs the line between market coordination and private authority.

The dominance of institutional investors is therefore both a consequence and a driver of the broader transformation of capitalism. As financial markets deepen, intangible assets expand, and global savings pools grow, institutional investors will continue to shape corporate strategies and economic priorities. The central challenge for policymakers and societies is to harness the stabilizing and innovative potential of institutional stewardship while mitigating the risks posed by excessive concentration, short-termism, and inequality. Striking this balance is essential for understanding and governing the political economy of the 21st century.

The Shadow Banking and the Rapid Growth of Private Equity

The expansion of shadow banking and the rapid growth of private equity and private credit represent two of the most consequential structural shifts in contemporary finance. Together, they signal a reconfiguration of financial intermediation away from publicly regulated banking and transparent capital markets toward private, opaque, and highly leveraged systems of credit creation. While these developments have expanded access to finance and diversified sources of capital, they have also increased systemic fragility, weakened accountability, and intensified extractive dynamics within modern capitalism.

Shadow banking refers to a broad set of institutions and practices that perform bank-like functions—such as maturity transformation, liquidity provision, and credit intermediation—without being subject to the same regulatory and supervisory frameworks as commercial banks. Money market funds, hedge funds, structured investment vehicles, securitization chains, and nonbank lenders now intermediate a substantial share of global credit. As Gary Gorton and Andrew Metrick argue, shadow banking replicates the core economic functions of traditional banking while lacking equivalent safety nets, such as deposit insurance and permanent access to central bank liquidity (Gorton and Metrick 2012). This structural asymmetry allows risks to accumulate outside the regulatory perimeter, often unnoticed until periods of stress.

Several interrelated forces have driven the growth of shadow banking. Post-2008 regulatory reforms constrained bank balance sheets and capital ratios, encouraging credit activity to migrate toward nonbank entities. At the same time, prolonged low interest rates pushed institutional investors to seek higher yields through alternative credit instruments. Financial innovation further enabled this shift by expanding securitization, repo markets, and collateralized lending structures that obscure risk transmission channels. According to the Bank for International Settlements, the size of nonbank financial intermediation has grown faster than traditional banking in many advanced economies, increasing interconnectedness and systemic opacity (BIS 2023).

These vulnerabilities become most visible during financial stress. Shadow banking institutions are particularly susceptible to runs, as short-term funding can evaporate rapidly when confidence deteriorates. Liquidity mismatches force asset fire sales, transmitting shocks across markets and amplifying volatility. During both the global financial crisis and the COVID-19 market panic, central banks were compelled to intervene beyond the traditional banking system, extending liquidity facilities to money market funds and repo markets. While these interventions stabilized markets, they also entrenched moral hazard by implicitly backstopping private risk-taking without imposing commensurate regulatory discipline (Adrian and Ashcraft 2016).

Parallel to the rise of shadow banking is the growing dominance of private equity and private credit in capital allocation. Capital formation has increasingly shifted from public equity and bond markets toward private investment vehicles, including private equity, venture capital, infrastructure funds, and direct lending funds. Firms remain private for longer periods, while leveraged buyouts have become a central mechanism of corporate restructuring. Private credit funds, in particular, have expanded rapidly by replacing banks as lenders to middle-market firms, offering flexible financing but at higher cost and with less transparency (Appelbaum and Batt 2014).

Proponents of private markets argue that these models enhance efficiency, reduce short-term pressures, and allow for active ownership. Empirical evidence, however, paints a more ambivalent picture. Private equity strategies often rely on aggressive leverage, dividend recapitalizations, and cost-cutting to generate returns, prioritizing financial extraction over long-term productive investment. Debt-loaded firms may appear profitable in the short run but become more vulnerable to downturns, increasing bankruptcy risk and employment instability. Private credit similarly exposes borrowers to elevated interest burdens, tightening financial constraints during periods of rising rates (Ivashina and Lerner 2019).

The private nature of these markets further erodes transparency and accountability. Unlike public companies, firms owned by private equity are subject to minimal disclosure requirements, limiting oversight by regulators, workers, and the public. Decision-making power is concentrated in the hands of fund managers and institutional investors, while the distributional consequences—job losses, pension exposure, and community impacts—remain largely externalized. As the notes, the growth of private capital markets raises significant concerns about governance, competition, and systemic risk that existing regulatory frameworks are ill-equipped to address (OECD 2022).

Taken together, the expansion of shadow banking and the rise of private equity and private credit reflect a broader transformation of finance from a publicly anchored intermediary into a privately governed system of credit creation and risk distribution. These developments have increased the reach and flexibility of capital but at the cost of stability, transparency, and social legitimacy. Rather than supporting productive investment, finance increasingly operates through hidden leverage, institutionalized opacity, and short-term extraction. The central challenge is not merely regulatory reform, but a deeper reconsideration of the role of finance in economies that have become structurally dependent on private credit and systemic risk concealment.

Debt Expansion and Debt Dependence

The expansion of debt and the emergence of debt-dependent growth regimes are among the defining structural features of contemporary capitalism. Across advanced and emerging economies, growth, consumption, and asset price appreciation increasingly rely on the continuous accumulation of debt rather than sustained productivity gains or broad-based income growth (Mian and Sufi 2014). Household borrowing, corporate leverage, and sovereign debt have all risen persistently over recent decades, transforming debt from a cyclical stabilizing instrument into a permanent pillar of economic functioning (Jordà et al. 2016). While this expansion has supported short-term stability and demand, it has also increased systemic vulnerability and narrowed the scope of effective public policy (BIS 2022).

At the household level, debt has become central to sustaining consumption amid stagnant real wages and rising living costs (Mian and Sufi 2014). Mortgages, student loans, credit cards, and consumer credit increasingly substitute for income growth, allowing households to maintain living standards that would otherwise be unattainable (Stiglitz 2012). Housing markets play a particularly important role in this process, as rising property prices depend on expanding credit availability (Jordà et al. 2016). Higher prices, in turn, justify larger mortgage loans, reinforcing a self-perpetuating cycle of leverage and asset inflation (Mian and Sufi 2014). This dynamic ties household balance sheets to asset markets, making consumption and financial stability highly sensitive to interest-rate changes and housing price corrections (Jordà et al. 2016).

Corporate debt has followed a parallel trajectory. Prolonged periods of low interest rates and accommodative monetary policy have encouraged firms to rely on borrowing rather than retained earnings to finance expansion, acquisitions, and shareholder distributions (Rajan 2010). A significant share of corporate debt has been used not for productive investment, but for stock buybacks, dividends, and leveraged mergers designed to boost short-term valuations (Lazonick 2014). As Hyman Minsky argued in his financial instability hypothesis, extended periods of stability generate increasingly risky financing structures, shifting firms from hedge finance toward speculative and Ponzilike positions in which debt servicing depends on favorable market conditions rather than robust cash flows (Minsky 1986). Contemporary corporate finance closely reflects this logic, particularly in highly leveraged sectors (Rajan 2010).

Sovereign debt has also expanded structurally. Governments increasingly rely on borrowing to finance social welfare systems, infrastructure, crisis responses, and macroeconomic stabilization (IMF 2023). Demographic aging, rising health care costs, and repeated financial and economic shocks have made persistent deficits a structural feature of modern states rather than an exception (IMF 2023). While low interest rates previously reduced the immediate burden of public debt, the normalization of monetary policy has exposed fiscal vulnerabilities, particularly in highly indebted economies (BIS 2022). Rising debt servicing costs increasingly constrain discretionary spending and long-term public investment (Stiglitz 2012).

Together, these developments have produced debt-dependent growth regimes in which economic stability itself relies on continuous refinancing and expansion of credit (Jordà et al. 2016). When credit growth slows or interest rates rise, economic activity weakens rapidly, prompting policy intervention to prevent deleveraging spirals (Mian and Sufi 2014). This dependence creates a structural bias toward monetary accommodation, as central banks are pressured to maintain low rates to sustain debt servicing across households, firms, and governments (Rajan 2010). The Bank for International Settlements has repeatedly warned that high debt levels amplify economies' sensitivity to monetary tightening and increase the risk that interest-rate normalization triggers financial instability rather than productive reallocation (BIS 2022).

Debt dependence also generates fiscal and monetary lock-ins that constrain public policy. On the monetary side, central banks face a dilemma between controlling inflation and preserving financial stability, as tightening policy risks destabilizing highly leveraged sectors. At the same time, prolonged accommodation fuels asset inflation and inequality (Rajan 2010). On the fiscal side, elevated public debt narrows political and economic space, as governments prioritize debt servicing and market confidence over long-term investments in infrastructure, climate transition, and social cohesion (IMF 2023). Policy autonomy is thus increasingly subordinated to the requirements of financial markets rather than democratic choice (Stiglitz 2012).

Moreover, debt-driven growth exacerbates inequality. Asset holders benefit disproportionately from credit-fueled asset inflation, while indebted households bear the risks associated with leverage and economic downturns (Mian and Sufi 2014). During crises, losses are frequently socialized through public bailouts, fiscal transfers, or monetary interventions, while gains accrued during expansions remain privatized (Stiglitz 2012). This asymmetry undermines the social legitimacy of debt-dependent systems and fuels political backlash against financial elites and institutions (Rajan 2010).

In sum, the expansion of debt and the entrenchment of debt dependence reflect a deeper transformation of modern economies in which credit substitutes for income growth, productivity, and inclusive development (Jordà et al. 2016). While debt has supported growth in the short run, it has also increased fragility, constrained policy space, and reinforced inequality (BIS 2022). Addressing these challenges requires not only prudent debt management and macroprudential regulation but also a fundamental rethinking of growth models that have become structurally reliant on leverage to function (Mian and Sufi 2014).

References

Aalbers, M. 2016. *The Financialization of Housing*. Routledge.

Adrian, T., and Ashcraft, A.B. 2016. "Shadow Banking: A Review of the Literature." *Annual Review of Financial Economics* 8, pp. 1–26. https://doi.org/10.1146/annurev-financial-041014-011840

Appelbaum, E., and Batt, R. 2014. *Private Equity at Work: When Wall Street manages Main Street*. Russell Sage Foundation.

Arner, D.W., Barberis, J., and Buckley, R.P. 2016. "The Evolution of FinTech: A New Post-Crisis Paradigm?" *Georgetown Journal of International Law* 47, no. 4, pp. 1271–1319.

Azar, J., Schmalz, M., and Tecu, I. 2018. "Anti-Competitive Effects of Common Ownership." *Journal of Finance* 73, no. 4, pp. 1513–1565.

Bank for International Settlements. 2022. *Global Liquidity: Vulnerabilities in a Changing Financial System*. BIS Quarterly Review.

Bank for International Settlements. 2023. *Global Liquidity: Vulnerabilities in a Changing Financial System.* BIS Quarterly Review.

Braun, B. 2022. "Asset Manager Capitalism as a Corporate Governance Regime." *Review of International Political Economy* 29, no. 3, pp. 567–593.

Brynjolfsson, E., and McAfee, A. 2014. *The Second Machine Age: Work, Progress, and Prosperity in a Time of Brilliant Technologies.* W. W. Norton.

Clark, G.L., and Monk, A. 2017. *The World's Largest Investors.* Oxford University Press.

Coffee, J.C., Jr. 2020. *The Future of Disclosure.* Columbia Law School.

Davis, G.F., and Kim, S. 2015. "Financialization of the Economy." *Annual Review of Sociology* 41, pp. 203–221. https://doi.org/10.1146/annurev-soc-073014-112402

Eccles, R.G., and Klimenko, S. 2019. "The Investor Revolution." *Harvard Business Review* 97, no. 3, pp. 106–116.

Epstein, G.A. (ed.). 2005. *Financialization and the World Economy.* Edward Elgar.

Epstein, G.A. (ed.). 2018. *The Political Economy of Financialization.* Edward Elgar.

Federal Reserve. 2023. Distribution of household wealth in the U.S. Federal Reserve.

Fichtner, J., Heemskerk, E.M., and Garcia-Bernardo, J. 2017. "Hidden Power of the Big Three? Passive Index Funds, Re-Concentration of Corporate Ownership, and New Financial Risk." *Business and Politics* 19, no. 2, pp. 298–326.

Gorton, G., and Metrick, A. 2012. "Regulating the Shadow Banking System." *Brookings Papers on Economic Activity* 2012, no. 2, pp. 261–312. https://doi.org/10.1353/eca.2012.0016

Gorton, G., and Zentefis, A.K. 2022. "GameStop and the Short Squeeze." *Journal of Economic Perspectives* 36, no. 2, pp. 187–210.

Hacker, J.S., and Pierson, P. 2010. *Winner-Take-all Politics: How Washington made the Rich Richer—and Turned Its Back on the Middle Class.* Simon & Schuster.

Haskel, J., and Westlake, S. 2018. *Capitalism without Capital: The Rise of the Intangible Economy.* Princeton University Press.

International Monetary Fund. 2023. *Global Debt Monitor: Debt Vulnerabilities and Policy Challenges.* IMF Publishing.

Ivashina, V., and Lerner, J. 2019. *Patient Capital? The Challenges of Long-Term Investment.* Princeton University Press.

Jordà, Ò., Schularick, M., and Taylor, A.M. 2016. "The Great Mortgaging: Housing Finance, Crises, and Business Cycles." *Economic Policy* 31, no. 85, pp. 107–152. https://doi.org/10.1093/epolic/eiv017

Krippner, G.R. 2005. "The Financialization of the American economy." *Socio-Economic Review* 3, no. 2, pp. 173–208. https://doi.org/10.1093/SER/mwi008

Lazonick, W. 2014. "Profits Without Prosperity." *Harvard Business Review* 92, no. 9, pp. 46–55.

Lazonick, W. 2014. "Profits Without Prosperity: Stock Buybacks Manipulate the Market and Leave most Americans Worse Off." *Harvard Business Review* 92, no. 9, pp. 46–55.

Mian, A., and Sufi, A. 2014. *House of Debt: How They (and you) Caused the Great Recession, and How We Can Prevent It from Happening Again.* University of Chicago Press.

Minsky, H.P. 1986. *Stabilizing an Unstable Economy.* Yale University Press.

Organisation for Economic Co-operation and Development. 2018. *A Broken Social Elevator? How to Promote Social Mobility.* OECD Publishing.

Organisation for Economic Co-operation and Development. 2020. *Productivity and Wage Trends.* OECD Publishing.

Organisation for Economic Co-operation and Development. 2022. *Private Equity and Corporate Governance: Risks and Policy Responses.* OECD Publishing.

Palan, R. 2013. *The Financialization of the Firm: Intangible Capital, Goodwill and the Dematerialization of Capitalism.* Routledge.

Pfeffer, F. 2018. "Growing Wealth Gaps in Education." *Demography* 55, no. 3, pp. 1033–1068.

Piketty, T. 2014. *Capital in the Twenty-First Century.* Harvard University Press.

Rajan, R.G. 2010. *Fault Lines: How Hidden Fractures still Threaten the World Economy.* Princeton University Press.

S&P Dow Jones Indices. 2023. *SPIVA U.S. Scorecard.* S&P Dow Jones Indices.

Saez, E., and Zucman, G. 2019. *The Triumph of Injustice: How the Rich Dodge Taxes and How to Make Them Pay.* W. W. Norton & Company.

Stiglitz, J.E. 2012. *The Price of Inequality: How Today's Divided Society Endangers Our Future.* W. W. Norton & Company.

Strange, S. 1996. *The Retreat of the State: The Diffusion of Power in the World Economy.* Cambridge University Press.

Tooze, A. 2022, October 21. "Liz Truss's Downfall and the Bond Market Revolt." Foreign Policy. https://foreignpolicy.com

Truman, E.M. 2019. *Sovereign Wealth Funds.* Peterson Institute for International Economics.

UN-Habitat. 2020. *World Cities Report.* United Nations Human Settlements Programme.

Zuboff, S. 2019. *The Age of Surveillance Capitalism: The Fight for a Human Future at the New Frontier of Power.* PublicAffairs.

CHAPTER 11

Investment in the Digital Age

From Innovation to Illusion

Algorithmic Capital Allocation and Market Automation

The contemporary financial system is undergoing a profound structural shift as markets shift from human-driven judgment to automated, data-intensive decision making. The rapid expansion of algorithmic and AI-driven investing, together with the dominance of passive index funds, signals a reconfiguration of how capital is allocated and where power resides within financial markets. These developments represent not merely technological progress but a transformation in the underlying logic of capitalism. Investment decisions that were once shaped by analysts, portfolio managers, and institutional committees are increasingly governed by algorithms, optimization routines, and large-scale index methodologies. As a result, markets become faster, more concentrated, and more sensitive to systemic flows and automated mechanisms than to firm-specific fundamentals.

The rise of algorithmic and AI-driven investing illustrates the growing computationalization of finance. High-frequency trading firms, quantitative hedge funds, and machine learning platforms rely on vast datasets and predictive modeling to identify signals that remain invisible to human observers. These systems operate at speeds far beyond human reaction times, enabling strategies that exploit tiny price discrepancies. As financial markets generate volumes of data that no individual analyst can process, machine-driven systems become the primary interpreters of market information. This development reflects a broader shift toward what

Andrew Lo describes as the adaptive markets hypothesis, in which market actors evolve in response to changing technological and informational environments increasingly shaped by algorithms rather than human cognition (Lo 2017).

AI-driven trading also introduces new forms of reflexivity within financial markets. Algorithms respond not only to price movements but also to the behavior of other algorithms, creating feedback loops that can accelerate volatility. Events such as the 2010 Flash Crash and the 2018 volatility spike illustrate how automated systems can trigger rapid and systemic disruptions in the absence of underlying economic shocks (Kirilenko et al. 2017). As reinforcement learning and adaptive modeling become more prevalent, machines begin to shape the very dynamics they are designed to analyze. Markets increasingly function as environments cocreated by interacting algorithms, where strategic behavior unfolds at speeds and scales that exceed human comprehension. Human discretion becomes marginal, while algorithmic logic moves to the center of market activity.

Parallel to the rise of AI-driven trading is the extraordinary expansion of passive investing. Index funds and exchange-traded funds now dominate global portfolio flows, directing capital through rule-based inclusion criteria rather than discretionary judgment. These flows are tied to major indices such as the S&P 500 and MSCI benchmarks (Morgan Stanley Capital International). Scholars such as John Bogle and researchers including Ben David, Franzoni, and Moussawi have documented the systemic effects of passive investing, including reduced price discovery, increased correlation across stocks, and a growing concentration of ownership in the hands of a small number of asset managers (Bogle 2017; Ben David et al. 2021).

The dominance of passive investing shifts capital allocation away from firm-level fundamentals. Inclusion in a primary index becomes a central driver of valuation, since passive funds must purchase the securities in their benchmarks regardless of earnings, strategy, or innovation. Market movements increasingly reflect automated inflows and periodic rebalancing cycles. As more investors favor passive vehicles for their low cost and perceived reliability, index-driven flows begin to outweigh discretionary investment decisions. Markets thus start to resemble mechanical systems that respond to the architecture of indices rather than to the distinctive characteristics of individual firms.

This automation of investment decision making also produces a significant centralization of power. Asset managers such as BlackRock, Vanguard, and State Street collectively oversee tens of trillions of dollars in assets, granting them unprecedented influence over corporate governance and market outcomes. Their index methodologies function as de facto regulators of global capital flows. As Fichtner, Heemskerk, and Garcia Bernardo argue, these firms have become the new giants of capitalism, exercising structural power not through active stock selection but through rule-based ownership across the entire economy (Fichtner et al. 2017).

The convergence of algorithmic trading and passive investing has created a hybrid market structure increasingly governed by automation. Algorithms dominate intraday price formation, while passive investment flows shape long-term capital distribution. Human judgment remains present, but it operates at the margins of a system in which computational logic embedded in trading algorithms and index methodologies determines most market behavior. Financial markets become less interpretive and more infrastructural, operating as automated networks that allocate capital according to encoded rules. This transformation raises serious concerns about systemic fragility and democratic oversight. Algorithms can amplify volatility, while passive concentration reduces market diversity. Economic power becomes embedded in data infrastructures and concentrated among a small group of asset managers, producing a form of financial centralization that is often obscured by claims of efficiency and objectivity. Although automation promises lower costs and broader market access, it also introduces opacity, concentration, and new forms of systemic vulnerability.

Cryptocurrencies: Institutionalized Speculation

The rise of cryptocurrencies marks one of the most revealing paradoxes of 21st-century capitalism. Introduced as tools of decentralization and financial emancipation, they have evolved into symbols of large-scale speculation, narrative-driven valuation, and institutionalized illusion.

While comparisons to Ponzi schemes are often dismissed as exaggerated, a structural perspective reveals notable similarities, as crypto assets generate returns not through productive activity but through the continuous entry of new participants and capital. Unlike classical frauds, however, this system operates openly and within legal frameworks, functioning as a normalized Ponzi sustained by technology, ideology, and the growing involvement of major financial institutions and states. What began as a marginal experiment has thus become a central component of digital capitalism.

Cryptocurrencies emerged from a libertarian ambition to create a decentralized and trustless monetary alternative beyond the authority of states and banks. Bitcoin's founding text envisioned a peer-to-peer financial system grounded in cryptographic verification rather than institutional trust (Nakamoto 2008). In practice, however, most crypto assets derive their value not from their function as currencies but from expectations of future price appreciation. This dynamic closely reflects George Soros's theory of reflexivity, in which market outcomes are shaped by self-reinforcing feedback loops between beliefs and prices (Soros 1987) (Figure 11.1). Anticipation of rising prices fuels demand, rising prices validate expectations, and belief sustains the cycle. Cryptocurrencies, therefore, function less as media of exchange and more as speculative narratives about a technological future that remains largely unrealized.

***Figure 11.1** Soros's theory of reflexivity emphasizes a circular causality between perceptions and fundamentals, whereby beliefs influence market outcomes and those outcomes, in turn, reinforce or destabilize prevailing beliefs.*

What distinguishes cryptocurrencies from earlier speculative episodes is the speed and depth of their institutional absorption. Assets once regarded as eccentric or utopian are now integrated into the portfolios and infrastructures of dominant financial actors. The approval of Bitcoin exchange-traded funds by firms such as BlackRock and Fidelity marked a critical moment by embedding speculative digital assets within regulated financial markets. Banks now offer crypto custody services, pension funds experiment with limited exposure, and governments explore central bank digital currencies that adopt blockchain aesthetics while reinforcing centralized authority. Institutional acceptance does not dilute the speculative foundations of crypto markets; instead, it formalizes and stabilizes them. Contemporary finance increasingly treats volatility itself as a source of value, transforming uncertainty into a tradable asset within a broader process of financialized instability (Gabor 2023). Cryptocurrencies thus gain durability not through fundamentals but through their incorporation into financial systems that are too interconnected and politically sensitive to abandon.

The speculative logic of crypto assets reflects a broader transition toward what has been described as the intangible economy, in which value is rooted in ideas, networks, and symbolic constructs rather than in physical production. Tokens have no intrinsic value; their value depends entirely on collective belief. In this respect, cryptocurrencies exemplify the hyperreal condition in which signs circulate independently of material referents and simulations exert greater influence than underlying reality (Baudrillard 1981). The crypto ecosystem monetizes belief itself, transforming faith in technological promise and digitally engineered scarcity into exchangeable assets. Bitcoin's fixed supply of 21 million coins is not a technical inevitability but an ideological decision that introduces scarcity into a medium defined by infinite reproducibility, illustrating the rise of artificial scarcity capitalism (Haskel and Westlake 2018).

Blockchain transparency is often cited as evidence that cryptocurrencies do not resemble Ponzi schemes. Yet transparency at the transactional level conceals opacity at the valuation level. Traditional Ponzi schemes relied on secrecy, whereas contemporary crypto Ponzi schemes rely on openly acknowledged belief. Many participants recognize that tokens lack intrinsic value, yet disbelief carries economic penalties. The defining feature of this system lies in its legitimized irrationality, as illusion becomes investable and consensus outweighs production as the primary source of value. As long as new participants continue to embrace the narrative, the structure remains intact.

The role of the state within this ecosystem is deeply ambivalent. Regulators warn of fraud, volatility, and systemic risk while simultaneously taxing crypto gains, approving institutional investment vehicles, and exploring digital currencies inspired by blockchain design. Cryptocurrencies have been described as the mother of all bubbles. Yet, governments often treat them as a controlled outlet for speculative energy that absorbs excess risk without destabilizing core financial systems (Roubini 2022). The result is a regulatory performance that reassures the public while essentially leaving speculative foundations untouched. The state becomes both overseer and beneficiary, critic and participant, rendering crypto markets too visible to condemn, too profitable to suppress, and too symbolically embedded in narratives of innovation to eliminate.

In this sense, cryptocurrencies are not an anomaly within capitalism but a reflection of its latest configuration. They reveal an economic system increasingly detached from material production, where wealth emerges from narratives, expectations, and symbolic scarcity. Capitalism, once constrained by physical limits, now flourishes in immaterial domains where belief and attention rival labor and output as sources of value. Cryptocurrencies persist not because they fulfill their promises of decentralization, but because they embody the core logic of contemporary capitalism: the conversion of illusion into infrastructure and speculation into a permanent, institutionalized condition of economic life.

The Rise of Meme Stocks

The rise of meme stocks stands out as one of the most revealing developments in contemporary financial markets. The term refers to stocks whose price movements are driven less by corporate fundamentals than by collective enthusiasm, viral attention, and digitally coordinated action across platforms such as Reddit, X, TikTok, and YouTube (Smales 2021). Speculative manias have appeared throughout financial history, but meme stocks are distinctive because they are deeply embedded in digital infrastructures, including zero commission trading platforms, social media ecosystems, and algorithmic amplification systems (Macey 2022). These forces have expanded market participation while simultaneously producing new forms of volatility, collective behavior, and cultural expression.

The most emblematic case remains the GameStop short squeeze of early 2021. Retail investors, coordinating broadly through the Reddit forum WallStreetBets, collectively bought shares and call options, driving prices sharply upward and inflicting significant losses on hedge funds that had taken large short positions (Ante et al. 2021). The episode triggered a wave of similar campaigns involving companies such as AMC Entertainment, BlackBerry, and Bed Bath and Beyond (Smales 2021). In each instance, online communities mobilized memes, antiestablishment rhetoric, and a shared sense of identity to sustain speculative momentum (Zuckerman 2022). The meme, once a lighthearted cultural artifact, became a financial instrument, collapsing the distinction between humor, protest, and market activity (Zuckerman 2022).

Digitalization enabled this phenomenon in several decisive ways. First, commission-free trading applications such as Robinhood dramatically lowered barriers to entry by removing transaction costs and encouraging more frequent participation (Macey 2022). Second, social media platforms served as decentralized spaces of collective meaning-making, where retail investors framed trading as entertainment, resistance, or self-expression rather than solely as calculation (Zuckerman 2022). Third, algorithmic amplification intensified these dynamics, as trending stocks received disproportionate visibility and attention, accelerating inflows and price movements (Lyócsa et al. 2021). This feedback loop generated extreme volatility, a pattern confirmed by empirical research linking social media activity to sudden price surges in meme stocks (Lyócsa et al. 2021).

Meme stocks expose more profound shifts in both cultural and financial logic. Conventional economic theory assumes that investors act rationally and base their decisions on earnings, productivity, and firm-level fundamentals (Eaton et al. 2022). Meme stocks diverge sharply from this model by blending digital subculture with financial speculation, allowing humor, affect, and identity to rival traditional valuation metrics

(Zuckerman 2022). For many participants, purchasing GameStop or AMC stocks was less an investment strategy than an expressive gesture signaling belonging, mockery of financial elites, or participation in a collective performance (Zuckerman 2022). In this sense, meme stocks demonstrate how cultural forces associated with digital life can reshape financial behavior (Smales 2021).

These dynamics also carry substantial risks. Collective enthusiasm that pushes prices upward can reverse abruptly, leaving late participants exposed to severe losses (Eaton et al. 2022). Digitally amplified herd behavior produces volatility that often bears little relation to underlying economic conditions (Lyócsa et al. 2021). Regulatory institutions face growing challenges as coordinated market behavior increasingly occurs through diffuse online networks beyond traditional monitoring frameworks (Eaton et al. 2022). The GameStop episode revealed the limits of narratives surrounding democratized finance when Robinhood temporarily restricted trading, a move widely interpreted as prioritizing systemic stability over retail autonomy. This incident underscored how digital finance remains deeply entangled with established structures of financial power.

From a sociological perspective, meme stocks can be interpreted through the lenses of risk society and network society theory. Financial risk is increasingly produced reflexively through the technologies and social arrangements that enable participation, rather than imposed from outside the system (Beck 1992). At the same time, meme stocks exemplify a networked market structure in which global flows of information, communication, and algorithmic amplification shape valuation outcomes (Castells 2011). A single viral post by an anonymous user can trigger massive shifts in market capitalization, highlighting how financial markets now operate as sociotechnical systems rather than isolated economic arenas (Castells 2011).

At a deeper cultural level, meme stocks reflect core features of postmodernity. The collapse of grand narratives helps explain how the traditional narrative of market rationality gives way to fragmented micronarratives produced within digital communities (Lyotard 1979). The efficient-market ideal is destabilized by actors who trade on irony, play, and social identity rather than on fundamentals (Zuckerman 2022). The concept of hyperreality further clarifies how meme stocks detach from economic referents, as prices become simulations of collective sentiment rather than reflections of material conditions (Baudrillard 1994). Meme stock participation also takes on a performative dimension, involving the public display of trades, the circulation of screenshots, and the production of memes that turn finance into spectacle (Jameson 1991).

Meme stocks are therefore not isolated curiosities but manifestations of broader transformations in culture, technology, and finance. They reveal a market environment in which narratives can overpower fundamentals, symbols can shape valuation, and online communities can challenge traditional financial hierarchies (Smales 2021). More broadly, they show how postmodern cultural sensibilities marked by play, fragmentation, irony, and spectacle now permeate even the most ostensibly rational domains of economic life. In doing so, meme stocks exemplify how digital capitalism generates new forms of financial behavior that are hybrid, performative, affective, and profoundly shaped by the infrastructures of the networked age (Castells 2011).

Platformization and the Expansion of Big Tech Finance

What began as companies offering search engines, online marketplaces, and social networking tools has evolved into an ecosystem in which a small group of firms, including Alphabet, Amazon, Apple, Meta, and Alibaba, exert growing influence over payments, credit, data, and investment flows. This transformation is commonly described as platformization, a process through which organizational models built around data extraction, network effects, and user lock-in expand across sectors (Srnicek 2017). As these platforms scale, they move beyond mediating economic activity and begin to shape financial infrastructures themselves. The result is the rise of Big Tech Finance, a new configuration of economic power that links digital services, monetary systems, and investment markets.

Platformization rests on three interrelated structural features. First, platforms operate as multisided markets that connect users, advertisers, merchants, developers, and service providers while retaining control over the rules governing interaction (Rochet and Tirole 2003). Second, they depend on continuous data collection, enabling predictive analytics, personalization, and behavioral targeting at scale (Zuboff 2019). Third, algorithmic systems coordinate transactions and optimize engagement, reinforcing dependency and enabling rapid expansion. Together, these features generate powerful network effects in which value increases with each additional user, making platforms difficult to displace. As economic activity becomes increasingly digitized, this architecture allows Big Tech firms to extend their reach from core digital services into financial intermediation.

The expansion of payment infrastructures offers one of the clearest examples of this shift. Apple Pay, Google Pay, Amazon Pay, Alipay, and WeChat Pay have embedded themselves into global payment systems by leveraging large user bases and integrating financial functions directly into devices and online marketplaces. These services reduce friction through one-click purchasing, biometric authentication, and seamless cross-platform integration. For merchants, they lower transaction costs while providing access to detailed consumer data. In China, platform-based payment systems have largely displaced cash, banks, and traditional card networks. Alipay and WeChat Pay process trillions of dollars annually and function as quasi-public utilities, illustrating how platform-controlled payment systems can rapidly become foundational elements of national financial infrastructure (Arner et al. 2017).

Credit markets follow a similar trajectory. Platforms draw on transactional, behavioral, and social data to generate alternative credit assessments, allowing them to evaluate consumer and merchant risk with a level of granularity that often exceeds traditional banking models. Amazon extends loans to sellers based on marketplace performance. Apple offers credit cards and installment plans integrated directly into its ecosystem through partnerships with financial institutions. In China, Ant Group's microcredit services, Huabei and Jiebei, rely on data-driven risk models rather than conventional collateral requirements (Didenko et al. 2020). This trend represents a shift from asset-based lending to information-based lending, where access to real-time user data enables dynamic pricing of risk. For Big Tech firms, credit provision is not an ancillary service but a logical extension of platform operations.

Platform dynamics are also reshaping investment activity. Retail trading applications such as Robinhood combine frictionless interfaces with real-time market data and gamified features that encourage continuous speculative engagement (Barber et al. 2022). At the same time, social media accelerates the spread of market sentiment, intensifying phenomena such as meme stock trading and amplifying volatility. On the institutional side, financial markets increasingly rely on cloud infrastructure from Amazon Web Services, Microsoft Azure, and Google Cloud to support algorithmic trading, fintech innovation, and decentralized finance systems. This phenomenon creates a form of structural dependence in which finance relies on Big Tech for computational power and data hosting. At the same time, Big Tech deepens its control by embedding itself within financial systems.

The growth of Big Tech Finance reshapes market organization in several important ways. It blurs sectoral boundaries by embedding financial functions into everyday digital interactions. It extends financialization into new domains as algorithms translate patterns of consumption, mobility, and social behavior into risk scores and financial signals (Langley and Leyshon 2021). It also concentrates on economic power, reinforcing winner-take-all dynamics in which a small number of firms control both digital markets and critical components of financial infrastructure.

These developments raise significant governance challenges. Existing financial regulation was designed for banks, insurers, and credit institutions with clear organizational boundaries and defined jurisdictions. Platform firms, by contrast, operate across borders, scale rapidly at low marginal cost, and accumulate vast reserves of behavioral data. They provide credit without functioning as banks, manage digital wallets without being payment institutions, and influence investment flows without operating as exchanges. This regulatory ambiguity complicates oversight and accountability. Recent responses include the European Union's Digital Markets Act and new regulatory initiatives in China and Singapore that introduce requirements for structural separation, algorithmic transparency, and capital adequacy for platform-based financial services (European Commission 2022; Huang 2020). Despite these efforts, regulation remains fragmented globally, enabling Big Tech firms to exploit jurisdictional gaps.

The broader consequences are structural rather than incremental. As platforms become embedded in financial infrastructure, economic activity becomes increasingly dependent on privately governed digital systems. Data concentration amplifies inequalities between firms, as dominant platforms gain unmatched capacity to price risk, shape consumer behavior, and access markets. What emerges is a new form of financial oligopoly rooted less in traditional capital accumulation than in technological dominance and control over digital infrastructures.

Green and ESG Finance: Reshaping Capital Allocation in the 21st Century

Green and ESG finance now play a central role in shaping capital allocation, influencing corporate conduct, and responding to systemic challenges such as climate change, inequality, and long-term sustainability. What began as a niche approach associated with socially responsible investing has become a mainstream feature of global finance. Trillions of dollars now flow into ESG funds, green bonds, and climate-focused exchange-traded funds, reflecting both societal pressure for ethical finance and growing awareness of the financial risks linked to environmental degradation and weak governance.

At the core of ESG finance is the incorporation of nonfinancial criteria into investment decisions. Environmental factors include carbon emissions, energy efficiency, and biodiversity impacts. Social criteria address labor standards, workplace diversity, and community relations. Governance focuses on transparency, executive compensation, and shareholder rights (Friede et al. 2015). Together, these dimensions broaden traditional risk-and-return analysis by embedding sustainability and accountability into assessments of firm performance. The rapid expansion of ESG ratings, indices, and benchmarks illustrates the extent to which investors now rely on these tools, even as methodological inconsistencies across providers persist.

Green finance, as a subset of ESG finance, concentrates specifically on environmental objectives. Green bonds provide a channel for governments, corporations, and multilateral institutions to raise capital for projects related to climate mitigation and adaptation. Since their first issuance by the European Investment Bank in 2007, green bonds have expanded rapidly, with global issuance exceeding $500 billion in 2021 (Climate Bonds Initiative 2022). Beyond financing renewable energy and sustainable infrastructure, these instruments serve as signals of commitment to low-carbon transitions. Carbon markets and emissions trading systems have also grown in prominence, creating financial incentives for firms to reduce greenhouse gas emissions and turning environmental performance into an economically relevant variable.

The expansion of ESG investing has likewise reshaped equity markets. Climate-focused exchange-traded funds and sustainable index products have grown rapidly, driven by investor demand and recognition of climate-related financial risks. Large asset managers such as BlackRock, Vanguard, and State Street have integrated ESG criteria across many portfolios, not only as a response to client preferences but also as part of fiduciary risk management (Krueger et al. 2020). By 2022, global ESG fund assets had surpassed $ 2.7 trillion, underscoring the scale of the shift from a niche strategy to a dominant investment approach (Morningstar 2022). Younger generations of investors have further reinforced this momentum by making sustainability central to their financial choices.

The rise of ESG finance reflects economic pragmatism as much as ethical concern. Climate change, resource scarcity, and social instability pose systemic risks to the global economy, including supply chain disruptions and the prospect of stranded assets in carbon-intensive industries. Empirical research suggests that firms with strong ESG performance often benefit from lower capital costs, reduced volatility, and more resilient long-term returns (Friede et al. 2015). As a result, ESG integration has become a tool for managing risk and identifying sustainable growth opportunities. This convergence of ethical considerations with financial logic marks a meaningful shift in contemporary capitalism.

Despite its growth, ESG finance faces significant challenges. One of the most prominent is greenwashing, in which firms overstate or misrepresent their environmental and social credentials to attract investment (Dyck et al. 2019). The absence of fully standardized reporting frameworks and wide variation among ESG rating agencies contribute to confusion and undermine credibility. High-profile cases illustrate these tensions, as companies may score well on environmental metrics while receiving poor evaluations for governance or labor practices. In response, regulators have begun to intervene. The European Union's Sustainable Finance Disclosure Regulation and the United States Securities and Exchange Commission's proposed climate disclosure rules aim to improve transparency, comparability, and accountability.

Another challenge involves balancing trade-offs among ESG priorities. Firms may perform strongly on emissions reduction while facing criticism for labor conditions or supply chain practices. Investors must therefore navigate competing objectives within a broader assessment of long-term value creation. Geopolitical developments further complicate ESG integration, as global capital flows intersect with divergent national regulations, energy dependencies, and political interests. The war between Russia and Ukraine highlighted these tensions by forcing investors to weigh energy security against decarbonization goals.

Even with these constraints, the direction of ESG and green finance remains clear. International agreements such as the Paris Agreement, widespread net-zero commitments, and intensifying climate risks create structural incentives for sustainable investment. New instruments, including sustainability-linked bonds whose interest rates vary according to ESG performance, demonstrate ongoing innovation in this area (OECD 2020). The expansion of impact investing, which explicitly targets measurable social and environmental outcomes alongside financial returns, further illustrates the alignment of finance with broader societal objectives. Green and ESG finance thus represents more than a passing trend. It signals a reconfiguration of global capital markets in which sustainability, accountability, and long-term resilience increasingly define value creation. While challenges related to greenwashing, standardization, and geopolitics remain unresolved, the integration of ESG criteria into mainstream finance appears durable and transformative.

Monetary Policy as Market Governance

Monetary policy is commonly presented as a technical tool employed by central banks to control inflation, smooth business cycles, and stabilize macroeconomic conditions. This conventional interpretation, however, understates its broader function within contemporary capitalism. In practice, monetary policy operates as a central mechanism of market governance. By shaping asset prices, structuring incentives, reallocating wealth, and influencing the balance of power among states, financial institutions, firms, and households, central banks actively participate in organizing economic life. Since the global financial crisis, this governing role has become more explicit, as central banking has shifted from a narrow focus on stabilization toward sustaining markets and supporting financialized growth trajectories (Gabor 2021).

At its core, monetary policy governs markets through the pricing of money. Interest rates influence borrowing costs, investment decisions, risk tolerance, and the allocation of capital across sectors of the economy (Mishkin 2019). Lower interest rates encourage leverage, asset accumulation, and speculative activity, while tighter monetary conditions restrain credit expansion and impose discipline on firms, governments, and households through higher financing costs. These effects are not neutral. Monetary policy systematically favors sectors such as finance and real estate while constraining others, thereby shaping the structure of economic activity rather than merely responding to it (Stiglitz 2015).

The adoption of unconventional monetary policies after the 2008 financial crisis marked a decisive shift toward direct market governance. Through quantitative easing, large-scale asset purchases, and forward guidance, central banks intervened deeply in bond markets, equity valuations, and credit spreads (Gorton and Metrick 2012). Institutions such as the Federal Reserve and the European Central Bank assumed the role of dominant market participants, effectively acting as buyers of last resort for government debt and key financial assets. While these interventions stabilized financial markets, they also entrenched a regime in which asset prices became increasingly dependent on monetary support rather than underlying productive dynamics (Borio 2014).

This transformation has significant distributive consequences. By inflating asset prices, accommodative monetary policy disproportionately benefits asset holders, institutional investors, and large corporations, while offering limited advantages to wage earners and younger households with restricted access to asset markets (Piketty 2020). In this sense, monetary policy functions as a concealed mechanism of redistribution, contributing to rising wealth inequality despite its presentation as politically neutral. The governance role of central banking is therefore not merely technical but deeply political, shaping social and economic outcomes without direct democratic authorization (Epstein 2005).

Monetary policy also governs markets by disciplining states. Governments dependent on bond markets face persistent pressure to maintain credibility in the eyes of central banks and investors. Interest rate expectations and sovereign bond spreads operate as disciplinary signals, constraining fiscal policy choices and limiting the scope of public spending (Blyth 2013). During the eurozone crisis, monetary interventions were explicitly linked to austerity measures, labor market reforms, and structural adjustment, illustrating how central banking can enforce market-conforming behavior at the national level (Streeck 2014).

In the contemporary financialized economy, monetary policy increasingly prioritizes stabilizing asset markets over promoting productive investment. Prolonged periods of low interest rates have encouraged debt-financed growth, stock buybacks, and speculative investment strategies, while discouraging long-term investment in productive capacity (Lazonick 2014). This pattern reflects a broader shift from industrial capitalism toward asset-based capitalism, in which economic stability depends less on expanding output and more on sustaining asset valuations (Davis 2017). Monetary policy thus functions as a governance tool that supports financial accumulation, even when this undermines long-term economic resilience.

The growing reliance on central banks as market governors raises essential questions of legitimacy and accountability. Institutions such as national central banks and the IMF exert substantial influence over economic outcomes while remaining insulated from electoral politics. This insulation is often justified on the grounds of expertise and credibility, yet it conceals the normative judgments embedded in monetary decisions (Tucker 2018). Choices regarding inflation targets, asset purchases, and financial backstops inevitably reflect value judgments about which interests deserve protection and which risks are acceptable. Monetary policy, therefore, should be understood not only as an economic instrument but as a central pillar of market governance in contemporary capitalism.

Financialization of Housing and Real Assets

Housing, land, and infrastructure were once primarily embedded in national welfare regimes, urban planning frameworks, and local economies. Over recent decades, however, these assets have increasingly been absorbed into global financial circuits, redefined as investment vehicles, collateral, and yield-generating instruments. This shift has profound implications for housing affordability, wealth distribution, urban governance, and social stability.

In housing markets, financialization manifests through the expansion of mortgage credit, securitization, real estate investment trusts, private equity ownership, and the integration of residential property into global capital markets (Aalbers 2016). Housing prices are no longer primarily anchored in local income levels, demographic demand, or construction costs. Still, they are increasingly influenced by interest rate regimes, global liquidity conditions, and portfolio allocation strategies (Fernandez and Aalbers 2016).

A key driver of housing financialization has been the transformation of mortgages into tradable financial assets. Mortgage securitization allowed financial institutions to pool housing debt and convert it into liquid securities, thereby expanding credit supply while dispersing risk across financial markets (Gorton 2010). While this process initially facilitated higher homeownership rates, it also linked housing systems to systemic financial instability. The global financial crisis of 2008 demonstrated how deeply housing had become embedded in speculative financial architectures, as the collapse of mortgage-backed securities precipitated widespread foreclosures, banking failures, and macroeconomic contraction (FCIC 2011).

Significantly, the crisis did not reverse the financialization of housing. Instead, it marked a reconfiguration of ownership structures. Institutional investors, including private equity firms, hedge funds, and asset managers, entered housing markets on an unprecedented scale, acquiring distressed properties and converting them into rental assets (Fields 2017). This shift represents a transition from mass homeownership toward a landlord model dominated by large-scale financial actors. Housing thus becomes less a means of social reproduction and more a source of rent extraction and capital accumulation.

The growing role of institutional investors has significant distributional consequences. Empirical research shows that financialized rental housing is associated with higher rents, increased eviction rates, and declining housing quality, particularly in low- and middle-income neighborhoods (Immergluck and Law 2014; Beswick et al. 2016). As investment strategies prioritize short-term returns and asset appreciation, housing provision becomes increasingly disconnected from social need. This dynamic contributes to affordability crises across major urban centers, reinforcing spatial segregation and displacement.

From a political economy perspective, the financialization of housing is closely linked to broader shifts in capitalism toward asset-based growth. In an environment characterized by declining returns in productive investment and prolonged low interest rates, capital increasingly seeks refuge in tangible assets as stores of value (Piketty 2014). Housing and land, due to their relative scarcity and durability, become prime targets for speculative investment. This process intensifies wealth inequality, as asset owners benefit from capital gains while nonowners face rising costs and exclusion from ownership (Ryan-Collins et al. 2017).

The financialization of tangible assets extends beyond housing to encompass infrastructure, land, and public services. Through privatization, public–private partnerships, and asset recycling schemes, infrastructure assets are transformed into financial products generating predictable cash flows for institutional investors (Flyvbjerg 2017). While often justified in terms of efficiency or fiscal necessity, these arrangements frequently shift long-term risks to the public sector while constraining democratic control over essential services. As a result, financial imperatives increasingly shape urban development, public investment priorities, and territorial governance. The financialization of housing reflects a more profound normative shift in how shelter is conceptualized. Housing is no longer treated primarily as a social right or a component of welfare provision, but as an asset class within diversified investment portfolios.

References

Aalbers, M.B. 2016. *The Financialization of Housing: A Political Economy Approach*. Routledge.

Aalbers, M.B. 2017. "The Financialization of Housing." *Annual Review of Sociology 43*, pp. 157–177. https://doi.org/10.1146/annurev-soc-060116-053315

Ante, L., Fiedler, I., and Steinmetz, F. 2021. "Trading Through a Pandemic: The Impact of COVID-19 on Retail Investors and the GameStop Short Squeeze." *Finance Research Letters 43*, p. 101948. https://doi.org/10.1016/j.frl.2021.101948

Arner, D.W., Barberis, J., and Buckley, R.P. 2017. "FinTech and RegTech in a Nutshell, and the Future in a Sandbox." *Journal of Banking Regulation 19, no.* 4, pp. 283–296. https://doi.org/10.1057/s41261-017-0034-7

Barber, B.M., Huang, X., Odean, T., and Schwarz, C. 2022. "Attention Induced Trading and Returns: Evidence from Robinhood Users." *The Journal of Finance, 77, no.* 1, pp. 1–53. https://doi.org/10.1111/jofi.13077

Baudrillard, J. 1981. *Simulacres et Simulation*. Éditions Galilée.

Baudrillard, J. 1994. *Simulacra and Simulation,* trans., S.F. Glaser. University of Michigan Press. (Original work published 1981)

Beck, U. 1992. *Risk Society: Towards a New Modernity*. Sage.

Ben-David, I., Franzoni, F., and Moussawi, R. 2021. "Do ETFs Increase Volatility?" *The Journal of Finance 76, no.* 6, pp. 2471–2535. https://doi.org/10.1111/jofi.13059

Beswick, J., Alexandri, G., Byrne, M., Vives-Miró, S., Fields, D., Hodkinson, S., and Janoschka, M. 2016. "Speculating on London's Housing Future: The Rise of Global Corporate Landlords in Post-Crisis Urban Landscapes." *City 20, no.* 2, pp. 321–341. https://doi.org/10.1080/13604813.2016.1145946

Blyth, M. 2013. *Austerity: The History of a Dangerous Idea*. Oxford University Press.

Bogle, J.C. 2017. *The Little Book of Common Sense Investing* (10th anniversary ed.). Wiley.

Borio, C. 2014. "The Financial Cycle and Macroeconomics: What have We Learnt?" *Journal of Banking & Finance 45*, pp. 182–198.

Castells, M. 2011. *The Rise of the Network Society* (2nd ed.). Wiley-Blackwell.

Climate Bonds Initiative. 2022. "*Sustainable Debt Global State of the Market 2021*." https://www.climatebonds.net

Davis, G.F. 2017. *Managed by the Markets*. Oxford University Press.

Didenko, A., Buckley, R.P., and Arner, D.W. 2020. "Regulating Digital Finance: FinTech, BigTech, and the Future of Financial Services." *Journal of Banking Regulation 21, no.* 1, pp. 1–14. https://doi.org/10.1057/s41261-019-00103-y

Dyck, A., Lins, K.V., Roth, L., and Wagner, H.F. 2019. "Do Institutional Investors Drive Corporate Social Responsibility? International Evidence." *Journal of Financial Economics 131, no.* 3, pp. 693–714. https://doi.org/10.1016/j.jfineco.2018.08.013

Eaton, G.W., Green, T.C., Roseman, B.S., and Wu, Y. 2022. "Retail Trader Sophistication and Stock Market Quality: Evidence from Meme Stock Trading." *The Review of Financial Studies 35, no.* 12, pp. 5723–5758. https://doi.org/10.1093/rfs/hhac032

Epstein, G.A. 2005. *Financialization and the World Economy.* Edward Elgar.

European Commission. 2022. *Digital Markets Act.* Publications Office of the European Union. https://eur-lex.europa.eu

Fernandez, R., and Aalbers, M.B. 2016. "Financialization and Housing: Between Globalization and Varieties of Capitalism." *Competition & Change 20, no.* 2, pp. 71–88. https://doi.org/10.1177/1024529415623916

Fields, D. 2017. "Unwilling Subjects of Financialization." *International Journal of Urban and Regional Research 41, no.* 4, pp. 588–603. https://doi.org/10.1111/1468-2427.12562

Financial Crisis Inquiry Commission. 2011. *The Financial Crisis Inquiry Report.* U.S. Government Printing Office.

Fichtner, J., Heemskerk, E.M., and Garcia-Bernardo, J. 2017. "Hidden Power of the Big Three?" *Business and Politics 19, no.* 2, pp. 298–326. https://doi.org/10.1017/bap.2017.6

Flyvbjerg, B. 2017. "Introduction: The Iron Law of Megaproject Management." In *The Oxford Handbook of Megaproject Management, ed.* B. Flyvbjerg, 1–18. Oxford University Press.

Friede, G., Busch, T., and Bassen, A. 2015. "ESG and Financial Performance." *Journal of Sustainable Finance & Investment 5, no.* 4, pp. 210–233. https://doi.org/10.1080/20430795.2015.1118917

Gabor, D. 2021. "The Wall Street Consensus." *Development and Change 52, no.* 3, pp. 429–459.

Gorton, G. 2010. *Slapped by the Invisible Hand.* Oxford University Press.

Gorton, G., and Metrick, A. 2012. "Regulating the Shadow Banking System." *Brookings Papers on Economic Activity* 41, pp. 261–312.

Haskel, J., and Westlake, S. 2018. *Capitalism Without Capital.* Princeton University Press.

Huang, H. 2020. "Regulating fintech in China." *Washington University Law Review 97, no.* 4, pp. 1269–1307.

Immergluck, D., and Law, J. 2014. "Speculating in Crisis." *Journal of Urban Affairs 36, no.* 1, pp. 1–19. https://doi.org/10.1111/juaf.12011

Jameson, F. 1991. *Postmodernism.* Duke University Press.

Kirilenko, A.A., Kyle, A.S., Samadi, M., and Tuzun, T. 2017. "The Flash Crash." *The Journal of Finance 72, no.* 3, pp. 967–998. https://doi.org/10.1111/jofi.12498

Krueger, P., Sautner, Z., and Starks, L.T. 2020. "Climate Risks for Institutional Investors." *The Review of Financial Studies 33, no.* 3, pp. 1067–1111. https://doi.org/10.1093/rfs/hhz137

Langley, P., and Leyshon, A. 2021. "Platform Capitalism." *Finance and Society 7, no.* 1, pp. 11–31. https://doi.org/10.2218/finsoc.v7i1.5496

Lazonick, W. 2014. "Profits Without Prosperity." *Harvard Business Review 92, no.* 9, pp. 46–55.

Lo, A.W. 2017. *Adaptive Markets*. Princeton University Press.

Lyócsa, Š., Baumöhl, E., Vyrost, T., and Molnár, P. 2021. "Fear of the Virus and Fear of Missing Out." *Finance Research Letters 40*, p. 101630. https://doi.org/10.1016/j.frl.2020.101630

Lyotard, J.-F. 1979. *La condition postmoderne*. Éditions de Minuit.

Macey, J.R. 2022. *The Death of Corporate Reputation*. Yale University Press.

Mishkin, F.S. 2019. *The Economics of Money, Banking, and Financial Markets*. Pearson.

Morningstar. 2022. "*Global Sustainable Fund Flows*." https://www.morningstar.com

Nakamoto, S. 2008. "*Bitcoin: A Peer-to-Peer Electronic Cash System*." https://bitcoin.org/bitcoin.pdf

OECD. 2020. "*Sustainable Finance and Investment*." https://www.oecd.org

Piketty, T. 2014. *Capital in the Twenty-First Century*, trans. A. Goldhammer. Harvard University Press.

Piketty, T. 2020. *Capital and Ideology*. Harvard University Press.

Rochet, J.C., and Tirole, J. 2003. "Platform Competition in two-sided markets." *Journal of the European Economic Association 1, no.* 4, pp. 990–1029. https://doi.org/10.1162/154247603322493212

Rolnik, R. 2019. *Urban Warfare*. Verso.

Roubini, N. 2022. *Megathreats*. Little, Brown and Company.

Ryan-Collins, J., Lloyd, T., and Macfarlane, L. 2017. *Rethinking the Economics of Land and Housing*. Zed Books.

Smales, L.A. 2021. "Investor Attention During COVID-19." *International Review of Financial Analysis 73*, p. 101616. https://doi.org/10.1016/j.irfa.2020.101616

Soros, G. 1987. *The Alchemy of Finance*. John Wiley & Sons.

Srnicek, N. 2017. *Platform Capitalism*. Polity Press.

Stiglitz, J.E. 2015. *The Great Divide*. W. W. Norton.

Streeck, W. 2014. *Buying Time*. Verso.

Tucker, P. 2018. *Unelected Power*. Princeton University Press.

Zuboff, S. 2019. *The age of surveillance capitalism*. PublicAffairs.

Zuckerman, E.W. 2022. "The GameStop Episode." *Socio-Economic Review 20, no.* 3, pp. 1031–1055. https://doi.org/10.1093/ser/mwac038

Index

Note: Page numbers followed by "f" and "t" refer to figures and tables.

www.ingramcontent.com/pod-product-compliance
Lightning Source LLC
LaVergne TN
LVHW050625100826
845148LV00011B/1731

* 9 7 8 1 6 0 6 4 9 6 4 3 5 *